Handbook of
Egyptian Mythology

TITLES IN ABC-CLIO'S
Handbooks of World Mythology

HANDBOOKS OF WORLD MYTHOLOGY

Handbook of Egyptian Mythology

Geraldine Pinch

ABC-CLIO

Santa Barbara, California • Denver, Colorado • Oxford, England

Library of Congress Cataloging-in-Publication Data
Pinch, Geraldine.
    Handbook of Egyptian mythology / Geraldine Pinch.
        p.   cm. — (Handbooks of world mythology)
    Includes bibliographical references and index.
    ISBN 1-57607-242-8 (alk. paper)—ISBN 1-57607-763-2 (ebook)
    1. Mythology, Egyptian.   I. Title.   II. Series.
BL2441.3.P56   2002
299'.31—dc21

                                                        2002004567

06 05 04 03 02   10 9 8 7 6 5 4 3 2 1

This book is also available on the World Wide Web as an e-book.
Visit abc-clio.com for details.

ABC-CLIO, Inc.
130 Cremona Drive, P.O. Box 1911
Santa Barbara, California 93116–1911
This book is printed on acid-free paper.
Manufactured in the United States of America

CONTENTS

4 Egyptian Myth: Annotated Print and Nonprint Resources, 215

CHRONOLOGY

Most of the dates for the kingdoms and periods into which Egyptian history is traditionally divided are only approximate.

This chronology mainly follows that given in I. Shaw and P. Nicholson, *British Museum Dictionary of Ancient Egypt* (London: British Museum Press, 1995). Abbreviations used are as follows: BCE = before common era (also known as BC); CE = common era (also known as AD); and c. = circa (the approximate time of).

Predynastic c. 5500–3200 BCE

Protodynastic c. 3200–3100 BCE (Dynasty 0)

Early Dynastic c. 3100–2686 BCE (Dynasties 1–2)

Old Kingdom c. 2686–2181 BCE (Dynasties 3–6)

First Intermediate Period c. 2181–2055 BCE (Dynasties 7–11)

Middle Kingdom c. 2055–1650 BCE (Dynasties 11–13)

Second Intermediate Period c. 1650–1550 BCE (Dynasties 14–17)

New Kingdom c. 1550–1069 BCE (Dynasties 18–20)

Third Intermediate Period c. 1069–747 BCE (Dynasties 21–24)

Late Period c. 747–332 BCE (Dynasties 25–30 and three Persian kings)

Greco-Roman Period 332 BCE–395 CE

(Macedonian Dynasty 332–310 BCE; Ptolemaic Dynasty 305–30 BCE; Roman rule 30 BCE–395 CE)

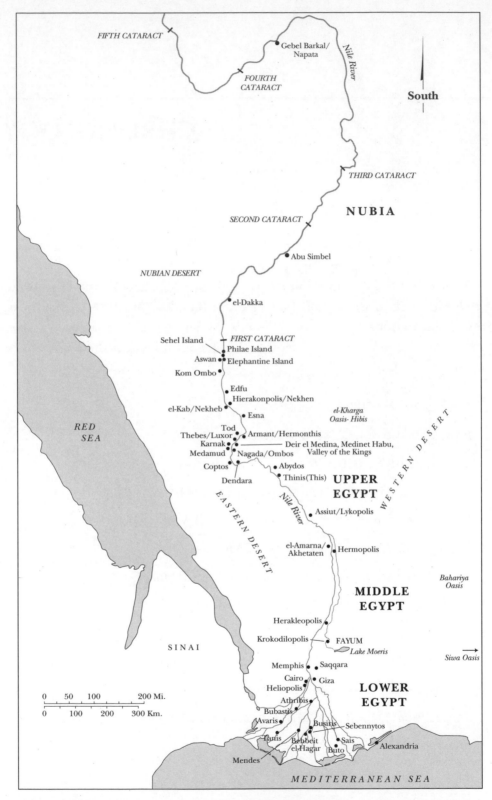

Map One. Ancient Egypt and Nubia. The Nile river flows from south to north, so Egypt's southern boundary on the First Cataract was thought of as the top of the country, and the Mediterranean coast as the bottom.

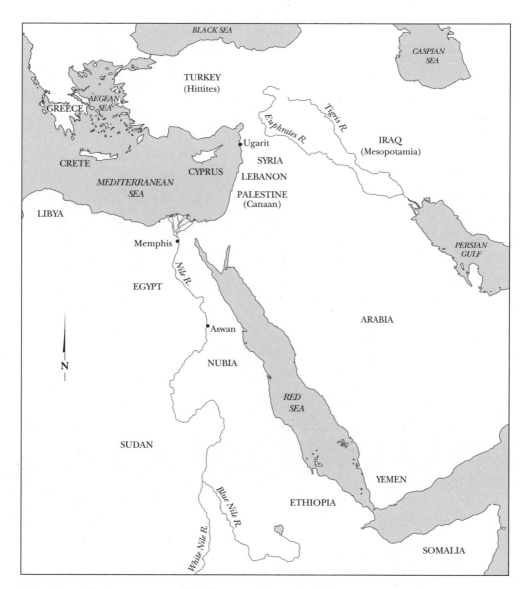

Map Two. The Egyptian World. This map shows the only countries and civilizations known to the Egyptians through direct contact up to the end of the second millennium BCE.

INTRODUCTION

WHAT IS A MYTH?

If asked this question, most people would reply that a myth is a story that is not true, even though you might want it to be. Scholarly arguments about the definition of a myth have been going on for more than 2,000 years. Many definitions have been proposed. Among the most common are that myths are stories about gods, myths are sacred stories, myths are stories that explain the way the world is, or myths are simply traditional stories that hand on collective knowledge or experience.

Writers from various disciplines and intellectual movements have interpreted myth in different ways. Myths have been seen as a "disease of language," as garbled memories of historical events, as a mode of prelogical thought, as expressions of the subconscious mind, as symbolic descriptions of the natural world or symbolic statements about the social order, and as the spoken part of ritual.[1] As theories to explain the whole of world mythology, these interpretations all have flaws, but each of them is applicable to some Egyptian myths.

In his book on the meaning and functions of myth, G. S. Kirk proposed three main categories of myths.[2] His first category is myths told for entertainment. This is a reminder that myths may be sacred, but they are not necessarily solemn. The validity of this category might be challenged, but some cultures do seem to have told one version of a myth for entertainment while another, more secret version, was used in rituals.[3]

Kirk's second category includes operative, iterative, or validatory myths. These are stories about things that may not have really happened, but the stories themselves are thought to have power to transform the real world. Such myths "tend to be repeated regularly on ritual or ceremonial occasions . . . to bring about a desirable continuity in nature or society."[4] Myths that are used to justify and maintain a particular institution or state of affairs are sometimes known as **charter myths**. In Kirk's third category are explanatory or speculative myths. These may be simple **etiological myths** that explain the origin of an object, custom, or natural feature,[5] or they may be complex myths that try to answer the questions that have always troubled humanity, such as why people die. Some myths seem to acknowledge that these questions may be unanswerable but provide strategies for coping with the sorrows and contradictions of human life. Examples of all these different categories of myths can be found within Egyptian mythology. In order to explore this mythology, we must first look at the geography and history of Ancient Egypt.

MYTH AND GEOGRAPHY

Egypt is a large country in the northeast corner of the continent of Africa, but modern geographical terms have little relevance to how the Ancient Egyptians saw themselves. They had no conception of the huge size of Africa. In the third millennium BCE the Egyptians' known world extended only from what are now Greece and Turkey in the north to what is now Ethiopia in the south, and from Libya in the west to what is now Iraq in the east (see Map Two). The Egyptians believed that they were set apart from the people who lived in these surrounding countries. The ancient word *Kemet* (usually translated as Egypt) literally means Black Land. This referred to the rich black soil of the land on either bank of the great river Nile, which flows through the center of Egypt. The Egyptians were claiming to be the people of the valley, but they had not always been so.

For many millennia North Africa enjoyed a moist climate. Vast areas that are now desert were then grasslands with large animal populations. Nomadic peoples, all with a fairly similar culture, ranged across the grasslands. From around the sixth millennium BCE on, the climate became drier and hotter, and the grasslands gradually turned into desert. The first Egyptians built villages on the edges of the Nile valley, where they mainly survived by hunting and fishing. By the fourth millennium BCE, agriculture-based communities were established in the Nile valley and **Delta**. This great climatic and cultural change may have shaped the idea found in Egyptian myth that the world had once been different.

Egypt had become one of the driest places on earth and a hard country to get in or out of. To the north there were marshes, saltwater lakes, and the Mediterranean Sea. The Ancient Egyptians were never enthusiastic seafarers and were one of the few coastal cultures to worship no deities of the sea. To the east, west, and south there were deserts that were dangerous to cross. These deserts made up about 90 percent of Egypt's territory. The Egyptians called them the Red Land in contrast to the Black Land of the valley.[6] The mountainous areas of the deserts contained gold, gemstones, and types of hard stone that could be used to make long-lasting buildings and artifacts. The south of the country often went without rain for many years at a stretch. When rain did

Figure 1. The Nile Valley (Black Land) seen from the desert hills (Red Land). (Courtesy of Geraldine Pinch)

come, it was in the form of violent desert storms that could lead to destructive flash floods. The usually cloudless skies made it particularly easy for the Egyptians to observe the stars and planets. Much early mythology may have developed to explain the movement of celestial bodies.

The habitable part of Egypt was effectively a giant oasis created by the Nile and its annual flood, which is known as the inundation. Every year a combination of melting snows and monsoon rains in the mountains of Ethiopia caused a huge increase in the amount of water in the Nile. When the swollen river reached Egypt, it flooded all the low-lying land in the Nile valley and Delta, depositing a thick layer of silt.[7] As the floods went down, the fields were planted, and crops such as emmer wheat and barley grew very quickly in the moist, fertile soil. In a good year, the Egyptians could grow more grain than they needed to feed the population. In bad years, the flood might not be high enough to reach all the fields, or it might be too high and sweep away villages and towns and drown thousands of people. The whole welfare of the country depended on this one phenomenon, and because of this the Ancient Egyptians seem to have felt both uniquely blessed and uniquely vulnerable.

Aspects of the inundation were personified as deities (see "Hapy" in "Deities, Themes, and Concepts"), but there was no god or goddess of the Nile.

The annual rising of the Nile was thought of as part of the divine order of things decreed by a creator deity. This divine order was known as **maat**, and the creator was often identified with the god of the sun. The sun was the great provider of the light and warmth necessary for life. Its rays were also powerful enough to blind or kill. From early times on, the Egyptians believed that they needed a spiritual leader who could treat with the dangerous world of the gods on behalf of humanity. This leader was usually a king with semidivine status.

In Egypt, concepts that might in other cultures belong to the realm of abstract philosophy were expressed by symbols, images, and, to a lesser extent, myths. The divine order envisaged by the Egyptians placed their country at the center of the created world. This world was still surrounded by the primeval waters (the *nun*) from which the creator had originally emerged. The ultimate source of the Nile and the inundation was believed to be in the *nun*. Foreign lands and the deserts that bordered the Nile valley were said to belong to the realm of chaos (*isfet*), the force that constantly threatened the divine order.

There was a tradition that the creator and the numerous gods and goddesses whom he/she had created originally lived in Egypt itself. At the beginning of history they withdrew up into the heavens or down under the earth, though their spirits might be persuaded to reside in shrines built for them by the king. The Egyptians believed that some supernatural beings could still be encountered in the wilder regions of the earth, such as the remote desert and the areas of untamed marshland on the edges of the Nile valley and in parts of the Delta.

Many of the key events in Egyptian myth, such as the burial of the murdered god Osiris, were supposed to have happened in specific places in Egypt or in its neighboring countries. Thus a mythical geography can be superimposed on the physical geography. Every major Egyptian temple was designed as a miniature cosmos in which the main events in mythical history were repeatedly played out, so there came to be many "tombs of Osiris." It is this kind of apparent contradiction that has led many distinguished scholars to write about Egyptian myth in a tone of baffled irritation. G. S. Kirk complained that a "liberalism of interpretation, amounting at times to a chaotic indifference to consistency and meaning, is characteristic of Egyptian thought."[8] Much of this confusion can be resolved if the myths are examined in the contexts in which they occur, rather than in isolation.

HISTORY AND THE SOURCES OF EGYPTIAN MYTH

Ancient Egyptian religion had no official holy book equivalent to the Bible or the Koran (Quran). The relationships between deities did not become fixed at one moment in time but went on changing and developing for thousands of years. Egyptian mythology was never gathered by priests into one "authorized version" or harmonized in any long literary work comparable to Hesiod's *Theogony*, an important source for the study of Greek mythology. Comparatively few literary treatments of myths survive from any stage of the Egyptian language.

The mythology of Ancient Egypt has to be laboriously pieced together from a variety of written and visual sources. The extent and nature of these sources varied greatly during the 3,500 years that the native Pharaonic culture dominated Egypt. The remainder of this chapter will give a historical overview of the sources for Egyptian myth.

PROTODYNASTIC (DYNASTY 0) AND EARLY DYNASTIC PERIODS (DYNASTIES 1–2): C. 3200–2686 BCE

According to a tradition found in ancient chronologies, Egypt was originally divided into separate kingdoms of **Upper** (southern) and **Lower** (northern) **Egypt**. A King Menes was said to have united these kingdoms and founded a new capital at Memphis to be the "balance of the Two Lands." Menes cannot easily be identified with any specific king known from contemporary records.

Early Kings

There is plenty of archaeological evidence for a series of powerful southern kings in the late fourth millennium BCE. The hieroglyphic system of writing may have been invented for administrative and ritual purposes at the court of these kings.[9] Two early towns were associated with their rule: Nagada, later known as Ombos, where the local god was Seth, and Nekhen, later known as Hierakonpolis, where a falcon god was prominent. This falcon god came to be identified with Horus, although Horus seems to have been a northern god in origin.

There is much less evidence for a unified northern kingdom at this time. The gods Seth and Horus were later presented as warring opposites in need of reconciliation. Some Egyptologists have argued that a historical war between Ombos and Hierakonpolis, or between the north and south of Egypt, was the origin of the myth of the conflict between Horus and Seth.[10] This kind of "historicizing" approach to myth has been out of fashion for many years but has recently been revived.

Objects from the late Protodynastic Period belonging to kings called Narmer, Aha, and Scorpion have been recovered from temple deposits at Hierakonpolis and Abydos. These kings may have been rulers of most of Egypt. They probably all contributed to the legend of Menes the Uniter. Their ritual objects belong to a formative stage in Egyptian art. Strict rules were being developed to govern the content and style of the art used in palaces, temples, or tombs. This formal court-based art rapidly replaced previous styles and became the standard canon for over 3,000 years.[11] Myths often focus on episodes of intense conflict or tragedy, but the Egyptian rules of "decorum" usually made it impermissible to illustrate such episodes in formal art. The images used in art were felt to have power to affect the real world, so order had to be shown triumphing over chaos and good over evil. Violent mythical episodes such as that in which Seth tears out the eye of Horus were not represented directly.

The King and the Gods

From the First Dynasty onward, every Egyptian king was called a Horus. The extent to which Egyptian rulers were regarded as divine is much disputed,[12] but the kings of the Early Dynastic Period certainly enjoyed more power and responsibility than anyone else in their culture. They were rulers of the first large nation-state in history. The king was the political, religious, and military leader of this state. Royal annals for the Early Dynastic Period partially survive in a copy on the Palermo Stone and related fragments.[13] The annals list the kings of Egypt, starting with a series of prehistoric kings.

Seal impressions and small bone or wood labels of the Early Dynastic Period portray kings engaging with a variety of deities.[14] Mesopotamian seals and sealings of a comparable date appear to show episodes or characters from myths set in the realm of the gods. The Egyptian pieces mainly show deities as "resident" in statues or cult objects in man-made shrines. The labels record (or anticipate) visits by kings to shrines in different parts of the country. The royal annals record many years for which the most important events were deemed to be the dedication of **cult images** or the king's participation in rituals, such as visiting the sacred lake of the god Heryshef ("He who is upon his lake") or "spearing the hippopotamus."[15]

There is plenty of evidence by the Early Dynastic Period for a complex pantheon of Egyptian deities who could be represented in a variety of human, animal, or semihuman forms. Whether myths about these deities were current at this stage is hard to say. The unification of the country and the subsequent patronage of local cults by each king must have led to some kind of organization of the pantheon at this time. Deities began to be grouped into pairs, groups, or hierarchies. The creation of relationships between deities who had previously been worshipped in isolation may have generated myths.

Among the earliest pairings of deities were the Two Ladies and the Two Lords. The Two Ladies were the goddesses Nekhbet and Wadjyt. In the symbolic language that had developed to express ideas about kingship, the Two Ladies represented Upper and Lower Egypt and were identified with the White Crown of the south and the Red Crown of the north. The Two Lords were Horus and Seth. Most Early Dynastic Period kings associated themselves with Horus by showing a Horus falcon on the *serekh* that enclosed their names. The names and titles taken by a king at the start of his reign identified the ways in which he manifested Horus and acted as a kind of policy statement.

During the Second Dynasty a king called Peribsen replaced the Horus falcon with the curious composite animal that represented the god Seth. Peribsen may have been trying to assert the primacy of his local god, but he seems to have lost his throne to a king called Khasekhemwy from Hierakonpolis. Khasekhemwy placed both the Horus falcon and the Seth animal above his name and included the phrase "the Two Lords are at rest in him" in his title. This seems to be an early example of the Egyptian tendency to present actual conflicts in mythological terms.

Two sculptures of Khasekhemwy wearing the White Crown may be the oldest known statues of a specific historical ruler from anywhere in the world. The king's enemies are shown as a chaotic mass of contorted figures under his feet, so the statues embody the triumph of order over chaos. The reign of Khasekhemwy seems to have marked a change in royal policy. Recent excavations have confirmed that he built several huge funerary complexes at several different sites. A greater proportion of the country's resources seems to have been diverted toward the royal mortuary cult. The emphasis was shifting from a system in which the king honored the gods and goddesses in their local shrines to one in which the gods and goddesses were brought together to help sanctify the king in life and the afterlife.

This trend developed further in the Third Dynasty. Some Egyptologists place the Third Dynasty at the end of the Early Dynastic Period, whereas others put it at the beginning of the Old Kingdom. Ancient Egyptian king lists gave particular prominence to a Third Dynasty ruler called Netjerikhet, later known as Djoser (Zoser). His reign was regarded as the beginning of a new era.

OLD KINGDOM (DYNASTIES 3–6) AND
FIRST INTERMEDIATE PERIOD (DYNASTIES 7–11):
C. 2686–2055 BCE

In later times the Egyptians looked back on the Old Kingdom as a golden age of stability and achievement. King Djoser was remembered for thousands of years as the king for whom the first pyramid was built. This was the step pyramid at Saqqara, one of the world's earliest great stone buildings. Early Dynastic kings had high-walled funerary enclosures in mud brick and separate tombs under great mounds. The two forms were put together at Saqqara, so the mound had to become higher to be visible above the great enclosure walls. A mound was also found as the focal point of some early temples, such as at Hierakonpolis. Such mounds may represent the Primeval Mound that features in Egyptian creation myths (see "Deities, Themes, and Concepts"), but there is no written evidence from this period to confirm this.

The Pyramid Builders

The man in charge of building the pyramid complex of Djoser was an official named Imhotep. At this period, literacy was mainly confined to such officials and their households. Many of these officials served as part-time priests in the cult places of deities and deceased kings.[16] Imhotep, who was a priest of the sun god at Heliopolis, was later credited with writing a book of wisdom. This earned him a place as the first of Egypt's great sages and eventual deification (see "Deities, Themes, and Concepts"). The tradition may reflect an actual advance in the uses of writing at this period.

The development of long, connected texts only seems to have taken place in Egypt centuries after the introduction of writing. An incomplete **naos** (inner shrine) from Heliopolis that dates to Djoser's reign is carved with some of the earliest known integrated texts and reliefs. The images of the gods shown in the carvings on the naos are accompanied by short speeches saying what they will do for the king. These images may be the oldest surviving representation of the Ennead of Heliopolis, a group of nine deities that was very important in the creation myths recorded in later times. Some of these myths could already have been current, but whether they were written down or existed only in oral form is not clear. A type of religious text that does seem to have developed in this period was the topographical list.[17] This listed deities according to their cult places and summarized their functions and qualities with epithets. Some epithets, such as Horus, "protector of his father," suggest the existence of a story behind them.

In the Fourth Dynasty the king's role was redefined as being "'the son of Ra," the deputy of the sun god on earth. Sneferu, the first king of the Fourth Dynasty, was one of Egypt's greatest builders. Three pyramids were completed in his reign, each with two temples for the funerary cult of the king. Later literary tradition was favorable to Sneferu but not to his successor Khufu (Cheops), the builder of the Great Pyramid at Giza (see under "Kings and Princes" and "Magicians" in "Deities, Themes, and Concepts"). Writing in the fifth century BCE, the Greek historian Herodotus reported a legend that King Khufu had been cursed by the gods for closing down their temples to divert resources to his pyramid.

Archaeological evidence suggests an element of truth to this tradition. Local temples seem to have received little royal support during the Fourth and Fifth Dynasties. The huge **pyramid complexes** of this era seem to concentrate wholly on the divinity of the king, but this is partly an accident of preservation. Reliefs and statues in the badly damaged pyramid temples did once show the king interacting with many of the deities of Egypt. Pyramid complexes have been interpreted as "resurrection machines" for the king and as models of the Egyptian cosmos, making them a kind of mythology in solid form.[18] The kings of the Fifth Dynasty had smaller pyramids, but several of them built magnificent temples for the sun god.

The favored elite who served Old Kingdom rulers were rewarded with beautifully decorated tombs in the royal cemeteries. Many of these tomb owners had personal names that linked them with deities, such as Ptah-hotep ("the god Ptah is satisfied"). The inscriptions in their tombs tell us that many of them were part-time priests in the temples and shrines of deities, but at this period it was not permissible to show even a statue of a deity in a private tomb. The prevailing reticence about religion in daily life makes it difficult to know much about the gods at this period. A rich new source of evidence appeared in the twenty-fourth century BCE, when hieroglyphic inscriptions were carved inside the pyramid tomb of King Weni (Unas). These inscriptions, composed in the language known as Old Egyptian, are now called the **Pyramid Texts**.

The Pyramid Texts

The Pyramid Texts are the oldest of the three principal collections of Egyptian funerary literature.[19] They are also among the earliest religious writings known from anywhere in the world. The texts are divided into sections; each is preceded by an Egyptian phrase meaning "words to be spoken" but sometimes translated

Figure 2. A section of the Pyramid Texts in the antechamber of the pyramid of King Weni. The antechamber represented the Akhet, the place where the dead king would be transformed and rise again like the sun above the horizon. (Courtesy of Princeton University)

as "spell" or "incantation." These incantations can be as short as a single sentence or many paragraphs long. The pyramid of King Weni contains around 300 incantations, but more than 800 are currently known. Pyramid Texts have been found in the pyramids of five Old Kingdom kings and three queens. No two pyramids have exactly the same selection.

No illustrations accompany the Pyramid Texts, though the ceilings of royal burial chambers were usually decorated with stars. Many hieroglyphic signs consist of images of living creatures. In the writing of the Pyramid Texts, potentially harmful creatures such as snakes, scorpions, and some kinds of birds and people are often shown dismembered or skewered with knives. This suggests that there was a strong fear of the latent power of images during this period.

The texts themselves seem to have been adapted from a variety of genres, such as hymns, lists of divine names and epithets, spells from the type of magic used in daily life, and the "recitations" that accompanied ritual actions. Many were composed in the first person and would have been highly dramatic when spoken or chanted aloud. Some of the incantations may have been passed down orally for many generations and only written down when the Pyramid Texts were first assembled. The majority of the texts probably belong to the "secret knowledge" written on leather or papyrus rolls, which is known to have been kept in the libraries attached to some Old Kingdom palaces and temples. The composing, copying, and reading out of these sacred books were the province of a special class of priests, known as **lector priests**. No actual books of this kind have survived from the Old Kingdom, and they are rare from later periods too. No major temple library has ever been discovered intact, and this gap is one of many in the sources for Egyptian myth.

The main purpose of assembling these texts and inscribing them inside pyramids was to help the body of the deceased king to escape the horror of putrefaction and his spirit to ascend to the celestial realm where he would take his place among the gods. Some of the texts were probably recited during the king's funeral or as part of the mortuary cult that continued after his death. Others may have been intended to be spoken by the deceased king as he entered the afterlife. In this type of incantation, the king took on the role of many different deities.

Around 200 deities are mentioned in the Pyramid Texts. Some are the major deities already known from cult temples, such the fertility god Min and the creator goddess Neith. Others are entities such as snake deities and celestial ferrymen who inhabit a complex and intensely imagined realm of the gods. The most frequently mentioned deities are Anubis, Atum, Geb, Horus, Isis, Nephthys, Nut, Osiris, Ra, Seth, Shu, and Thoth (see "Deities, Themes, and Concepts"). These include most of the deities who make up the Ennead of Heliopolis, and it is often argued that the Pyramid Texts largely represent the theology of the solar temple at Heliopolis. A stellar element was also important in the Pyramid Texts. The king was destined to join the "imperishable stars," and the god Osiris was identified with the constellation of Orion and the goddess Isis with the Dog Star, Sirius.[20] The cult of Osiris is hardly known before the Fifth Dynasty, but he gradually became the most important funerary god.

One thing the Pyramid Texts are not is a collection of narrative myths. They do contain numerous allusions to myths, many of which are difficult to interpret. Some passages include what have been called "mythical statements." These give the bare outlines of an event that has taken place in the divine realm, such as "Horus comes and Thoth appears. They raise up Osiris from upon his side and make him stand erect in front of the two Enneads."[21]

Many of the most important themes of Egyptian mythology, such as the journey of the sun god in his solar barque, the murder of the good god Osiris, and the violent conflict between Horus and Seth, are already present in the Pyramid Texts. These texts are also the earliest source for the complex array of myths and symbols that the Egyptians constructed on the theme of creation. The gods as depicted in the Pyramid Texts often seem violent, hostile, and terrifying beings, and this is a consistent picture in Egyptian funerary texts.

Near the end of the Sixth Dynasty, sections of the Pyramid Texts began to be used in the tombs of important but nonroyal people in various parts of Egypt.

This has been seen as one of the symptoms of a breakdown of royal authority that led to the fall of the Old Kingdom.[22] In the twenty-second century BCE, Egypt entered a time of disunity, which historians call the First Intermediate Period.

There were still kings ruling from Memphis, but they did not control the whole country. A rival dynasty emerged from a place called Herakleopolis. One of these kings was traditionally credited with writing the remarkable work known as the Teaching for King Merikare. This text mentions a brutal civil war in which the king had been involved. Later Egyptian literature generally portrayed the First Intermediate Period as a time of chaos and misery when the gods had withdrawn their blessing.

Only one First Intermediate Period king had a pyramid inscribed with Pyramid Texts, but they continued to be used in some private burials.[23] A group who benefited from the relaxation of royal authority was the **nomarchs** (provincial governors). These nomarchs had close ties with their local temples, and it was probably among the priesthood of these temples that an innovative new body of funerary texts began to develop. The independence of the nomarchs and the period of disunity were brought to an end in the late twenty-first century BCE by a king called Nebhepetra Montuhotep (Mentuhotep), who came from the southern city of Thebes.

MIDDLE KINGDOM AND SECOND INTERMEDIATE PERIOD (DYNASTIES 11–17): C. 2055–1550 BCE

Once Nebhepetra Montuhotep was established as king of all Egypt, he ruled from Memphis, but he built shrines for important gods all over the country. He was eventually buried at western Thebes in a mortuary complex whose chief feature seems to have been a representation of the Primeval Mound, the place where creation began.

In the twentieth century BCE, kings of the Twelfth Dynasty built a new royal residence called Itjtawy and were buried under pyramids at various desert sites. None of these royal tombs was inscribed inside. Elaborate temples for the royal mortuary cult were built near these pyramids, but none of them has survived in good condition. Nor have many of the temples built for deities during this period survived. One tantalizing text known as the Ramesseum Dramatic Papyrus seems to be the script for a religious ritual in which the king took part in the reenactment of mythical events, such as the coronation of the god Horus (see Figure 3).[24]

More is known about the religious life of the government officials and their families who formed the elite of Egyptian society. In their decorated tombs, no-

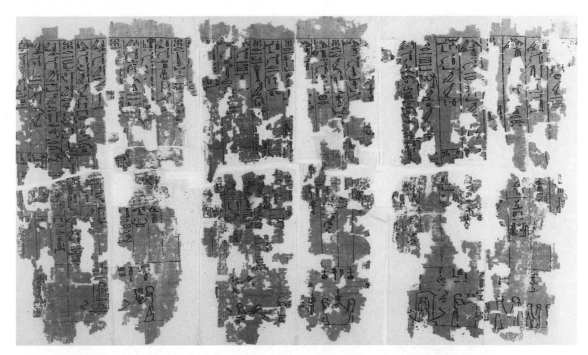

Figure 3. A page from the Ramesseum Dramatic Papyrus. This Middle Kingdom papyrus contains the script for a royal ritual based on mythical events. (British Museum)

marchs could be shown presiding over religious festivals and venerating sacred objects. Other modes of religious activity and belief could be presented in encoded ways.[25] Short hymns to deities, of the type that might have been sung at festivals, start to be written on tomb walls or funerary **stelae**. The coffins in elite burials of this period were sometimes painted with texts and scenes that formed part of the second of the major collections of funerary literature: the **Coffin Texts** (CT).

The Coffin Texts

Coffin Texts is a modern name for the diverse body of spells or recitations used on burial equipment during the Middle Kingdom. These texts were mainly painted on wooden coffins, but they also appeared on tomb walls and on funerary items such as stelae and **canopic** chests. The Coffin Texts were composed in Middle Egyptian, a form of the Egyptian language that became standard for literary works. The texts were usually written in cursive (simplified) hieroglyphs, but some examples are in **hieratic**, a script developed for administrative and lit-

Figure 4. Outer coffin of Gua. Middle Kingdom coffin painted with a map showing the safest routes for the soul to take through the underworld. Such maps formed part of the Book of Two Ways. (British Museum)

erary uses. Modern editors of the Coffin Texts have so far assembled 1,185 different spells. Only a small selection of these was used in any one burial.

Many spells in the Coffin Texts are also known from versions in the Pyramid Texts. Both collections may derive from an archive of mortuary texts written on papyrus that does not survive. Some of the Coffin Texts spells are given titles that define their function, such as Spell for Navigating in the Great

Barque of Ra, or include instructions for the rituals that should accompany them. A few spells incorporate elaborate glosses to explain obscure passages. These may reflect the way that religious knowledge was expounded among the elite. Some spells are monologues spoken in the person of a deity, beginning with phrases such as "I am the Inundation-deity who provides food"(CT 320); others are dialogues between deities that amount to miniature religious dramas. A few sections of the Coffin Texts have **vignettes**: illustrations that form an integral part of the spell. The most elaborate of these are the maps that belong to a section of the Coffin Texts known as the Book of Two Ways (see Figure 4). [26]

These maps, which were usually painted on the floor of coffins, are the earliest known maps from any culture. The Book of Two Ways was nothing less than an illustrated guidebook to the afterlife. It claimed to give two routes (by water and by land) through a sinister divine realm beyond the horizon and to provide the deceased with the spells they would need to get past the monstrous guardians they would meet on the way. The deceased had to pass through the mysterious region of Rosetau, where the body of Osiris lay surrounded by walls of flame. If the deceased man or woman proved worthy, he or she might be granted a new life in a paradise called the Field of Offerings. The Book of Two Ways has been described by Erik Hornung as representing "the results of government-funded research into the hereafter,"[27] but research may be too academic a word. The extraordinary visual detail in which the afterlife is presented has a hallucinatory quality similar to that of the "spirit voyages" induced by shamans in many cultures. [28]

Although they are not narratives, some spells in the Coffin Texts describe major events in the Egyptian creation story and even provide evidence for Egyptian views about the end of the world (see "Return to Chaos" under "Linear Time" in "Mythical Time Lines"). The creator god Atum-Ra and his offspring Shu and Tefnut are particularly prominent. Many texts deal with transformations of the sun god into various forms. A new element is a stress on the dangers faced by the sun god during his celestial voyages, such as attacks by the chaos monster Apophis. The prominence of the solar cult leads some Egyptologists to believe that the Coffin Texts were, like the Pyramid Texts, mainly generated by the priests of Heliopolis. Other Egyptologists point to the huge range of deities that feature in this collection and see the Coffin Texts as being more representative of regional traditions.[29]

Coffin Texts spells have been found in sites all over Egypt, but the majority come from the geographical region known as **Middle Egypt**. The local deities of Middle Egypt, such as Thoth and the group of primeval beings later known as the Ogdoad of Hermopolis, feature in many of the spells. Thoth also appears in many of the spells that allude to the conflict between Horus and Seth and the rescue of the body of Osiris. By the time of the Coffin Texts, all the elite dead could be identified with Osiris, the god who died and rose again.

Literature

The same learned class of priest-officials who composed or used the Coffin Texts were also the writers and readers of Middle Kingdom literature. The hymns that were sung to deities each dawn in temples and when statues of deities left their sanctuaries during festivals can contain beautiful poetry.[30] Such hymns were sometimes copied onto papyrus to be enjoyed as literature or inscribed on stelae dedicated by pious individuals. Middle Kingdom hymns mainly consist of sequences of divine epithets, but these can be helpful in reconstructing the myths that may have been current about deities in this period.

Popular in the Middle Kingdom were texts in which a father instructs his son on the right way to behave in life. These are often known as Instruction or Wisdom Texts. One of the topics Instruction Texts deal with is the proper relationship between humanity and the gods, so they sometimes allude to mythical events, such as the sun god's decision to destroy rebellious humanity. Other literary works that deal with ethical issues are in the form of prophecies or dialogues between a man and a supernatural being.[31]

In a text comparable to the biblical Book of Job, a man named Ipuur (Ipuwer) questions the Lord of All about why suffering and injustice are rife in Egypt. The god's replies are not very well preserved in the only surviving manuscript, but the gist is that people must accept responsibility for their own actions.[32] Some Egyptologists assign the Dialogue of Ipuur to a genre of pessimistic literature that describes Egypt as a society in chaos. It used to be thought that these texts were written during the turbulent First Intermediate Period or very shortly afterward, but they have now been redated to the high Middle Kingdom or even to the Second Intermediate Period. The texts mythologize the past in order to praise the present or predict the future. They see Egypt as a battleground in a continuing cosmic struggle between order and chaos.

Literary narratives had developed by this period, though only a few have survived. There was almost certainly a parallel tradition of oral storytelling. Most Egyptian texts were intended for reading aloud, and stories could have passed from an oral tradition into a written one and back again, as they have in Arab storytelling in more recent times.[33] In some Middle Kingdom stories, gods feature as characters. If the definition of myth as "stories about gods" is accepted, these narratives might count as myths, but they are really about people who happen to encounter gods. Another common definition of myth is "stories about the world of the gods," but these Middle Kingdom tales are set in the human world, sometimes in a specific historical period.

A series of linked stories set in the Third and Fourth Dynasties describes marvels performed by the magicians of this era, such as transforming a wax crocodile into a real one.[34] In the framing story, five deities disguise themselves as people to help a mortal woman who is about to give birth to triplets destined to be kings. An incomplete story tells of an alarming encounter between a herdsman and a seductive goddess.[35] Another relates how an official sent on a mission was shipwrecked on a mysterious island.[36] There he encounters a giant serpent who seems to be a form of the creator sun god.

One Middle Kingdom narrative that only features divine characters is a fragmentary story about the attempted seduction of Horus by Seth, an event alluded to in the Pyramid Texts. Some Egyptologists refuse to class this as a genuine myth because it may have formed part of a spell used in healing magic.[37]

Magic and Popular Religion

Heka, the Egyptian term usually translated as "magic," was one of the forces used by the creator to make the world. Humans were permitted to use magic in daily life to protect themselves or to heal others. Knowledge of written magic was confined to the literate elite, so it is not surprising that some spells have a distinct literary quality. Healing spells often identify the doctor-magician with a deity skilled in the use of *heka*, such as Isis or Thoth; the patient with a deity who suffered in myth, such as Horus the Child (see "Deities, Themes, and Concepts"); and the disease or problem with a hostile supernatural force.

These identifications were sometimes extended into a narrative of the misfortune that befell the deity and its ultimate resolution. A complex story about the poisoning of the sun god, known as the True Name of Ra (see "Period of Direct Rule by the Creator Sun God" under "Linear Time" in "Mythical Time Lines"), is an example that may have been composed as early as the Middle Kingdom. By creating these links, the doctor-magician hoped to mobilize cosmic forces to act on behalf of the patient as they once had on behalf of the deity. J. F. Borghouts, who has edited and translated many of the magical texts, commented that although some mythical themes that occur in spells are not known from other sources, "There is, however, not a shred of proof that a specific kind of 'unorthodox' mythology was especially coined *à bout portant* for this genre."[38] Indeed, the efficacy of such spells may have partly depended on the patients' being familiar with the story of which they were being made a part.

Similar links between human and divine events were created in visual form on magical objects of the Middle Kingdom and Second Intermediate Period. Ivory wands that were used to protect newborn children and their mothers show a wide array of divine beings, some in monstrous forms (see Figure 30). Many of these have been identified with the deities of Middle Egypt who feature in the Coffin Texts. Brief inscriptions on some of the wands state that these deities have come to fight on behalf of a particular child. The wands seem to be based on a myth of an endangered divine child hundreds of years before such a myth is clearly delineated in narrative sources. Some of the creatures shown on the wands, such as the griffin, feature in Egyptian animal fables known from much later periods.

The wands suggest an almost lost world of oral traditions concerning the gods. They were also among the first private objects to include depictions of deities, although most of these are not in the formal style found in temples. The late Middle Kingdom and the Second Intermediate Period were times of intellectual and religious change. At the height of the Twelfth Dynasty, the power and influence of the provincial elites had been suppressed by the crown. This seems to have been one of the factors that led to a decline in the use of the Coffin Texts.

By the Thirteenth Dynasty royal authority was also in decline, and this may have led to greater freedom of expression in religious art and literature. Images of deities started to be shown on votive objects dedicated by nonroyal people, particularly in the holy city of Abydos. Middle Kingdom inscriptions tell of festivals at Abydos in which large numbers of people joined in ceremonies that reenacted key events in the myth of Osiris.[39] It was around this time that an ancient royal tomb at Abydos was reidentified as the burial place of Osiris. This merging of mythical and physical geography was to become increasingly characteristic of Egyptian culture.

That culture seemed to suffer a setback when a Palestinian dynasty took control of the Delta region of northern Egypt during the seventeenth century BCE. These foreign rulers, known as the Hyksos, established a capital at Avaris, a region where Seth was the leading deity. Seth was equated with the Palestinian god Baal, and the worship of foreign goddesses such as Astarte and Anat (see "Deities, Themes, and Concepts") seems to have been introduced into Egypt at this time.

Hyksos kings called themselves Sons of Ra, but one of them bore the name of Ra's archenemy Apophis.[40] A legend tells how King Apophis picked a quarrel with the Egyptian ruler of the Theban area by complaining that the roaring of the hippopotami kept 500 miles away in Thebes was disturbing his sleep.[41] This New Kingdom story restates the political conflict in mythological terms by making it into a fight between the Followers of Horus (the Thebans) and the hippopotamus-worshipping Followers of Seth (the Hyksos). The Theban rulers who made up the Seventeenth Dynasty gradually drove the Hyksos out of Egypt. Under the Seventeenth Dynasty, a new collection of funerary texts developed that was to become the famous Book of the Dead. The expulsion of the Hyksos was completed by King Ahmose I (c.1550–1525 BCE). The Egyptians considered him to be the first king of a new dynasty and a new era.

NEW KINGDOM (DYNASTIES 18–20) AND THIRD INTERMEDIATE PERIOD (DYNASTIES 21–24): C. 1550–747 BCE

Ahmose, and the other warrior kings of the early Eighteenth Dynasty, took Egyptian armies as far as the Euphrates. They established an empire in Syria and Palestine and took control of much of Nubia. In the late sixteenth century BCE, the royal court moved back to Memphis, but Thebes became the religious capital. Most New Kingdom rulers were buried there in underground tombs in the desert wadi now known as the Valley of the Kings (see Figure 5). The offering cults for the dead kings were carried out in separate mortuary temples some way from their tombs. Amun, who had been the most important god in Thebes since the Middle Kingdom, united with the sun god and became the King of the Gods. The temple of Amun at Karnak in eastern Thebes developed into the biggest and richest temple complex in Egypt.

The Eighteenth Dynasty is often considered the high point of Egyptian culture. Much great art and architecture was produced during the reigns of Queen Hatshepsut (c. 1473–1458 BCE); her nephew and stepson, King Thutmose (Tuthmosis) III (c. 1479–1425 BCE); and the latter's great-grandson, Amenhotep (Amenophis) III (c. 1390–1352 BCE). Hatshepsut's famous mortuary temple at Deir el-Bahri in Thebes had many innovative features, such as an open court for solar worship inscribed with a summary of the ruler's secret knowledge about the sun god.[42] Both Hatshepsut and Thutmose III built special shrines where ordinary people could come to pray to deities such as the goddess Hathor in her cow form or Amun "of the Hearing Ear."[43] Amenhotep III enlarged or founded numerous temples, and many of the features introduced by his architects remained standard for c. 1,500 years. He commissioned huge numbers of divine statues to stress his identification with all the deities of Egypt. Amenhotep III sometimes gave himself the attributes of a lunar deity while his chief wife, Queen Tiy, was identified with the goddesses who could play the role of the **solar eye** (see "Eye of Ra" in "Deities, Themes, and Concepts").[44]

Figure 5. View of the desert hills at western Thebes showing the pyramid-shaped mountain peak that overlooks the Valley of the Kings. (Courtesy of Richard Pinch)

Amenhotep III and Tiy were the parents of Amenhotep IV (c. 1352–1336 BCE), who early in his reign changed his name to Akhenaten. King Akhenaten and his chief wife, Nefertiti, were dedicated to the cult of Aten, a form of the sun god represented by the solar disk. Akhenaten built huge temples for Aten that were open to the sky. He established a new capital and a new royal burial ground at Akhetaten (modern Tell el-Amarna). Akhenaten suppressed the cult of Amun, but the idea that he closed down all of Egypt's temples seems to be an exaggeration.[45] In Akhenaten's theology the worship of Aten as the creator sun god and the king as his representative on earth made other deities and their myths superfluous. Belief in a separate realm of the dead ruled by Osiris was replaced by the idea that spirits of the dead could live on in the Aten temples.

Akhenaten's religious and political policies were not popular, and under the boy king Tutankhamun (Tutankhamon) (c. 1336–1327 BCE), Thebes was reestablished as the religious capital and Amun-Ra as the national god. Horemheb (c. 1323–1295 BCE), the last king of the Eighteenth Dynasty, presented Akhenaten's reign as a time of chaos in which the gods had abandoned Egypt. Horemheb was succeeded by his vizier Rameses (Ramses, Ramesses), the founder of the Nineteenth Dynasty. Rameses' son, Seti (Sety) I (c. 1294–1279 BCE), was a vigorous king who reestablished Egyptian authority over parts of Syria, but the art of his reign has a serene beauty. Seti's son Rameses II ruled Egypt for sixty-seven years and became a legend in the ancient world for his grandiose achievements. His battles against the Hittite empire were celebrated in narratives, poetry, and pictures on the walls of the numerous temples he constructed in Egypt and Nubia. Rameses eventually made peace with the Hittites and married two Hittite princesses. He constructed a new capital in the eastern Delta, but he did not neglect Thebes. The 21-meter-high columns of the central hall at Karnak built under Seti I and Rameses II give a sense of limitless power.

After Rameses' long and prosperous reign, the international situation became more difficult for Egypt. His son Merenptah had to fight off invasions by the Libyans and the mass migration known as the Sea Peoples. The same enemies in even greater numbers faced Rameses III (c. 1184–1153 BCE), the second king of the Twentieth Dynasty. He defeated them by sea and land in battles that are recorded on the walls of his fortresslike mortuary temple at Medinet Habu. This whole temple is a monument to the triumph of order over chaos, but Rameses III was the last great temple builder of the New Kingdom.

Temples and Kings

Throughout the New Kingdom much of the wealth generated by the empire and by the exploitation of Egyptian and Nubian gold fields was spent on building and endowing temples. All over the country the small, mainly mud-brick, temples that had been common in earlier periods were replaced by large stone structures whose walls were carved with hieroglyphic texts and scenes of kings with deities. Major temples were like small towns, with their own granaries, slaughterhouses, workshops, offices, schools, libraries, and housing. Large numbers of priests, some working full-time, were needed to run such temples.[46]

Like the pyramid complexes of the Old Kingdom, New Kingdom temples were models of the Egyptian cosmos.[47] The undulating mud-brick walls that surrounded temples may have represented the primeval waters that were thought to surround the inhabited world. Sacred lakes were used for reenactments of myths of the emergence of the creator from the primeval waters or for the pacification of his fiery daughter, the Eye goddess. In the outer courtyard the king was represented in reliefs or colossal statues as the champion of *maat*. The battles that he was shown fighting were sometimes real and sometimes imaginary, but the foreign enemies always represented the forces of chaos.[48] The massive **pylon** gateways resemble defensive structures, but they also stood for the mountains of the eastern horizon, between which the sun rose. The plant-shaped columns of the inner halls formed a stone replica of the marsh where gods were born or reborn. The innermost sanctuary that contained the

Figure 6. The Osireion at Abydos was built to represent both the Primeval Mound and the tomb of the god Osiris. (Courtesy of Richard Pinch)

cult statue was said to be built on the Primeval Mound, the very place in which the creator first brought forth life.

Each temple was dedicated to one main deity, but in the New Kingdom it became common to group deities into divine "families," with subsidiary temples for the chief deity's consort and child. So at Karnak, for example, Amun was worshipped as part of a triad, with Mut as his consort and Khonsu as his son. Not all these groupings seem to have been based on existing myths, but some of them eventually generated myths to explain features of their cult. The relationships between deities could be expressed by moving divine statues between temples during religious festivals. These processions, in which the god was carried inside a boat-shaped shrine, gave ordinary people their only chance to get close to the sacred images of their deities.

The names of some of the festivals listed in temple calendars suggest that reenactments of myths were involved, but such reenactments were rarely depicted. The majority of New Kingdom temple reliefs show a ritualized exchange between the king representing humanity and a deity representing the divine realm. The king makes offerings or performs rituals. The god responds with a gesture or an object that symbolizes the bestowal of divine gifts, such as long life or power. Among exceptions are scenes that form a narrative sequence about the divine conception and birth of rulers such as Hatshepsut, Amenhotep III, and Rameses II.[49]

It is typical of Egyptian pictorial narratives that some incidents or details are only found in the text whereas others are shown only in the reliefs. The text, for instance, describes a sensuous encounter between a queen and the god Amun, who has taken the form of her husband in order to sleep with her. The accompanying relief complies with the strict rules of Egyptian art and shows the god, in his usual appearance, barely touching the queen's hand (see Figure 20). The queen gives birth to the future ruler surrounded by deities who will nurse and protect the child and its spirit-double, the *ka*. This royal birth scene may be based on mythical prototypes, but it predates all the known depictions of the birth of infant gods. Greek myth has equivalent stories of Zeus's disguising himself to seduce mortal women, but their focus is on very human emotions of lust and jealousy. The seductions by Zeus are set in a mythical age of heroes, and the god's behavior may be criticized. In Egypt, such stories were a solemn part of the myth of divine kingship and were told about living people.

Each Egyptian king was the "son" of the supreme creator god Amun-Ra but also Horus, the avenger of his father, Osiris. Some New Kingdom rulers took a renewed interest in the holy city of Abydos and the cult of Osiris. Ironically, the finest temple at Abydos was built by Seti I, a king who was named after Seth, the great enemy of Osiris.[50] This temple of Seti I is so large and well preserved that its scenes and inscriptions have been used to reconstruct the daily ritual that went on in every Egyptian temple. This ritual was influenced by the concept of the daily rebirth of the sun god and by the myth of the death and resurrection of Osiris.[51]

Some episodes from the Osiris myth are shown in the temple of Seti I, with the king in the role of Horus. These include a very rare depiction of Isis in bird form magically conceiving Horus by sexually arousing her murdered husband. This was a moment of triumph and hope, but it was still not intended to be seen by any but the highest grade of priests. The murder of Osiris was not shown on the walls of Seti's temple, but he was celebrated as a dead god in a remarkable building known as the Osireion (see Figure 6).[52] This was built in the style of an ancient royal tomb. A long passage leads down to an underground hall where a sarcophagus once stood on an artificial island surrounded by water, providing a symbolic tomb for the king. An adjoining chamber is inscribed with the images and texts that form the Book of Nut, a major source for reconstructing Egyptian **cosmology**.

A hymn inscribed on a New Kingdom private stela from Abydos provides the most detailed account in Egyptian of the Osiris myth.[53] After the usual lists of divine epithets, there is a section of narrative verse that begins with Osiris "appearing on his father's throne" and ends with Horus being acclaimed as his rightful successor. If this were our only source for the myth, the story would be very difficult to follow because the actual death of Osiris is not mentioned and his enemy is only identified as "the disturber." Rules still prevented explicit images of those moments when *maat* was threatened by terrible events. There was one place in which it did become permissible to show the forces that daily threatened the divine balance, and that was in New Kingdom royal tombs. In the great crisis of death, the king needed to identify with gods in crisis and share in their triumph in overcoming the forces of destruction.

Underworld Books

Underworld Book is a general term for a type of mortuary text used in royal tombs and cenotaphs of the New Kingdom. It is taken from an Egyptian term for the genre to which these books belonged: "that which is in the underworld." The earliest of these books, the Book of the Hidden Chamber (now known as the Amduat), may be derived from solar rituals performed by the king at Heliopolis and other temples. The versions on the walls of the tomb of Thutmose III and his successor Amenhotep II look as if they have been directly copied from a papyrus scroll (e.g. Figure 45). This gives us an idea of what these temple copies must have been like.

By the end of the New Kingdom about twelve different books were in use.[54] They were painted on the walls or ceilings of the tomb or inscribed on important items of burial equipment such as shrines and shrouds. The books were composed in Middle Egyptian, but the later ones show considerable influence from Late Egyptian, a form of the language current in writing from the late Eighteenth Dynasty onward. The texts are all written in hieroglyphs, but sometimes in ways that make them difficult to read. These books contained very restricted knowledge, which was supposed to be known only to the king and people who held high-ranking priestly offices.

The purpose of the Underworld Books was to maintain the cosmos and, secondarily, to aid the king's transition to the afterlife through his identification with the sun god. Their common theme was the daily journey of the sun god, Ra-Atum. Most concentrated on his perilous passage through the night sky, which was equated with the underworld. The dangerous journey is probably the world's oldest narrative motif, but the Underworld Books are not presented as stories. The structure of the books is provided by the passing of time[55] or by the geography of the underworld, which was imagined as divided into caverns or regions separated by guarded gates. Every Underworld Book presents a different view of the topography of the afterlife, yet from the late Eighteenth Dynasty on, royal tombs included more than one book in their decoration.[56]

The pictorial element is dominant in most of the Underworld Books. With a few exceptions, the text is mainly in the form of captions to the images. Underworld Books such as the Book of Gates and the Book of Caverns are essentially more detailed forms of the maps of the underworld found on Middle Kingdom coffins. Each hour or gate or cavern is represented by giant tableaux of hundreds of deities, demons, and monsters. Some Egyptologists have called such groupings "image-clusters." Individual symbols can modify their meaning when incorporated into one of these clusters.

These secret books admit the vulnerabilty of the divine order and illustrate the ordeals faced by the creator sun god. Virtually the entire cast of Egyptian mythology is drawn in to crew the sun boat and defend the sun god from Apophis and the other chaos monsters. Even more remarkably, the corpses of Osiris and the rest of the dead can be shown waiting for their temporary revival by the sun god in the sixth hour of the night. The Osireion at Abydos was probably constructed as a setting for this mystical union between Ra and Osiris.

In two compositions that are often counted as Underworld Books, the Book of the Heavenly Cow and the Litany of Ra, the genre develops in different directions. The former is centered on a complex image of the sky goddess in cow form (see Figure 26), but part of the text is a lively narrative about why Ra felt driven to leave earth after crushing a rebellion among humanity (see "The Destruction of Humanity" under "Linear Time" in "Mythical Time Lines"). This story may have originated in a dawn myth first recorded in the Pyramid Texts,[57] but by the New Kingdom it had changed into something more profound. Ra is credited with human emotions of anger, bitterness, and pity, and the story answers the important question of why creation includes pain and death.

In contrast, the book known as the Litany of Ra conveys the utter mysteriousness of the creator sun god through heightened language and powerful visual images. The sun god is evoked as the animating force behind the universe in seventy-five nocturnal manifestations. These manifestations range from major deities such as Horus and Isis to obscure entities such as the "Great Tom Cat" and "He of the Cave," yet part of the Egyptian title for this book was "adoring the united one in the west." The characteristic acts of independent beings that are the mainspring of mythical narratives become almost irrelevant in such a context.

New Kingdom hymns, such as those preserved in Papyrus Leiden I 350, explore the idea that all deities are aspects of the creator. They speculate on the miraculous process by which the one creator, usually named as Amun-Ra, was able to divide himself into many.[58] The worship of the creator sun god as the maintainer of the universe was widespread among the Egyptian elite. Solar hymns celebrating the day and night voyages of Ra were inscribed at the entrances to some New Kingdom private tombs or on statues of priests and officials. By the end of the New Kingdom, a version of the Litany of Ra was appended to the mortuary texts known as the Book of the Dead.

The Book of the Dead

The Egyptian **Book of the Dead** is a term coined in the nineteenth century CE for a body of texts known to the Ancient Egyptians as the Spells for Going Forth by Day. After the Book of the Dead was first translated by Egyptologists, it gained a place in the popular imagination as the Bible of the Ancient Egyptians. The comparison is very inappropriate. The Book of the Dead was not the central holy book of Egyptian religion. It was just one of a series of manuals composed to assist the spirits of the elite dead to achieve and maintain a full afterlife.

The collection was used for over a thousand years and eventually consisted of more than 190 spells or "formulas." Individual copies of the Book of the Dead vary greatly in the number and selection of spells they include. The order of the spells did not become fixed until around 650 BCE. In the New Kingdom, spells from the Book of the Dead were occasionally inscribed on items of funerary equipment such as shrouds and coffins or on the walls of royal tombs and mortuary temples. The majority of copies were on papyrus. These were included in the burials of wealthy priests, priestesses, and officials.

The spells in the Book of the Dead were most commonly written out in hieroglyphs or in a cursive (simplified) form of the hieroglyphic script. The majority of the spells are in Middle Egyptian. By the New Kingdom, the spoken language had changed considerably, so the number of people who could understand texts in archaic Middle Egyptian would have been very restricted. This may be one of the reasons why the vignettes to the Book of the Dead became increasingly important. By the end of the New Kingdom nearly every spell had its traditional vignette. In some copies the illustrations alone are used to represent the spells they should accompany. The vignettes can also occur as tomb decoration, since from the fourteenth century BCE onward it became acceptable to show deities on the walls of private tombs.

Copies of the Book of the Dead have been found all over Egypt, but the temples of Thebes seem to have been the main center of production. Many of the spells were adapted from earlier funerary literature, particularly the Coffin Texts. In Spell 17, quotations from the Coffin Texts are interspersed with com-

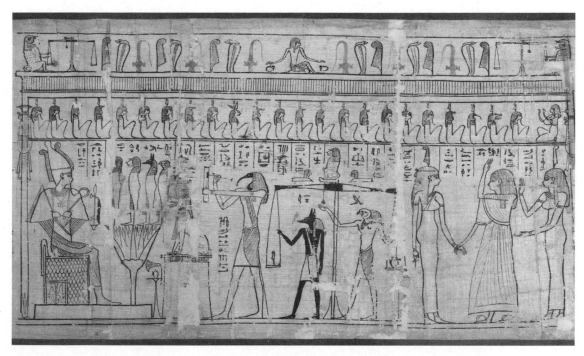

Figure 7. Vignette to Spell 125 of the Book of the Dead. From right to left, a dead woman is brought into the Hall of the Double Maat *by the two goddesses of truth; her heart is weighed against the feather of truth by Horus and Anubis; the result is recorded by Thoth and announced to the Ammut monster, the four sons of Horus, and Osiris. (Gift of Martin Brimmer, Courtesy Museum of Fine Arts, Boston. Illustration by Peter Manuelian used with permission.)*

mentaries headed "this means." In these explanatory passages, ancient creation myths are reinterpreted in terms of later theology. This is a clear example of the way in which the meaning and functions of Egyptian myths could change from period to period.

Many deities are mentioned or depicted in the Book of the Dead, but the afterlife that the spells envisage is dominated by two gods, Ra and Osiris. Some of the spells concerning Ra were adapted from solar hymns used in temples. The spirits of the dead could join the "crew" of the sun boat or seek a place at the court of Osiris, the ruler of the underworld. Most of the spells designed to help nourish and protect the spirit on its journey to these destinations were based on earlier prototypes, but there was a new emphasis on judging the past life of the deceased.

This is seen most clearly in Spell 125, the formula for "descending to the great hall of the Double *Maat*." Before the throne of Osiris, the deceased had to face a jury of gods and goddesses and declare himself or herself innocent of forty two specific sins. Most of the sins in this negative confession are offenses against deities, temples, or ritual purity, so Spell 125 may derive from an initiation ritual for priests.[59] The vignette for Spell 125 supplements rather than illustrates the text. In one of the most famous of all Egyptian images, the heart of the deceased person is shown being weighed against the feather that represents Maat, the goddess of truth. If the heart were found to be heavy with sin, it would be devoured by a monster.

In origin, this trial was just one of a series of perils that could be overcome by magic, but the popularity of Spell 125 in the later New Kingdom coincided with a new emphasis on god as a just but forgiving judge. In prayers of this period, people turn to gods such as Thoth and Amun to help them survive in an unjust society. Other individuals humbly acknowledged that their sufferings were a just punishment for actions such as breaking an oath sworn in a god's name.[60] These "penitential texts," like much of our knowledge of religion in daily life, come from Deir el-Medina, the village of the artists who built and decorated the Theban royal tombs. This exceptionally well preserved desert site was also the place where most New Kingdom literature was found.[61]

Mythology in Literature

Only about ten Late Egyptian narratives survive from the New Kingdom. The authors of these stories obviously assumed that their readers would have a detailed knowledge of Egyptian myth.

A story about a prince who is doomed by seven goddesses to be killed by a snake, a crocodile, or a dog has been called the world's oldest fairy tale. The ending of the story is missing, but the prince was probably saved by the spirited princess whose hand he wins in a jumping competition. The story known as Truth and Lies has been interpreted as an allegorical version of the Osiris myth, with the deities transformed into a dysfunctional human family.[62] The plot involves a son who grows up to avenge his father, Truth, and defeat the enemy, Lies. In contrast to Isis, the hero's mother is presented as lustful and heartless.

The female characters also prove to be evil in the story of the Two Brothers. The hero is falsely accused of attempting to rape his brother's wife and then betrayed by the woman given to him as a wife by the gods. Many mythological themes appear in semidisguised form in this story.[63] The two brothers have the same names as two gods (Anubis and Bata) and exhibit some superhuman powers. The story is set in a time when, just beyond the borders of Egypt, it was still possible to encounter gods and monsters. The motif of the sea's attempts to seize a beautiful female occurs both in the Two Brothers and in another New

Kingdom tale about Seth's fight with a god of the sea to save the goddess Astarte. This seems to be a partially Egyptianized version of a foreign myth (see "Astarte" in "Deities, Themes, and Concepts"). Even more fragmentary tales involve a woman who turns into a lioness and the god Heryshef's recruitment of a human to help him in his war with a divine falcon.[64]

The most controversial of the stories that date to the New Kingdom is the Contendings of Horus and Seth. This is the longest narrative to survive about the conflict between the two gods and its eventual resolution. That does not mean that it should be taken as the most important or the standard version of the myth. As many scholars have emphasized, a myth consists of all its versions. This text is in narrative form because it appears to have been read aloud for entertainment. It combines a retelling of the ancient myth with a satire on the difficulties of obtaining justice in the New Kingdom legal system and perhaps with veiled comments on recent problems with the royal succession.[65]

Some Egyptologists believe that the comic treatment of many of the characters and events in the Contendings of Horus and Seth disqualifies it from being a true myth, but a robust, often cruel, sense of humor is displayed in the myths of many cultures. Some of the story's more scandalous episodes, such as Seth's failed attempt to seduce his nephew Horus or Horus cutting off his mother's head in a tantrum, are also found in funerary and magical texts.

A devoted but dominating mother who gets her way through cunning and magic, Isis is the first fully realized character in Egyptian myth. A New Kingdom **ostracon** gives part of a story in which Isis and her attendant scorpions take shelter with a fisherwoman (see "Serqet" in "Deities, Themes, and Concepts"). This story was used hundreds of years later on magical statues and stelae as part of a sequence of spells to drive out poison. Many of the myths now known only from magical texts were probably adapted from other types of source material or from oral tradition. Quite a number of spells survive on papyri of the later New Kingdom. The Harris Magical Papyrus, now in the British Museum, contains a sequence of anticrocodile spells that is full of allusions to myths such as the rape of Isis.

Myths are often thought of as communal artifacts, but in Egyptian culture they had many personal applications. Another example was the use of lists of lucky and unlucky days, based on calendars of temple festivals. In the so-called Cairo Calendar, each day of the year is associated with a particular deity or mythical event.[66] These associations were believed to affect what could be done on a day, making the calendars rather similar to horoscopes. For example, the twenty-ninth day of the second month of Peret (spring) was the day on which the "children of Geb" had rebelled against the creator. "Do nothing on this day," the calendar warns. Some entries summarize well-known mythical incidents, such as the reconciliation of Horus and Seth; in contrast, others allude to very obscure myths, such as that of "the lost children of Bedesh."

The End of the New Kingdom

By the eleventh century BCE, the kings, who lived in the eastern Delta, seem to have had little influence over the south of the country. The last king of the Twentieth Dynasty, Rameses XI (c. 1099–1069 BCE), had a tomb cut in the Valley of the Kings but was probably never buried in it. In the Theban area, power had fallen into the hands of one family whose members served as generals in the army and high priests in the temple of Karnak. Several members of this family gave themselves royal titles, even after a new line of kings, the Twenty-First Dynasty, took control in the north. A series of marriages between the two families kept the peace.

Some of the most beautifully illustrated Books of the Dead were made for royal and aristocratic women who served as priestesses in the temples of Thebes during the eleventh and tenth centuries BCE (see, for example, Figure 24). It became the custom for elite burials to include a selection of spells from the Book of the Dead and a papyrus based on one or more of the royal underworld books. During this period most of the royal **mummies** were moved from their original resting places by the Theban priesthood, so the secret Underworld Books on the walls of their tombs became available for copying.[67]

The papyri based on Underworld Books are often referred to as "mythological papyri." They can consist almost entirely of drawings, with just a few brief captions. Mythological episodes known from texts of the third millennium BCE onward, such as the creator's engendering life or the separation of the earth and the sky, are illustrated for the first time on papyri and coffins of this period (see for example, Figure 42). These extraordinary papyri illustrate the Egyptian tendency to think in images. Language is rarely adequate to express the numinous. Instead the Egyptian priesthood devised a complex system of visual symbols to convey difficult concepts without the use of words.

In the ninth century BCE the production of funerary papyri suddenly stopped. This may have been the result of disruptions in temple life caused by a civil war between the Thebans and a new dynasty of kings in the north. The kings of the Twenty-Second Dynasty were of Libyan descent, but they seem to have completely adopted Egyptian religion. They favored the cult of the feline goddess Bastet and rebuilt part of her temple at Bubastis. Reliefs in the Festival Hall of Osorkon II (c. 874–850 BCE) show all the deities of Egypt gathering at

Bubastis to honor the king's jubilee. Bastet was one of the goddesses who could take the role of the Eye of Ra, the fiery protector of the sun god and of every king. The cycle of myths associated with the Eye goddess became increasingly prominent during the first millennium BCE.

Most of the northern kings were buried in the city of Tanis, in tombs within the temple of Amun-Ra. Some of these tombs have versions of New Kingdom Underworld Books, such as the Book of the Day and the Book of the Night, inscribed on their walls.[68] The temples of Tanis were adorned with Middle and New Kingdom statues brought from all over Egypt. This was probably more than an economy measure. The reuse of old royal statues gave new structures an instant past and invoked the protective presence of the royal ancestors.

In spite of this tendency to look back on past glories, innovations did appear among small objects. A wide range of **amulets** in the form of deities was introduced during the Third Intermediate Period. These were probably used to protect the health and safety of the living as well as the bodies of the dead. Some of the amulets depict mythological episodes such as those in which Horus harpoons Seth or Isis nurses the baby Horus in the marshes.[69] The choice of such amulets suggests a widespread knowledge of the stories behind these images. Until the Third Intermediate Period, scenes of nursing goddesses had always shown a king playing the role of Horus. As Horus the Child ceased to be so closely identified with the living king, he developed an important role in mythology and popular religion.

By the eighth century BCE, Egypt was split up into a number of regions ruled by petty kings and chieftains. The Theban area was under the control of a line of royal high priestesses known as the Divine Adoratrices of Amun. In temple rituals these priestesses acted the mythological role of the Hand of Atum, the partner of the creator.[70] Egypt's divisions were eventually brought to an end by invaders from the south.

LATE PERIOD AND PTOLEMAIC PERIOD (DYNASTIES 25–30 AND THE PTOLEMIES): 747–30 BCE

The first millennium BCE saw the rise and fall of a series of great empires. Egypt suffered invasions and occupations by the Nubians, the Assyrians, the Persians, and the Greeks; so for most of this period the country was either ruled by a foreign power or fighting for its independence. Egypt's culture was under pressure from new ruling elites, yet many of the best sources for Egyptian myth date to this era. Indeed, some scholars do not recognize that Egypt had a developed mythology before the Late Period. It is a common cultural phenomenon that after a change of rulers, religion, or language, native people or scholarly incomers become anxious to record a country's traditions before they disappear. This often involves codifying these beliefs and traditions for the first time.

Respect for ancient traditions was a policy of the Nubian kings who ruled Egypt as the Twenty-Fifth Dynasty. These kings came from an area of Nubia known as Kush. Their culture combined Nubian and Egyptian elements. The chief religious site in Kush was the holy mountain of Gebel Barkal near ancient Napata, where there was a temple for Amun-Ra and Hathor as the Eye of Ra. King Piye (Piankh) and his brother King Shabaqo (Shabaka) were the first two kings of this dynasty to rule Egypt. A victory inscription of King Piye (c. 747–716 BCE) is full of references to Egyptian deities and myths. It records that he seized the capital Memphis "like a desert storm, just as Amun-Ra had commanded me." [71] Some pyramid tombs of Nubian kings near Napata are inscribed with extracts from Old Kingdom Pyramid Texts. In Thebes, priests appointed by the Nubian kings revised and codified the Book of the Dead. Some of the spells they added contain passages that are probably in the Nubian language.[72] Also dating to this Nubian period is the Shabaqo Stone with a copy of the text known as the Memphite Theology (see Figure 8).

The Memphite Theology

This text tells how the earth god Geb judged between the rival gods Horus and Seth and how Osiris was established as ruler of the underworld. It reconciles the separate creation myths of Atum of Heliopolis and Ptah of Memphis and includes a first-person account by Ptah of how he created all life through his powers of thought and speech. This section has often been compared to the famous opening of St. John's gospel: "In the beginning was the Word, and the Word was with God and the Word was God." The whole text may have been read aloud during religious festivals.

King Shabaqo (c. 716–702 BCE) claims to have had the Memphite Theology copied onto stone because the original was "eaten by worms." The new version, which was set up in the temple of Ptah in Memphis, was to prove equally unlucky. The slab on which it was inscribed was eventually reused as a millstone, so parts of the text have been ground away. The preface to the Memphite Theology states that Shabaqo thought this text worthy of preservation because it was found "to be a work of the ancestors." In the past, Egyptologists accepted

Shabaqo's word that this was a very ancient text and assigned it to the Old Kingdom or even the Early Dynastic Period. Recent work has shown that the Memphite Theology cannot be earlier than the late New Kingdom. It was probably re-written under Shabaqo using a deliberately archaic style to give the contents added authority.[73]

Figure 8. The 'Memphite Theology' inscribed on the Shabaqo Stone. The inscription was damaged when the stela was reused as a grindstone. (Courtesy of Geraldine Pinch)

Much of the Memphite Theology is similar to accounts of creation in the so-called Bremner-Rhind Papyrus, which dates to around the fourth century BCE (see "BRP" in "Appendix: Primary Sources").[74] Among the texts inscribed on this papyrus are rituals designed to attack the enemies of the king, the state, and the cosmos and render them harmless. The Book of Knowing the Transformations of the Sun and of Overthrowing Apophis gives instructions on making models and drawings of enemies and destroying them by methods such as stabbing, trampling, burning, and burying. These sections are prefaced by speeches from the creator god describing the creation of life and the establishment of the divine order. This identifies the ritual as part of the continuing cosmic struggle. Until recently, the Bremner-Rhind Papyrus **cosmogony** has received much less attention from scholars than the Memphite Theology, partly because the former conforms to modern ideas of what a religious text should be like, whereas the latter was seen as belonging to the primitive world of magic. Of the two, it is probably the Bremner-Rhind Papyrus that is more characteristic of the way in which mythology was used in Egyptian culture.

In the seventh century BCE, most Egyptians must have felt that the forces of chaos had triumphed when their country endured a series of brutal invasions by the Assyrians. Unlike most invaders, the Assyrians showed little respect for Egypt's gods. They looted the temples of Heliopolis and Thebes, taking away vast quantities of treasure. The Nubian kings were driven out of Egypt, but they continued to reign over Kush for almost a thousand years.

The Assyrians did not have enough manpower to leave a large army in Egypt. They appointed Egyptians to govern the country on their behalf and collect tribute. A family from the region of Sais in the Delta collaborated with the Assyrians for awhile. As soon as the Assyrians were occupied with problems elsewhere in their empire, this family made Egypt independent again and ruled as the Twenty-Sixth Dynasty. Under these kings, Greek merchants were allowed to trade and settle in the Delta.

The cult center of the goddess Neith at Sais became one of the most important temples in Egypt. According to a later tradition, the secret of how the soul can unite with God was inscribed in hieroglyphs in the sanctuary at Sais.[75] At this time a script known as **Demotic** was introduced to write texts in the contemporary form of the Egyptian language. It soon replaced hieratic for most purposes.

Persians and Greeks

In 525 BCE the Persian king, Cambyses, conquered Egypt and executed most of the Egyptian royal family. It is probably only a legend that Cambyses showed his contempt for Egyptian gods by stabbing the sacred Apis bull (see "Deities, Themes, and Concepts"). The Persians did not try to impose their own religion on Egypt, and they were willing to honor Egyptian deities. The innovative reliefs in the temple of Hibis in the western desert were mainly carved under Darius I, one of the Persian kings who made up the Twenty-Seventh Dynasty (see Figure 33). The reliefs include some very unusual forms of deities. These forms and the epithets used in the captions, such as Atum "scarab who appeared at the First Time," help to define the deities' mythological roles.[76]

It was during the first period of Persian rule that the Greek historian Herodotus of Helicarnassus (c. 484–420 BCE) seems to have visited Egypt. Book Two of his *Historia* is a description of the geography, history, customs, and marvels of Egypt. Some Classicists and Egyptologists think that Herodotus made up his account from travelers' tales, but others believe him to be a reliable eyewitness and take everything that he writes very seriously.[77] Herodotus claims to have talked with Egyptian priests in several important religious centers, but his information mainly seems to derive from Memphis and the eastern Delta. He argued that the priests' knowledge was important to humanity because, unlike the Greeks, the Egyptians had access to very ancient and continuous records.

Herodotus thought it possible to identify many Egyptian deities with Greek ones, so he calls Osiris, Dionysus, and Horus, Apollo. It became a general practice among Classical writers to use Greek names for Egyptian deities, but these cross-cultural identifications are not always consistent. Herodotus says more about religious architecture and rituals than about mythology. "As for the stories told by the Egyptians," he wrote, "let whoever finds them credible use them."[78] He does not relate the full Osiris myth because he saw it as comparable to the Greek Mystery cults, which devotees had to vow to keep secret.

Herodotus does outline some brief myths to explain curious features of buildings or statues, such as why the temple grounds at Buto contained a floating island or why Amun could be shown with a ram's head. These are not unlike the kinds of tales told to gullible tourists by unofficial Egyptian guides at the monuments today. The bizarre legends Herodotus relates about some Egyptian kings, such as a tale of King Mycerinus (Menkara) raping his own daughter and burying her inside a cow, may have reflected contemporary folktales. The Egyptians had a long tradition of telling unflattering stories about past kings.

Between 404 and 343 BCE, several dynasties of Egyptian-born kings were able to keep the Persians out of Egypt. The three kings of the Thirtieth Dynasty instituted a style of art and architecture that was to continue under their foreign successors. A Thirtieth Dynasty mythological text about the reigns of Shu and Geb defines a ruler's duties as defending Egypt from foreign enemies, maintaining the country's defensive walls and irrigation systems, and rebuilding the temples of the gods.[79] A huge granite temple was begun at Behbeit el-Hagar for the goddess Isis, whose cult was becoming increasingly important. Later legend claimed that it was the failure of King Nectanebo II (360–343 BCE) to complete a temple for the god Onuris-Shu that led to his defeat when the Persians invaded again.[80] This time the Persians seem to have punished the Egyptians by destroying some important temples.

The second period of Persian rule was brief because the Persian empire was soon under attack from the Greeks, led by the young king of Macedonia, Alexander the Great. Alexander "liberated" Egypt in 332 BCE and was crowned king in the temple of Ptah at Memphis. During his stay in Egypt, he declared himself a living god and founded the city of Alexandria on the Mediterranean coast. After Alexander's death, one of his generals, a Macedonian called Ptolemy, made himself ruler and then king of Egypt. The Ptolemy family were to rule Egypt for around 300 years.

Alexandria and Memphis

Under the Ptolemies, the country was governed from Alexandria, and nearly all the important posts in the government went to Greek settlers rather than to Egyptians. In the third century BCE, King Ptolemy II (285–246 BCE) founded a great library. The contents of the famous Library of Alexandria have been lost, owing to fires, earthquakes, and tidal waves, but its 700,000 book-scrolls probably contained little about Egyptian mythology. Greek philosophy, science, and literature were the main interests of the scholars at the Mouseion, a kind of protouniversity attached to the library.

Most members of the Ptolemy family never learned the Egyptian language, but they were conscious that they were ruling a multicultural society and that they needed the support of influential Egyptians. As a symbol of cultural fusion, the Ptolemies established the cult of a new god, Serapis, who combined features of the Egyptian deities Apis and Osiris with aspects of Greek deities such as Zeus and Dionysus. Many of the Ptolemies were crowned in the temple of Ptah at Memphis, and they often contributed to the cost of religious ceremonies in the ancient capital.

Ptolemaic kings and queens were happy to identify themselves with Egyptian deities and to rule in their names. They encouraged the Egyptians to worship them as divine rulers. The Memphis decree of King Ptolemy V (205–180 BCE) ordered the setting up of Egyptian-style statues of "Ptolemy who has preserved Egypt" in every temple. In the decree, Ptolemy refers to slaughtering rebels just as Ra and Horus, son of Osiris, had slaughtered those who rebelled against them "in the First Time." The Memphis decree is best known from the copies in Greek and two forms of Egyptian on the Rosetta Stone (see Figure 10).[81]

Among the cults supported by the Ptolemies was that of the Apis bull, who lived in a special enclosure at the temple of Ptah. When an Apis bull died, it was mummified and given a funeral as elaborate and expensive as that of a king. A papyrus of the first century BCE summarizes the rituals to be performed, including mythological dramas. The conflict between Horus and Seth and the victory of Ra over Apophis were acted out on boats on the lake of the temple of Ptah. This is typical of the way in which Egyptian rituals lifted events out of ordinary time and made them part of the whole sequence of mythological history.

Two young women, preferably twin sisters, played the roles of Isis and Nephthys to mourn the Apis bull as if he had been Osiris himself. Versions of the types of laments that they sang have survived in the Bremner-Rhind Papyrus and other sources.[82] The laments are notable for their emotional intensity. Osiris is mourned not just as a king but as a beloved husband and brother. Anthropologist Claude Lévi-Strauss has pointed out that although poetry is notoriously difficult to translate from one language to another, myths often pass easily between languages and cultures because their content is far more important than the way in which they are told.[83] Greeks and other immigrants found the joys and sorrows of Isis to have meaning for their lives. Isis and Osiris came to be the most famous Egyptian deities among foreigners, but the native Egyptians continued to worship a multiplicity of deities.

Priests and Temples under the Ptolemies

The Ptolemies undertook massive temple rebuilding programs to legitimize their rule in the eyes of the Egyptians and their gods.[84] Native Egyptian society was more temple centered than ever, and the priesthood became the custodians of Egyptian culture. Working for a temple was virtually the only form of advancement available to talented Egyptians. The priesthood turned into a hereditary caste, jealous of its rights and privileges. Yet this was not a period of decadence. Egyptian art, literature, and theology continued to flourish and develop.

The architecture of the Ptolemaic temples reflects their use by the general population. Inside the enclosure walls there were sanatoria where people could visit statues with healing powers or spend the night in the hope that a deity would come to them in a dream and tell them how their illness could be cured. Crowds took part in the annual festival of Osiris and left miniature mummy figures of Osiris in special shrines. Many temples kept large numbers of the type of animal that was sacred to the main deity of the temple. People could pay for these animals to be ritually sacrificed and then mummified to act as messengers to the realm of the gods. Wealthier temple visitors continued the Late Period practice of dedicating beautifully made bronze images of deities (see, for example, Figure 13). An area of the temple that may have been a particular focus for women was the **mammisi** (Birth House). These structures were decorated with texts and scenes describing the conception and birth of a deity, most usually a form of Horus.[85]

By the Ptolemaic Period, religious texts, such as detailed festival calendars, cycles of hymns, and the scripts for rituals, were commonly inscribed on temple walls. This was thought to allow the temple to function even if there was nobody to perform the rites. Some of the most interesting texts are found in the extraordinarily well preserved temple of Horus at Edfu, which was built between 237 and 57 BCE. Scenes and inscriptions on the walls have allowed scholars to reconstruct annual ceremonies such as the Festival of the Beautiful Union, which celebrated the coming together of Horus and Hathor. The Festival of Victory commemorated the triumph of Horus over Seth and his followers (see Figures 31 and 32). This conflict seems to have been acted out on and around the temple lake.[86] A second mythological drama, the Legend of the Winged Disk, has Horus defending Ra against his enemies, a role usually taken by the Eye goddess. The foundation of the temple is traced back to the First Time in a series of texts sometimes known as the Edfu Cosmogony.[87]

Every major Ptolemaic temple seems to have had its own creation myth, with the principal deity of the temple playing the role of creator. Texts of this type, such as the Khonsu Cosmogony at Karnak,[88] use wordplay to incorporate the myths of other creator deities and show them as aspects of the same phenomenon. At some temples members of the priesthood used their knowledge of history and legend to devise stories to support their claims to land and privileges. The Famine Stela on Sehel island in the First **Cataract** and the Khonsu Stela at Thebes are examples of Ptolemaic charter myths in which deities interact with historical figures (see "Khnum" and "Khonsu" in "Deities, Themes, and Concepts").

Among the inscriptions found on the walls of Ptolemaic temples are lengthy lists of all the sacred places in the forty-two **nomes** (districts) of Egypt. The richness of this mythical geography is brought out by Papyrus Jumilhac, an illustrated selection of the myths and legends of the Jackal nome, the seventeenth district of Upper Egypt.[89] There were probably similar collections for other regions. Most of the brief narratives are about the conflict between Horus and Seth, with a particular emphasis on the struggle to protect the body of Osiris (see Figure 21). Episodes from this cycle become etiological myths to explain topographical features, or elements of ritual, such as why Egyptian priests wear leopard skins. These are national gods localized, rather than local gods universalized.

Papyrus Jumilhac was not just an antiquarian collection, as its texts seem to have been recited during religious festivals. The first Egyptian to write about Egyptian religion purely as a scholarly exercise may have been a priest called Manetho who lived in the late fourth and early third centuries BCE. Manetho was one of the educated elite who could understand the hieroglyphic script and earlier forms of the Egyptian language, but he also learned Greek. His ambition was to explain and justify Egyptian culture to outsiders, particularly the Greeks. He is famous for writing a history of Egypt that only survives in excerpts in later Classical writers.[90] Manetho was credited with at least seven other works, including books on Egyptian festivals, rituals, and "ancient religion." Sadly, no manuscripts of these books have yet been found.

In general, less literature has survived from the first millennium BCE than from the Middle and New Kingdoms. One virtually complete Late Period story written in hieratic is antiestablishment in tone and features a cowardly and lustful king and greedy and heartless priests. The hero, Meryra, enters the underworld in his king's place and is helped by a goddess to avenge himself on those who have betrayed him.[91] There are fragments of mythological tales in Demotic, including at least one about the crowning of Horus and Seth.[92] Some interesting mythological narratives survive from the Late and Ptolemaic Periods inscribed in hieroglyphs on special types of statues and stelae used in healing magic.

Isis and Horus

Magical statues and stelae usually feature a carved figure of Horus in child form overcoming dangerous animals (see, for example, Figure 16). Such stelae are known as **cippi** or "Horus on the crocodiles stelae." The most famous object of this type is the Metternich Stela, now in the Metropolitan Museum of Art, New York.[93] This is inscribed with a collection of spells for driving away dangerous animals and reptiles or curing their poisonous bites and stings. These creatures were both hazards of daily life and symbols of the chaos that constantly threatened the divine order. Surrounding the central figure of Horus on most *cippi* is a grotesque array of deities in their most terrifying and powerful forms. These images complement the text of the spells but do not illustrate them.[94] The power of the words and images could be absorbed by drinking or bathing in water poured over the stela.

Most of the spells center on a briefly stated mythical event, such as Ra-Atum transforming himself into a mongoose to kill Apophis. A few are fleshed out into narratives with lively dialogue. In the longest of these dramatized spells, Isis is imprisoned by Seth but escapes to the marshes of Chemmis, where she gives birth to Horus. Isis is depicted as oppressed by powerful males, struggling with poverty, and in constant fear of losing her child. This was probably the lot of most ordinary women in Ancient Egypt. The *cippi* texts raise the question that must be answered by every religion: If god is good, why do innocent children suffer? An angry attitude toward divine indifference is put in the mouth of Isis. Her challenge to the sun god to help her dying child is one of the most powerful emotional passages in all of Egyptian literature. Ra responds by sending Thoth to cure Horus. Isis as everywoman has triumphed, and the spell promises that every child will be saved because Horus was saved.

Cippi have been found in houses and tombs, but large examples such as the Metternich Stela would originally have been set up in an outer area of a temple. Ptolemaic Period temples are decorated with endless scenes of gods and **pharaohs**, but the absence of specific royal names from some cartouches gives a clue that it was often difficult for the priests to know who was in charge of the country or for how long. From the second century BCE onward there were frequent wars between rival members of the Ptolemy family as well as rebellions by native Egyptians. In the first century BCE, one of the feuding Ptolemies unwisely sought help from Rome, the city that was becoming the greatest military power in the ancient world. The Romans were eager for an excuse to get hold of the gold and the grain that Egypt produced.

The Greek writer Diodorus Siculus (of Sicily) visited northern Egypt in the mid first century BCE. In his description of the country he picked out elements of Egyptian religion that he found bizarre, such as the reverential treatment of sacred animals. Diodorus summarized the myth of Osiris, including his murder by his brother, Typhon (Seth). He explained the symbolic tombs of Osiris found in temples all over Egypt by a myth in which Isis deceives the priests in each temple into thinking that they have the true body of the god. This literal-minded interpretation points up the differences between Greek and Egyptian thought.

Soon after Diodorus's visit, Rome was interfering in Egyptian affairs. The Roman general Julius Caesar took part in a civil war and secured the position of the last great member of the Ptolemy family, Queen Cleopatra VII (51–30 BCE). After Julius Caesar returned to Rome, Cleopatra gave birth to a son, Ptolemy Caesarion. Cleopatra used Egyptian myth to political advantage by identifying herself with the goddess Isis and her fatherless son with Horus the child. A few years later Cleopatra joined forces with another Roman general, Mark Antony, to try to establish a new empire of the east. Mark Antony's patron deity was Dionysus, the Greek god generally identified with Osiris. In 30 BCE Antony and Cleopatra were defeated by Octavian, who subsequently became the first emperor of Rome under the title of Augustus. Egypt was reduced to being a province of the Roman empire.

ROMAN PERIOD: 30 BCE–395 CE

For a time, Roman rule had relatively little impact on the religious life of the country. Roman emperors replaced Ptolemaic kings on the temple walls. Strabo, a geographer who visited Egypt in the early Roman Period, stressed the country's past glories but was able to describe flourishing cult temples.[95] Under Augustus, and later under Trajan (98–117 CE) and Hadrian (117–138 CE), new temples were built for Egyptian and Nubian deities. The language of temple inscriptions was still neo–Middle Egyptian, written in a form of the hieroglyphic script that was increasingly difficult to read.[96]

The long tradition of speculation about the First Time continued. The temple of Khnum at Esna, which largely dates to the first century CE, is inscribed with hymns detailing the roles of Khnum and the goddess Neith as creator deities. Chaeremon, an Alexandrian who became one of Emperor Nero's tutors, described the Egyptian priests of his day as pious philosophers who were the custodians of an esoteric knowledge sought by people of many races.[97] One of the seekers who made good use of such knowledge was the Greek writer and thinker Plutarch (c. 46–126 CE).

Plutarch's Osiris

Plutarch is best remembered as a historian whose biographies of leaders such as Coriolanus and Mark Antony formed the main source for several of Shakespeare's plays. Plutarch was fascinated by Egyptian religion and wrote a book on this topic called "Concerning Isis and Osiris." He could not speak or read any form of the Egyptian language, so he had to rely on conversations through interpreters and speculations about Egyptian deities found in the works of earlier Classical writers. Plutarch's narrative of the life and death of Osiris and the wanderings of his widow, Isis, is the one commonly used in popular books on Egyptian mythology.

Figure 9. The columned hall of the temple of Hathor at Dendara, built during the Roman Period. (Courtesy of Richard Pinch)

Plutarch had few reservations about describing in detail the murder of Osiris and the mutilation of the god's body. Much of Plutarch's Osiris narrative must have been based on stories and customs that were current in Egypt during the first century CE, but this does not make it a reliable source for earlier periods. The myth of Osiris had been developing and changing for over 2,500 years before Plutarch was born, but Plutarch's written sources could only take him back about 600 years. Plutarch himself gave alternate versions of parts of the story, some of which he thought might be more authentic than others.

His stated purpose in writing the book was to seek the universal truths that he believed to lie behind the myths and beliefs of all cultures. He quotes other writers' far-fetched allegorical interpretations of Egyptian myth. His own comments on the nature of myth often sound surprisingly modern. He did not believe that myths described events that had actually happened. He is scathing about people who interpreted all myths in terms of natural phenomena such as crop cycles or eclipses: "One should take the greatest heed and care not unconsciously to reduce and resolve the divine to terms of winds, fluxes, sowings, ploughings, terrestrial occurrences and seasonal changes, like those who explain Dionysus as wine and Hephaestus as flame."[98]

Plutarch saw the mythology of Isis in particular as a profound expression of the benevolent face of the divine. It is to his credit as a scholar that he related some incidents, such as one in which Isis strikes a child dead with her glance, that do not easily fit with this view. Roman Period hymns in Greek and Egyptian speak of all gods and goddesses as merely forms of the great creator Isis. One of the things that made the cults of Osiris and Isis popular with foreigners was the promise of a happy afterlife for all the virtuous dead, whatever their status had been in life. This was not a concept that was very common among ancient religions.

Vignettes of the judgment of the dead feature prominently in the Book of Breathing, a condensed version of the Book of the Dead placed in burials during the Ptolemaic and Roman periods. A new text known as the Book of Traversing Eternity was sometimes combined with the Book of Breathing. This contained spells to allow the spirit of a dead person to return to earth to visit temples and take part in the festivals of Osiris[99] The scholar-priests who compiled these books were presumably drawing on ancient texts preserved in temple libraries,[100] but there is evidence that such priests were also open to influences from outside Egyptian culture.

Demotic Literature

Under the Roman administration, Greek remained the chief language of intellectual and literary life. Huge numbers of Roman Period papyri have survived, particularly from the Fayum region and the town of Oxyrhynchus. Among these are literary papyri in Greek and Demotic from temple libraries or priests' houses. Much of this literature may originally have been composed in the Ptolemaic Period. Some of the Demotic literature shows foreign influence. A fragmentary tale of a war between an Egyptian prince and an Amazon queen has been compared with Greek myths such as the combat of Achilles and Penthesilia or the conquest of the Amazon queen Hippolyta by Theseus. The Demotic version is told from the point of view of the "queen of the land of women." She appeals to Isis to help her against the Egyptian prince, who is compared with the chaos monster Apophis.[101]

The war between order and chaos is the underlying theme of the myth of
the Eye of the Sun, also known as the myth of the Distant Goddess (see "The
Distant Goddess" under "Linear Time" in "Mythical Time Lines"). The outline
of this myth can be pieced together from rituals inscribed on the walls of
Ptolemaic and early Roman Period temples. A literary version in Demotic is the
longest mythical narrative in Egyptian to survive from any period.[102] The Eye of
the Sun text seems to have been put together from many different sources and
was probably read aloud to entertain people. It includes passages of virtuoso
descriptive writing, elaborate praises of Egyptian culture that would have gone
down well with a native audience, and animal fables. These short moral tales
are told by the god Thoth as part of his plan to lure the angry goddess back to
Egypt to resume her place in the divine order as the sun god's chief defender.
Thoth's story of a lion helped by a mouse has the same plot as a shorter fable attributed to Aesop, a Greek slave thought to have lived in the sixth century
BCE.[103] Incidents from other fables in the Eye of the Sun have been recognized in
drawings dating to the late second millennium BCE, so Egypt seems to have had
a tradition of animal fables centuries before Aesop.

Another genre with a long history in Egypt was stories about magicians.
These were usually set in the past, like the Middle Kingdom sequence of stories
about Old Kingdom magicians in Papyrus Westcar. One badly preserved
Demotic story cycle tells how the Third Dynasty official Imhotep used magic to
help the armies of Egypt.[104] Very similar stories are told about Nectanebo II in
the Greek "Alexander Romance" of the second century CE, which is probably
based on a lost Egyptian original. Another story cycle was centered on a prince
called Setna, a character based on an actual son of Rameses II, Prince
Khaemwaset. Part of one of these stories is known from the fourth century BCE,
but the most complete versions come from the early Roman Period (see
"Appendix: Primary Sources"). The proper uses of magic and other types of secret knowledge form one of the main themes of these stories.

Land of Magicians

By the Roman Period, Egypt was renowned as a land of priest-magicians. The
ancient city of Memphis was thought to be the place where they learned their
secret craft. In the first of the stories about Setna, the prince steals the magical
Book of Thoth from an ancient tomb near Memphis. He ignores the warnings of
the ghosts who inhabit the tomb and is punished by horrible hallucinations until he gives back the forbidden book. Several manuscripts ranging in date from
the first century BCE to the second century CE preserve parts of an actual Book

of Thoth.[105] This begins with a dialogue between a person seeking divine wisdom and Thoth, the god of wisdom and secret knowledge. The seeker hopes to gain some of the very powers mentioned in Setna's magic book, such as understanding the speech of birds and animals and seeing Ra in his sun boat. The Setna story seems to be a warning against trying to use such knowledge to gain earthly power rather than spiritual enlightenment.

In the second story in the cycle, Setna is allowed to pay a brief visit to the underworld to see Osiris judging the dead. Such a spirit voyage also forms part of the Book of Thoth, where it acts as a kind of initiation rite.[106] In the Demotic story, the scenario of the traditional underworld books is fictionalized into a personal journey. Some of the horrors Setna sees, such as souls tormented by tasks they can never complete, seem to be based on Greek visions of the afterlife. In the third story, Setna's son Sa-Osiris ("son of Osiris") turns out to be a reincarnation of a great magician of the past, a concept that may be more Greek than Egyptian. A battle against malevolent Nubian sorcerers reflects contemporary fears of the powerful Nubian kingdom to the south, which the Romans never succeeded in conquering.

A number of magical papyri of the Roman Period have survived, mainly from Thebes. Most of their spells are in Greek, but four papyri of the third century CE contain elaborate spells in Demotic.[107] The Demotic spells often utilize Egyptian deities in their traditional mythical roles for dubious purposes. So, for example, the myth of the rape of the goddess Tefnut is invoked in a spell to separate a woman from her husband. The spells in Greek are populated by figures borrowed from Egyptian, Greek, and Roman myth and Aramaic and Jewish religion. Egypt was a cosmopolitan country, and the Roman Period was an age of religious synthesis. This is also apparent in the Greek texts known as the **Hermetica**.[108]

Like the Book of Thoth, Hermetic texts were usually in the form of a dialogue between a disciple and a deity or a revered sage. The deity is most commonly Hermes, the Greek god identified with Thoth. Some Hermetica feature Isis or Asclepius, the Greek god of medicine identified with the deified Egyptian sage, Imhotep. The instructing deity sometimes relates myths about the beginning or the end of the world. Many spells in the magical papyri claim the power to summon visions of deities. In the Hermetica, such visions can lead to a truer understanding of the meaning of life and the nature of the divine.

The Hermetica were principally a development of Greek philosophy. It used to be argued that the Hermetica were written and read only by Greeks until some Hermetic texts in Coptic were found. Coptic was a form of the Egyptian language used from the second century CE onward. It was written in the Greek alphabet with the addition of six signs borrowed from the Demotic script. Most scholars now agree that the traditional wisdom of the Egyptian priests and their knowledge of Egyptian myth were among the elements that made up the Hermetica.

Some of the Hermetica have much in common with the teachings of **Gnosticism**, which promised salvation through *gnosis* (knowledge) of the self. Gnostics rejected the material world as evil, a point of view that was alien to traditional Egyptian thought, which had always celebrated the created world as part of the divine order. Manicheism, a religious movement that originated in Iran, was more sympathetic. Its emphasis on a perpetual struggle between the forces of darkness and light could be seen by Egyptians as a version of their unending war between chaos and order. The real challenge to traditional Egyptian beliefs, however, was to come from another new religion: Christianity.

At first Christianity was just one of many religions thriving in Egypt. During the second and third centuries CE, Christians were brutally persecuted for refusing to acknowledge that the Roman emperors were gods. Some early Christian writers, such as the second-century CE Bishop Clement of Alexandria, are useful though hostile witnesses on Egyptian religion. During the fourth century CE, Christianity became the dominant religion of the Roman Empire. The date usually given for the end of Pharaonic culture is 395 CE. This was the year when the Roman Empire was divided into two. Egypt became part of the eastern, or Byzantine, Empire, and most of its pagan temples were closed down by order of the emperor.

The Isis temple at Philae on Egypt's southern border stayed open until the sixth century CE because it was protected by Nubian tribes who still revered the goddess. The latest known hieroglyphic texts are from Philae. When there was no longer anyone left who could read the ancient texts, knowledge of the Egyptian gods and their myths gradually died out. This change of religion was far more significant for Egyptian culture than all the previous changes of government.

POST-PHARAONIC EGYPT

The three centuries in which Egypt was predominantly a Christian country are often referred to as the Coptic Period. It was in the deserts of Egypt that Christian monasticism first developed, and the great monasteries partially took the place of temples in Egyptian society. Christian chroniclers provide evidence that some Egyptians clung to the old beliefs as late as the sixth century CE. A few magical texts of this period still mention the myths of Isis and the Horus

Figure 10. The Memphis Decree of 196 BCE inscribed in three scripts on the Rosetta Stone: top, hieroglyphic; center, demotic; bottom, Greek. (British Museum)

child, but most replace them with anecdotes about the Virgin Mary and Baby Jesus. The last stories about the gods of Egypt are those that tell of their defeat by Coptic saints.[109]

In the seventh century CE, Egypt was invaded first by the Persians and then by the Arabs. The Arabs brought with them the Muslim religion, but many of the native Egyptians (the **Copts**) remained Christian. The Coptic language fell out of general use around 1000 CE, but it has continued to be used in the liturgies of the Coptic church right up to the present day. For centuries Egypt was part of an Arab empire ruled by caliphs in Damascus or Baghdad. The most famous of these caliphs was Haroun al-Rashid, who features in the Arabian Nights Entertainment, a vast collection of stories compiled in medieval Egypt. Egypt's greatest medieval leader was Saladin (1169–1193 CE), who defended Egypt and Palestine against the Christian crusaders. Arabic literature flourished in Egypt, and one of its themes was the lost treasures and secrets of the ancient pagan sites.[110]

Medieval Christian pilgrims who visited Egypt because it was a Bible land brought back descriptions of the pyramids, which they generally identified with the granaries of Joseph. A crucial part of the Renaissance, which began in fourteenth-century CE Italy, was the rediscovery of Classical texts. During the fifteenth and sixteenth centuries CE, Hermetica from Egypt were wrongly thought to be the world's most ancient religious documents. This aroused great interest in Egyptian religion and its relationship to Judaism and Christianity. The myths of Osiris, Isis, and Horus became the subject of sermons and essays. From the sixteenth through the eighteenth centuries CE, there were many attempts to decipher Egyptian hieroglyphs.[111]

Up to the end of the eighteenth century CE, most of Egypt was a difficult and dangerous place for Western travelers to visit. When the French leader Napoleon Bonaparte invaded Egypt in 1798, he took many scholars and artists with him. The survivors wrote and illustrated a multivolume *Description of Egypt*, which contributed to a Europe-wide fascination for all things Egyptian. Among the antiquities found during Napoleon's campaign was the Rosetta Stone. This was one of the documents used by the brilliant French linguist Jean-Francois Champollion to decipher the hieroglyphic script. The rage for collecting Egyptian antiquities meant that papyri and inscribed objects ended up in museums and private collections all over the world. A fashion for holding mummy-unwrapping parties inspired Gothic novels, such as Jane Webb's *The Mummy* (1827), which were forerunners of the modern horror genre.

Most major Egyptian religious and literary texts were translated into Western languages during the second half of the nineteenth century CE. Some of these sources, particularly E. A. Wallis Budge's translation of the Book of the Dead, were drawn on by occult writers such as the Theosophist Madam Blavatsky and the self-styled Great Beast, Aleister Crowley. Sigmund Freud, the founder of psychoanalysis, was attracted by the symbolic qualities of Ancient Egyptian art, and his colleague Carl Jung was fascinated by Egyptian solar mythology.[112] Sir James Frazer, the "Father of Anthropology," devoted several chapters of his influential book *The Golden Bough* to the myths of Osiris and Isis, which he interpreted as primarily relating to the annual growth and decay of vegetation.[113] Other twentieth-century CE anthropologists and historians of religion used Ancient Egyptian religion to argue that myths were always linked with rituals or even that all myths evolved to explain existing rituals. Extreme advocates of the latter school derived all the world's myths from prehistoric Egyptian kingship rituals.[114] Equally controversial in recent times has been Martin Bernal's work on the Egyptian contribution to Greek mythology and culture.[115] One offshoot of the feminist movement has been a new interest in goddesses, and Isis is now worshipped again in many parts of the world.

Egyptian mythology has never been a key part of Western literature in the way that Greek mythology has. Egyptian funerary religion and archaeology have provided more inspiration to writers than Egyptian myths. The reanimated mummy is the image that has captured the modern imagination, but the deities of Ancient Egypt have appeared as peripheral characters in horror stories by writers such as Théophile Gautier, Arthur Conan Doyle, Edgar Allen Poe, H. Rider Haggard, Bram Stoker, H. P. Lovecraft, and Sax Rohmer (see "Egyptian Myth: Annotated Print and Nonprint Resources").[116]

The sensational discovery of the tomb of Tutankhamun in 1922 encouraged the cinema's fascination with "the curse of the mummy."[117] The plot of the recent Hollywood blockbuster *The Mummy*, in which a mercenary searches for a magical golden book in a haunted city, is very close to that of the Setna story. Like Setna, the hero has to learn that seeking the secret knowledge of the Ancient Egyptians can be a risky business. You have been warned.

NOTES

1. For summaries of these and many other interpretations, see G. S. Kirk, *Myth: Its Meaning and Functions in Ancient and Other Cultures* (Cambridge and Berkeley, 1970); or W. G. Doty, *Mythography: The Study of Myths and Rituals*, 2d ed. (Tuscaloosa, AL, and London, 2000).

2. Kirk, *Myth*, 252–261.

3. For examples, see Clyde Kluckhohn, "Myths and Rituals: A General Theory," *Harvard Theological Review* 35 (1942): 45–79.

4. Kirk, *Myth*, 254–255.

5. It is a feature of etiological myths that, factually speaking, the explanation given is nearly always wrong.

6. In Ancient Egyptian color symbolism, black was a "good" color standing for fertility and rebirth, whereas red was a "bad" color standing for danger and sometimes for evil.

7. Because of the Nile flood, all permanent settlements had to be built on banks or mounds of high ground within the floodplain or in the desert hills that flank the Nile valley. The annual flood is now controlled by the huge Aswan Dam.

8. Kirk, *Myth*, 208–209.

9. For an accessible account of recent discoveries about the origins of Egyptian writing, see Vivian Davies and Renée Friedman, *Egypt* (London, 1998), chap. 1.

10. The main historical interpretations of the myth are summarized by J. G. Griffiths in *The Conflict of Horus and Seth from Egyptian and Classical Sources* (Liverpool, 1960). H. te Velde has pointed out that even if there is any truth to these theories, the function of the story of Horus and Seth in Egyptian culture was as a religious myth. See te Velde, *Seth, God of Confusion* (Leiden, 1977), 74–80.

11. For a very detailed study of these rules about the content and style of art, see Heinrich Schäfer, *Principles of Egyptian Art*, rev. ed., trans. and ed. John Baines (Oxford, 1986). Those with less time to spare should consult the first two chapters in Gay Robins, *The Art of Ancient Egypt* (London, 1997).

12. A variety of views on divine kingship can be found in D. O'Connor and D. Silverman (eds.), *Ancient Egyptian Kingship* (Leiden, 1995). See also L. Bell, *Mythology and Iconography of Divine Kingship in Ancient Egypt* (Chicago, 1994).

13. This copy may date to the twenty-third century BCE. See D. B. Redford, *Pharaonic King-lists, Annals, and Day-books: A Contribution to the Study of the Egyptian Sense of History* (Mississauga, Ontario, 1986).

14. For a comprehensive list of all the deities recorded in the Early Dynastic Period, see Toby A. H. Wilkinson, *Early Dynastic Egypt* (London and New York, 1999), chap. 8.

15. In most periods the hippopotamus was a sacred animal of Seth. Several Early Dynastic labels show a king harpooning or even wrestling with a hippopotamus. Such representations may have been the origin of a late tradition that King Menes was killed during a hippopotamus hunt.

16. During all of the third and much of the second millennium BCE, Egyptian temples were mainly staffed on a rota basis. People were organized into "phyles" or crews that performed ritual duties in temples for one month in every ten. Temple archives, which show how this rota system worked in practice, have survived from the Old Kingdom. See Mark Lehner, *The Complete Pyramids* (London, 1997), 233–235.

17. Early examples of such topographical lists are discussed and interpreted by John Baines in "An Abydos List of Gods and an Old Kingdom Use of Texts," in *Pyramid Studies and Other Essays Presented to I. E .S. Edwards*, ed. John Baines (London, 1988), 124–133.

18. For a summary of recent theories about pyramid complexes, see Dieter Arnold, "Royal Cult Complexes of the Old and Middle Kingdoms," in *Temples of Ancient Egypt*, ed. Byron E. Shafer (Ithaca, 1997), 31–85.

19. For a full bibliography of translations and interpretations of the Pyramid Texts and all the other funerary texts mentioned in this chapter, see Erik Hornung, *The Ancient Egyptian Books of the Afterlife*, trans. David Lorton (Ithaca and London, 1999).

20. Recent research has suggested that the stars and planets were thought of as forming part of the great cycle of the sun's progression through the sky, so it was not contradictory to claim that the deceased king was joining both the sun and the stars.

21. These statements are from Pyramid Text 477. This is typical of the way in which the death of Osiris was alluded to (he has "fallen upon his side") but never clearly described. The belief that this terrible event should not be directly shown or narrated persisted right until the end of Egyptian culture.

22. This provincial use may only be evidence for the gradual spread of literacy and an increasing availability of artists outside the capital. Some parts of the Pyramid Texts were probably recited at private funerals long before they were first written down on private tomb walls and coffins.

23. Extracts from the Pyramid Texts occur on tomb walls and coffins right down to the Ptolemaic Period (332–30 BC). It is a remarkable testament to the longevity of Egyptian culture that educated people living in this period could read and appreciate texts composed over 2,000 years earlier.

24. See Kurt Sethe, *Dramatische Texte zu altägyptischen Mysterienspielen* (Leipzig, 1928). Egyptologists have been unable to agree on the nature of the rituals recorded in this text. They have been interpreted as a coronation ceremony, or as part of the *sed* **festival** at which a king's power was renewed by the gods, or a royal funeral.

25. For a persuasive interpretation of the religious symbolism of Middle Kingdom tomb decoration, see Janice Kamrin, *The Cosmos of Khnumhotep II at Beni Hasan* (London and New York, 1999).

26. For a translation and study of the Book of Two Ways, see Leonard H. Lesko, *The Ancient Egyptian Book of Two Ways* (Berkeley, 1972).

27. Hornung, *The Ancient Egyptian Books of the Afterlife*, 11.

28. See Mircea Eliade, *Shamanism: Archaic Techniques of Ecstasy*, trans. W. R. Trask (New York, 1964).

29. Both views about the Coffin Texts are represented among the essays in H. Willems (ed.), *The World of the Coffin Texts* (Leiden, 1996).

30. The services in Egyptian temples did not include a congregation. Only priests were allowed to enter the sanctuary and touch the image of the deity. Hymns were sung by temple musicians as part of the process of "waking" a deity each morning. For temple music, see Lisa Manniche, *Music and Musicians in Ancient Egypt* (London, 1991), chap. 4. For a selection of Middle Kingdom hymns, see Miriam Lichtheim, *Ancient Egyptian Literature*, vol. 1, *The Old and Middle Kingdoms* (Berkeley, Los Angeles, and London, 1973), pt. 3, sec. 4.

31. See Richard B. Parkinson, "Individual and Society in Middle Kingdom Literature" and "Types of Literature in the Middle Kingdom," in *Ancient Egyptian Literature: History and Forms*, ed. Antonio Loprieno (Leiden and New York, 1996), 137–156, 297–312.

32. The text is translated by Richard B. Parkinson in *The Tale of Sinuhe and Other Ancient Egyptian Poems 1940–1640 BC* (Oxford, 1997),166–199.

33. In his *Folktales of Egypt* (Chicago, 1980), Hasan M. El-Shamy argues that "book stories" and oral folk stories develop in parallel, but he cites a number of "crossovers."

34. For translations of these tales, see "Appendix: Primary Sources" under P. Westcar.

35. The story is translated and discussed by Hans Goedicke in "The Story of the Herdsman," *Chronique d'Égypte* 45 (1970): 244–266; and by Parkinson in *The Tale of Sinuhe*, 287–288.

36. For a translation of the story see Lichtheim, *Ancient Egyptian Literature* 1:211–215. See also John Baines, "Interpreting the Story of the Shipwrecked Sailor," in *Journal of Egyptian Archaeology* 76 (1990): 55–72.

37. This is particularly true of Jan Assmann in "Die Verborgenheit des Mythos in Ägypten," *Göttinger Miszellen* 25 (1977): 7–43. See also J. Zeidler, "Zur Frage der Spätentstehung des Mythos in Ägypten," *Göttinger Miszellan* 132 (1993): 85–109.

38. J. F. Borghouts, *Ancient Egyptian Magical Texts* (Leiden, 1978), xi.

39. Reconstructing the myth of Osiris from the reticent accounts on these stelae is like trying to reconstruct the Gospels from brief descriptions of Easter services, but see "Les Fetes D'Osiris À Abydos Au Moyen Empire Et Au Nouvel Empire" by Marie-Christine Lavier and "La Stéla D'Ikhernofret (Berlin No. 1204)" by Jacques Guiter in *Egypte: Afrique et Orient*, no.10 (August 1998): 27–38.

40. Names linked to the opponents of Ra were sometimes given to criminals and foreign enemies as part of a procedure to obliterate their identities in life and the afterlife. It is possible that this Hyksos ruler continued to use a name that was given to him as an insult when he first came to Egypt.

41. For a translation of this story, see W. K. Simpson (ed.), *The Literature of Ancient Egypt: An Anthology of Stories, Instructions, and Poetry* (New Haven and London, 1973), 77–80.

42. This inscription is sometimes called the "King as Sun Priest text." It may derive from the scripts for Middle Kingdom rituals. The text is discussed and translated in J. Assmann's *Egyptian Solar Religion in the New Kingdom: Re, Amun, and the Crisis of Polytheism*, trans. Anthony Alcock (London and New York, 1995), 18–21.

43. Some offerings suggest that temple visitors were familiar with deities' mythological roles, but whether this knowledge came through stories or images is unclear. See G. Pinch, *Votive Offerings to Hathor* (Oxford, 1993).

44. For the influence of solar and lunar mythology on the art and architecture of Amenhotep III's reign, see "Designing the Cosmos" in A. P. Kozloff and B. M. Bryan, *Egypt's Dazzling Sun: Amenhotep III and His World* (Cleveland, 1992), 73–124.

45. For modern myth making about Akhenaten and Nefertiti, see D. Montserrat, *Akhenaten History, Fantasy, and Ancient Egypt* (London and New York, 2000).

46. At a large temple such as the one at Karnak, there were four "shifts," so no one had to spend more than a quarter of their time on ritual duties. For all aspects of the priesthood, see David Lorton's new translation of S. Sauneron's *The Priests of Ancient Egypt* (Ithaca and London), 2000.

47. More specifically, the temples were models of the cosmos as it was newly created "in the First Time." For a summary of the symbolic aspects of temples, see "The Temple as Cosmos," in E. Hornung, *Idea into Image: Essays on Ancient Egyptian Thought* (Princeton, 1992), 115–130; or "Worlds within Worlds," in R. H. Wilkinson, *The Complete Temples of Ancient Egypt* (London, 2000), 52–79.

48. Greek visitors such as Diodorus Siculus later interpreted such scenes as representing a mythical battle between gods and giants set in the far past, but the Egyptians used contemporary enemies as characters in their defining myth of the war between order and chaos.

49. Hatshepsut's scenes are at Deir el-Bahari and Amenhotep III's at Luxor temple. The scenes involving Rameses II are only known from a few stray blocks.

50. Seth was the local deity of the part of the eastern Delta from which Seti and his family came. At Abydos, a picture of Osiris sometimes replaces the picture of Seth, which should be used to write the king's name.

51. For example, every cult image was treated as if it were the mummified body of Osiris, which could be restored to life by offerings symbolizing the powerful Eye of Horus. See A. R. David, *A Guide to Religious Ritual at Abydos* (Warminster, England, 1981).

52. The Osireion was probably begun under Seti I and finished by his grandson Merenptah.

53. The hymn is found on the stela of the official Amenmose (Louvre Museum C 286). See in "Appendix: Primary Sources."

54. The majority of the Underworld Books first appear in the late Eighteenth and early Nineteenth Dynasties, perhaps as a counterreaction to Akhenaten's efforts to abolish the realm of Osiris. For summaries of all the Underworld Books, see Hornung, *The Ancient Egyptian Books of the Afterlife*.

55. The Egyptians seem to have been the first people to divide the day into twenty-four hours: twelve for the day and twelve for the night.

56. The tomb of Rameses VI (c. 1143–1136 BCE) includes all or part of seven Underworld Books. This alone suggests that they were not to be taken as factual descriptions of the afterlife. Underworld Books were true in the sense that they were thought to be effective in bringing about a desired state.

57. In a forthcoming book, *Crowns in Egyptian Funerary Literature—Symbols of Royalty, Rebirth, and Destruction,* Katja Goebs suggests that the myth of the destruction of mankind evolved from a myth of the sun god's reabsorption of the powers of all the other celestial beings, just as the sun appears to swallow up the stars at dawn.

58. For translations of a selection of these hymns, see "Hymns and Prayers to Amun-Re: The Apogee of Ancient Egyptian Religious Thought,'" in J. L. Foster, *Hymns, Prayers and Songs: An Anthology of Ancient Egyptian Lyric Poetry,* ed. Susan Tower Hollis (Atlanta, 1995), 55–79. The problem of the nature of the relationship between the one creator deity and the myriad other gods and goddesses continued to fascinate Egyptian thinkers long after Akhenaten's solution had been rejected. See Assmann, *Egyptian Solar Religion In the New Kingdom.*

59. J. Assmann, "Death and Initiation in the Funerary Religion of Ancient Egypt," in J. P. Allen et al., *Religion and Philosophy in Ancient Egypt,* Yale Egyptological Studies 3 (New Haven, 1989), 150–152. For the possible influence of Egyptian concepts of divine judgment on other religions, see S. G. F. Brandon, *The Judgement of the Dead: An Historical and Comparative Study of the Idea of Post-mortem Judgement in the Major Religions* (London, 1967).

60. For example, a man named Neferabu describes how the goddess Meretseger struck him down like a savage lioness because he had sinned against her. This seems to be a reference to the myth told in the Book of the Heavenly Cow of humanity's being punished for its sins by the unleashing of a terrible lioness. For a translation of Neferabu's stela, see "Appendix: Primary Sources."

61. Owing to the occupation of the villagers, there was an unusually high literacy rate in Deir el-Medina. Even so, most of the artists probably could not read the texts of the Underworld Books they copied onto the walls of the royal tombs. For the religious life of the villagers, see L. H. Lesko (ed.), *Pharaoh's Workers* (Ithaca and London, 1994).

62. See John Baines, "Myth and Literature," in Loprieno, *Ancient Egyptian Literature,* 373–374.

63. The mythological basis for the story is explored by S. Tower Hollis in *The Ancient Egyptian "Tale of Two Brothers": The Oldest Fairy Tale in the World* (Norman, OK, and London, 1990).

64. For a discussion of all these New Kingdom stories and fragments, see S. Quirke, "Narrative literature," in Loprieno, *Ancient Egyptian Literature,* 263–276. Most of the stories are translated in Simpson, *The Literature of Ancient Egypt.*

65. For varying interpretations of this story, see C. Oden, "A Structural Interpretation of the Contendings of Horus and Seth," *History of Religions* 18, no. 2 (1979): 352–369; and S. A. Allam, "Legal Aspects in the 'Contendings of Horus and Seth,'" in *Studies in Pharaonic*

Religion and Society in Honour of J. Gwyn Griffiths, ed. A. B. Lloyd (London, 1992), 137–145.

66. The Ancient Egyptian year was divided into three seasons, each lasting four months. The months were mainly named after deities. For a translation of the Cairo Calendar, see "Appendix: Primary Sources."

67. The ostensible reason for moving the royal mummies was to save them from tomb robbers, but it also allowed the high priests to recycle the treasure buried with these rulers. The mummies were gathered together and hidden in two separate tombs, where they were rediscovered in the nineteenth century CE.

68. The burial equipment from these tombs, which includes splendid jewelry with mythological motifs, is displayed in the Cairo Museum. Hardly any royal tombs from the rest of the first millennium BCE have survived in Egypt, but it is known that Underworld Books continued to be used on royal sarcophagi.

69. For examples of such amulets, see C. Andrews, *Amulets of Ancient Egypt* (London, 1994), pls.80, 101.

70. For the myth of Atum's creating life with his hand, see "Creation" under "Linear Time" in "Mythical Time Lines." The word for hand was feminine in Egyptian. For further information on these powerful royal women, see G. Robins, *Women in Ancient Egypt* (London and Cambridge, MA, 1993), chap. 8.

71. For a translation of this inscription, see Miriam Lichtheim, *Ancient Egyptian Literature*, vol. 3 *The Late Period* (Berkeley, Los Angeles, and London, 1980), 66–84; and for the full story of these remarkable kings, see R. G. Morkot, *The Black Pharaohs: Egypt's Nubian Rulers* (London, 2000). Note that in some chronologies all or part of the Twenty-Fifth Dynasty is counted as part of the Third Intermediate Period.

72. See L. H. Lesko, "Nubian Influence on the Later Versions of the Books of the Dead" in *Abstracts of Papers: Eighth International Congress of Egyptologists* (Cairo, 2000), 111.

73. For translations of the Memphite Theology, see MT in "Appendix: Primary Sources;" for the discussion of its date, see F. Junge, MDAIK 29 (1973): 195–204; and H. Schlögl, *Der Gott Ta-tenen*, Orbis Biblicus et Orientalis 29 (Freiburg and Göttingen, 1980).

74. This papyrus is now in the British Museum, London (PBM 10188). For a full translation, see "Appendix: Primary Sources." For a commentary on the creation myths, see J. P. Allen, *Genesis in Egypt: The Philosophy of Ancient Egyptian Creation Accounts*, 2d ed., Yale Egyptological Studies 2 (San Antonio, TX, 1995), 27–30.

75. This inscription is mentioned by the neo-Platonist philosopher Iamblichus in his book *Mysteries of Egypt*, written around 300 CE. The major temples and royal tombs of Saïs now lie beneath a marshy area that has not been fully excavated.

76. See "Appendix: Primary Sources" under Hibis texts. The temple of Hibis has now been dismantled and is going to be rebuilt on a drier site.

77. The truth about Herodotus probably lies somewhere between these opposing viewpoints. For a very detailed study of this topic, see A. B. Lloyd, *Herodotus Book II*, 3 vols. (Leiden, 1975–1988).

78. As translated by David Grene in *The History Herodotus* (Chicago and London, 1987).

79. The text is from the Ismailia Naos, also known as El-Arish Naos. See "Appendix: Primary Sources."

80. The implication is that Egypt was defeated because this warrior god had withdrawn his protection.

81. One version of the Memphis decree is in the contemporary Demotic language and script; the other is in a classicizing neo–Middle Egyptian language written in hieroglyphs. The Rosetta Stone played an important role in the decipherment of the hieroglyphic script in the nineteenth century CE. The Memphis decree is translated by R. S. Simpson in R. Parkinson, *Cracking Codes: The Rosetta Stone and Decipherment* (London, 1999).

82. Among these other sources are a Ptolemaic copy of the Book of the Dead and texts for Osiris rituals inscribed on temple walls. For translations, see "Appendix: Primary Sources" under Lamentations.

83. Lévi-Strauss, "The Structural Study of Myth," in *Myth: A Symposium,* ed. T. A. Sebeok (Bloomington and London, 1955), 85–86.

84. See the excellent survey by R. B. Finnestad, "Temples of the Ptolemaic and Roman Periods: Ancient Traditions in New Contexts," in *Temples of Ancient Egypt,* ed. B. E. Shafer (London and New York, 1998), 185–237.

85. The birth of Isis was celebrated at Dendara. This is an example of how a type of myth that originally applied to only one god was adapted for other deities who had become important. The classic publication on temple birth houses is F. Daumas, *Les mammisis des temples égyptiens* (Paris, 1958).

86. Followers of the theory that drama was born from the coming together of myth and ritual have cited the Festival of Victory as one of the world's oldest plays. See H. W. Fairman, *The Triumph of Horus: An Ancient Egyptian Sacred Drama* (London, 1974).

87. For discussions of all these sources, see R. B. Finnestad, *Image of the World and Symbol of the Creator* (Wiesbaden, 1985); or B. Watterson, *The House of Horus at Edfu* (Stroud, England, 1998).

88. See L. Lesko, "Ancient Egyptian Cosmogonies and Cosmologies," in Shafer, *Religion in Ancient Egypt,* 105–107.

89. For a French translation and commentary, see PJ in "Appendix: Primary Sources." A few episodes from Papyrus Jumilhac are translated into English by Hollis as an appendix to *The Ancient Egyptian "Tale of Two Brothers,"* 171–176.

90. Manetho's scheme of dividing Egyptian history into thirty dynasties is still used today.

91. For a French translation, see PV in "Appendix: Primary Sources."

92. This story about the crowning of Horus and Seth is yet another variation on the myth about how the Two Lords were reconciled. For these fragmentary tales, see W. J. Tait, "Demotic Literature: Forms and Genres," in Loprieno, *Ancient Egyptian Literature,* 175–190.

93. The Metternich Stela dates to the reign of Nectanebo II (360–343 BCE). Versions of some of its spells were used 800 years earlier on a statue of Rameses III.

94. The divine forms on *cippi* and magical statues may derive from pattern books of amuletic images kept in temple libraries. See L. Kákosy, "A New Source of Egyptian Mythology and Iconography," in *Proceedings of the Seventh International Congress of Egyptologists*, ed. C. Eyre (Leuven, Belgium, 1998), 619–624.

95. Strabo gave a particularly vivid account of watching sacred crocodiles being fed, an event that had become something of a tourist attraction.

96. For most of Egyptian history there were about 750 hieroglyphic signs in use. By the Roman Period the number of signs had risen to around 7,000, and the old signs were often used in new ways. See "Figurative Hieroglyphs, or 'Cryptography,'" in Parkinson, *Cracking Codes*, 80–87.

97. See "Manetho and Chaeremon," in G. Fowden, *The Egyptian Hermes: An Historical Approach to the Late Pagan Mind* (Princeton, 1986), 52–95. Other accounts of Egyptian priests make them venal and quarrelsome.

98. Translation by J. G. Griffiths, from his *Plutarch's De Iside et Osiride* (Swansea, Wales, 1970), 223.

99. For these two books, see M. Smith, *The Liturgy of the Opening of the Mouth for Breathing* (Oxford, 1993); and F. T. Herbin, *Le Livre de parcourir l'éternité* (Leuven, Belgium, 1994).

100. Other examples of continuing knowledge of ancient religious texts in the Roman Period are provided in a version of the New Kingdom Book of Nut in Papyrus Carlsberg I and the use of part of the Book of the Heavenly Cow in a compilation known as the Book of the Fayum. For translations, see BofN and BHC in "Appendix: Primary Sources."

101. This tale is part of a series of stories (the Petubastis cycle) set in the Third Intermediate Period. Some commentators believe that Homer's *Iliad* was an influence on this cycle. By the Roman Period the Egyptians were claiming that Homer had been born in Thebes and was a son of the god Thoth. For a translation of the Amazons' story, see Lichtheim, *Ancient Egyptian Literature*, 3:151–156.

102. See EofS in "Appendix: Primary Sources." Part of a direct Greek translation of this version survives and is thought to have had an influence on the development of Ancient Greek fiction. See W. J. Tait, "Egyptian Fiction in Demotic and Greek," in *Greek Fiction*, ed. J. R. Morgan and R. Stoneman (London, 1994), 212–213.

103. The moral given in Aesop is that "a change of fortune can make the strongest man need a weaker man's help" (translation by S. A. Handford, *Fables of Aesop* [London, 1954], 41); in the Egyptian version the moral is "it is beautiful to do good to him who does it in turn" (translation by Lichtheim, *Ancient Egyptian Literature* 3: 159).

104. At this point, Imhotep had been worshipped as a god for well over a thousand years, but he was still treated as a historical figure in literature. This suggests that the Egyptians were not prone to confuse historical and mythical characters.

105. For a summary of this important text, see R. Jasnow and K. T. Zauzich, "A Book of Thoth?" in Eyre, *Proceedings of the Seventh International Congress of Egyptologists*, 607–618. It has no connection with Aleister Crowley's *The Book of Thoth*, which is about Tarot cards.

106. Such magical initiation rites are described in "How to Become a Magician: The Rites of Initiation," in F. Graf, *Magic in the Ancient World* (Cambridge, MA, and London, 1997), 89–117. For translations of the Setna stories, see Setna cycle in "Appendix: Primary Sources."

107. One of the four papyri also contains the most complete version of the Demotic Eye of the Sun myth. The largest collection of spells is in the London-Leiden Magical Papyrus. See J. H. Johnson, "Introduction to the Demotic Magical Papyri," in *The Greek Magical Papyri in Translation*, ed. H. D. Betz (Chicago and London, 1992), lv–lviii.

108. For surveys of the background to these difficult texts, see Fowden, *The Egyptian Hermes*; and the introduction to B. P. Copenhaver, *Hermetica* (Cambridge, 1992).

109. For a fascinating account of the long, slow decline of Egyptian "paganism," see D. Frankfurter, *Religion in Roman Egypt: Assimilation and Resistance* (Princeton, 1998).

110. The Arabic literature also referred to the terrifying guardians of such pagan sites—for example, the Great Sphinx. See U. Haarmann, "Medieval Muslim Perceptions of Pharaonic Egypt," in Loprieno, *Ancient Egyptian Literature*, 605–628.

111. All these attempts were fruitless because of their reliance on misleading information in Classical authors such as Plutarch and Horapollo. See E. Iversen, *The Myth of Egypt and Its Hieroglyphs in European Tradition* (Princeton, 1993).

112. Freud's collection of figurines of Ancient Egyptian deities can be viewed at the Freud Museum in London. In his autobiography, *Memories, Dreams, Reflections* (London, 1963), Jung wrote of the Horus myth: "It is a myth which must have been told after human culture—that is consciousness—had for the first time released men from the darkness of prehistoric times" (translated by Richard and Clara Winston).

113. See Frazer, *The Golden Bough: A Study in Magic and Religion*, abridged ed. (London, 1922), 477–507.

114. For the arguments for and against this thesis, see the anthology *The Myth and Ritual Theory*, edited by R. A. Segal (Malden and Oxford, 1998).

115. See his *Black Athena: The Afroasiatic Roots of Classical Civilization*, 2 vols. (London, 1987–1991). These books have contributed to a new interest in Ancient Egyptian history and mythology among African American writers and artists.

116. Some of these stories are reprinted in C. Frayling, *The Face of Tutankhamun* (London and Boston, 1992).

117. The fact that most of the excavators of Tutankhamun's tomb survived to old age has proved no impediment to the curse legend. For a survey of "Mummy" movies, see A. Lant, "The Curse of the Pharaoh, or How Cinema Contracted Egyptomania,"' in *October* 59 (1992): 86–112.

MYTHICAL TIME LINES

T he Egyptians did not think of time as moving at the same rate for all classes of beings or in all parts of the cosmos. For the dead, an hour in the presence of the sun god was said to be equivalent to a lifetime in Egypt. Nor was time always thought of as a linear progression. Historical Egyptians lived in linear time, experienced by each person as past, present, and future—like points on a straight line. King lists reflect this view of time, sometimes arranging kings or dynasties one after another even when they reigned contemporaneously. Yet the standard dating system started again with the reign of each new king because the Egyptians also thought of time as moving in cycles.

In these cycles, time appears to loop back on itself, and patterns of events are repeated, often at fixed intervals. In this view of time the roles of cause and effect can appear to be reversed, creating temporal paradoxes. Egyptian kings, for example, were sometimes said to be their own fathers.

The main part of this mythical time line consists of a linear mythical "history" in which I have laid out the principal events of Egyptian myth in the order in which they should logically occur. It is important to bear in mind that although everything in this section is drawn from original sources, no Ancient Egyptian text that we know of attempts this kind of synthesis. I then look at how the same events recur in different patterns in cyclical time.

LINEAR TIME

The mythical story of Egypt can be divided into seven stages: chaos (pre-creation), the emergence of the creator, the creation of the world and its inhabitants, the reign of the sun god, the period of direct rule by other deities, the period of rule by semidivine kings (history), and the return to chaos.

Chaos

Summary: Before creation there was a state of chaos that contained the potential for all life. This inchoate state was imagined as a dark watery domain of unlimited depth and extent. Elements and qualities of chaos could be personified as gods and goddesses. Some of these deities had to change or die to begin the creative process.

The origin of the universe was an intellectual problem that came to fascinate the Egyptians. Texts that allude to the unknowable era before creation define it as the time "'before two things had developed."[1] The cosmos was not yet divided into pairs of opposites such as earth and sky, light and darkness, male and female, or life and death.

The Egyptians speculated that the primeval substance was watery and dark and had no form and no boundaries. These primeval waters, known as the *nu* or the *nun*, continued to surround the world even after creation and were thought of as the ultimate source of the Nile. When personified as a deity, Nun could be called the father and mother of the creator, because the creator was thought of as coming into existence within the *nun*.

After creation, qualities of the primeval state, such as its darkness, were retrospectively endowed with consciousness and became a group of deities known as the Eight or the Ogdoad of Hermopolis (see "Deities, Themes, and Concepts"). The Eight were imagined as amphibians and reptiles, fertile creatures of the dark primeval slime. They were the forces that shaped the creator or even the first manifestations of the creator. In order to become "the fathers and mothers" of life, they had to change or, in some accounts, to die. Several temples claimed to be the burial place of these primeval deities.

Amun and his female counterpart Amunet were often regarded as part of the Eight and personified hidden power. When Amun became a national god, a new theology made Amun the invisible, unknowable force that began the movement toward independent life. In some accounts the Eight join together to be fertilized by the "seed" of the serpent Amun Kem-atef, the "first primeval god who gave birth to the primeval gods."[2]

The serpent may have been considered an appropriate form for the spirit of the creator because of its undivided body or because it periodically renewed itself by shedding its skin. When creator gods such as Amun or Atum are spoken of as serpents, they usually represent the positive aspect of chaos as an energy force, but they had a negative counterpart in the great serpent Apophis. Apophis represented the destructive aspect of chaos that constantly tried to overwhelm all individual beings and reduce everything back to its primeval state of "oneness." So, even before creation began, the world contained the elements of its own destruction.

Emergence of the Creator

Summary: The creator attains consciousness and becomes lonely. He/she differentiates the elements of chaos by speaking their names. The first light or the first sound begins the process of creation. The creator appears as the sun god. He may be born to a cow, emerge from a lotus on the water or from an egg, or alight in the form of a bird on the first mound of solid land.

The creator was the "unique one in the *nun*" who existed in this womblike environment as "one who is in his egg." The creator was in an inert state, yet this state contained the potential for all life. Passages in the Coffin Texts stress that the "self-created god" came into being alone. For a group-oriented culture such as that of the Egyptians, such loneliness must have been almost unimaginable. The creator remained alone until his/her "heart became effective" and he/she began to think and feel.

In Coffin Texts spell 76, the creator (here named as Atum) brings eight gods into existence "by speaking with the *nun*," presumably separating the elements of chaos by the process of naming them. Other texts refer to the creator's driving back the primeval waters, perhaps by the power of spoken command, to create a space in which to begin the work of creation.

Images of Emergence.   The "primal event" of the emergence of the creator to dispel the watery silent darkness could be represented in many different ways. No single image or narrative was considered sufficient to express such a wonder. Egyptian cosmogonies (creation accounts) often combine several different traditions about the creator, but rarely in any kind of temporal framework.[3]

The first act of the creator might be an exhalation of breath or a great cry. The first light came with the first appearance of the creator as the life-giving power of the sun. This manifestation could be pictured as an eye, a child, or a fiery bird. In Coffin Texts spell 75, although the creator is still alone in the *nun*, he/she sends out his/her eye to illumine the darkness and search for other life. Another image of the first sunrise was a blue lotus rising above the surface of the *nun* (see "Lotus" in "Deities, Themes, and Concepts"). From the New Kingdom onward, a naked child or a ram-headed figure was shown sitting in the lotus to represent the newborn sun.

The fertile aspect of the *nun* could be personified as the goddess Mehet-Weret, whose name means the Great Flood or the Great Swimmer. She was usually shown as a cow and was considered the mother of all the primeval beings, including Apophis. Mehet-Weret was envisaged as giving birth to the sun child and lifting him up on her horns. A New Kingdom hymn tells us that with the first light the sky became like gold and the primeval waters like lapis-lazuli.

Figure 11 . A pyramidion from a Late Period tomb showing the creator god Atum with the primeval benu *bird. The pyramidion itself may represent the Primeval Mound. (Courtesy of Geraldine Pinch)*

The sun might also be thought of as emerging from a "cosmic egg" laid by a primeval bird (see under "Birds" in "Deities, Themes, and Concepts") or, less often, by a snake or a crocodile. The role of the primeval bird could also be to break the silence. Some cosmogonies allude to a goose known as the Great Honker or Cackler whose strident cry was the first sound. The shining *benu* bird (see "*Benu* Bird" in "Deities, Themes, and Concepts") brought both the first noise and the first light to the *nun*. The creation myths inscribed in the Edfu temple give this role to a falcon, who alights on a floating mass of vegetation.

Alternatively, the first bird was said to have found a resting place on the first mound of dry land. The creator could not become fully active until there was a place in which to exist. At this stage, the *nun* was thought of as a great swamp from which the first land, the Primeval Mound, suddenly emerged. This mound could be personified as the god Tatjenen, "the rising land." Tatjenen, who was often identified with Ptah, could also be called the "father" of the creator.[4] One of the sacred books at Edfu was the Book of the Mounds of the First Time. This presents a primeval landscape of mounds, water, and reeds

that is close to what the Nile valley must have looked like before it
was settled by the first Egyptians.[5]
The creator could now begin the
work of creating the world and its
inhabitants.

Creation

Summary: At different periods and
in various theological centers, a
number of deities could be identified with the creator who emerged
from the primeval waters. These
creator deities include the gods
Atum, Ra (often combined as Ra-
Atum), Shu, Ptah, Khnum, and

Figure 12. Plaque with a Wedjat *(Sacred Eye). The Eye
of Ra and the Eyes of Horus could all be shown in this
way. (British Museum)*

Amun-Ra and the goddesses Neith, Hathor, and Isis. Important stages in the
creation process were the establishment of *maat,* the divine order; the division
of beings into male and female; and the separation of earth and sky.

The Egyptian cosmos consisted of a divine realm in the upper sky; the
earth, with Egypt its center; and the *Duat* (or *Dat*), the underworld that was to
become the realm of the dead. The creator produced other deities and then
lesser beings such as people and animals.

The One Who Made Himself into Millions.   In many Egyptian sources the creation of life involves three elements: the creation of a body, the transfer to that
body of some part of the divine essence of the creator, and the animation of the
body by the breath of life. Some creator deities were more strongly associated
with one of these elements than with the others. Khnum, for example, was
chiefly a creator of bodies, whereas Shu and Amun-Ra were both gods of the unseen breath of life. The second element, the transfer of the divine essence, eventually led to the concept that all deities, or even all living beings, were not just
made by a transcendent creator but were in some sense *forms* of the creator.
From the New Kingdom onward, this was a distinctive feature of Egyptian religious thought.

The creator was sometimes referred to as "the One Who Made Himself into
Millions" or "He Who Made Himself into Millions of Gods."[6] Creation could
be seen as a process of differentiation, in which one original force was gradually

divided (without necessarily diminishing itself) into the diverse elements that made up the universe. The ways in which this could have happened were the subject of much speculation.

The Heart and the Tongue.   The intellectual powers that enabled the creator to bring himself/herself into existence and to create other beings were sometimes conceptualized as deities. The most important of these were the gods Sia, Hu, and Heka. Sia was the power of perception or insight, which allowed the creator to visualize other forms. Hu was the power of authoritative speech, which enabled the creator to bring things into being by naming them. In Coffin Texts spell 335, Hu and Sia are said to be with their "father" Atum every day. In the illustrated Underworld Books of the New Kingdom, these two deities were often shown accompanying the creator sun god.

The power by which the thoughts and commands of the creator became reality was Heka (Magic). In Coffin Texts spell 261, the god Heka claims to have been with the creator even in the primeval era. In the cosmogony of Neith recorded in the Roman Period temple at Esna, this goddess creates the whole world with seven magic words. When Isis came to be worshipped as a creator deity during the same period, she was called the Mistress of the Word in the Beginning.

From at least as early as the New Kingdom, the god Ptah could represent the creative mind. Then Sia and Hu were identified as the heart and tongue of Ptah. This concept is expounded in the so-called Memphite Theology and in various hymns to Ptah. The Ancient Egyptians believed that the heart was the organ of thought and feeling. So Ptah was said to have made the world after planning it in his heart. It was "through what the heart plans and the tongue commands" that everything was made. Typically, the Memphite Theology also mentions other models of creation, such as the concept of the creator as Divine Craftsman or as the biological source of all life. The Egyptians did not take any one of these theories too literally. They were diverse but complementary attempts to convey something of the ultimately unknowable mystery of creation.

The Divine Craftsman.   Two deities, Ptah and Khnum, were sometimes credited with physically "fashioning" the world and its inhabitants. Ptah was the patron god of craftsmen and artists. He was particularly associated with sculpture and metalworking. Ptah was said to have invented the **Opening of the Mouth** ritual in which an adze and other tools were used to "bring to life" statues and mummies.[7] Hymns to Ptah speak of him designing and crafting the world and "smelting the Two Lands" (Egypt). He was also said to make bodies for kings out of electrum (an alloy of gold and silver), copper, and iron.

Presumably these were the bodies that kings hoped to inhabit in the divine realm.

The shaping of royal bodies was a task more usually attributed to Khnum. Khnum was represented by a ram, an animal renowned for aggressive virility. He was sometimes described as "begetting" the gods, but as a creator he was usually celebrated as the divine craftsman who "formed everything" on his potter's wheel. Craftsmen were valued and well treated in Egyptian society, but few of them attained high social status. Khnum's original role seems to have been as the divine potter who made things at the command of the creator. When he became a form of the universal creator, Khnum's name was usually linked with those of more established creator deities such as Ra or Ptah.

The Hand of Atum. Before creation begins there is no division into genders. The creator seems to include both the male and female principles. Creator deities were commonly called "the father and mother of all things." Deities who were normally regarded as male, such as Atum, are described as "giving birth" to other deities during the creative process.[8]

The actual means by which the creator reproduced were sometimes left vague and sometimes described in terms of blunt sexual imagery. Pyramid Texts (PT) spell 527 says that Atum took his penis in his hand and masturbated "and so were born the two siblings, that is Shu and Tefnut." In PT 600, Atum-Khepri is said to be the one who spat out Shu and Tefnut.[9] Several passages in the Coffin Texts refer to Shu being exhaled from Atum's nose and Tefnut being spat from his mouth.

These apparently contradictory statements are clarified in later sources, such as the Bremner-Rhind Papyrus and the Memphite Theology. Atum excites his penis with his hand and takes the semen into his mouth. The vignettes to some mythological papyri illustrate this moment in graphic detail. The mouth of the creator acts as a substitute womb. Atum uses his powers of thought and utterance to transform the seed into the first two gendered deities, who are expelled from his mouth or through the nose and mouth.

The combination of biological and intellectual methods of creation is stressed in the Memphite Theology, which states that the Ennead of Atum (the first nine deities created) "came into existence through his seed and his fingers, but the Ennead is the teeth and lips in this mouth that spoke the name of every thing and from which Shu and Tefnut came forth."

Once the twins had been born, the sexual identity of Atum becomes fixed as a father. A further development was the personification of the Hand of Atum as a goddess, thus giving him a sexual partner. Since the Hand goddess came directly from the creator, she was his "daughter" as well as his consort. This goddess was often identified with Hathor, who came to be regarded as the female creative principle.

The twins sometimes appear to be the male and female aspects of Atum. He embraces them to transfer his *ka* (vital essence) to them. In Coffin Texts spell 80, Shu and Tefnut are described as living with their father in the primeval waters. The three deities cling tightly to each other as if they were still one entity. For creation to continue, Shu and Tefnut had to become fully differentiated from the creator.

The Lost Children.   There are some allusions in the Coffin Texts to Atum becoming separated from his children. Shu and Tefnut seem to have drifted away from their father and become lost in the darkness of the primeval waters. In Coffin Texts spell 76, Shu is made to say that "Atum once sent his Sole Eye searching for me and Tefnut, my sister. I made light in the darkness and it found me." This eye is usually called the daughter of Ra, rather than of Atum, because she is part of the creator's solar aspect.[10] The Sole Eye is the disk of the sun envisaged as a goddess. She can function separately from the sun god but remains a part of him. The search for the lost children in Coffin Texts spell 76 is one of the many myths about the first sunrise. Shu, the god of air, creates a void in the primeval waters so that the solar eye can shine for the first time.[11]

A fuller version of this myth found in the Bremner-Rhind Papyrus has a different emphasis. The Lord of All recounts how Shu and Tefnut were nurtured by the god of the primeval waters, "with my Eye (following) after them from the time they became separated from me." When the creator came fully into existence on the Primeval Mound, Shu and Tefnut rejoiced and returned with the Eye. "Then she became furious after she had come back and found that I had put another in her place." The creator has apparently grown a new eye/disk.

To appease his angry "daughter," the creator transforms her into the first snake, the *uraeus* cobra, and puts her in the place of honor on his forehead.[12] This is one of several myths about the anger and appeasement of the solar eye. The creator's relationships with the aspects of his being that are embodied as daughter-goddesses are crucial to this stage of creation.

The Divine Order and the Separation of Earth and Sky.   In Coffin Texts spell 80, new identities are given to Shu and Tefnut. Atum names Shu as Life and Tefnut as *Maat* (Truth, Justice, Order). By naming these qualities, the creator brings them into existence. Atum embraces the two forms of his daughter, Tefnut and Maat.[13] Nun, the god of the primeval waters, tells Atum to kiss Maat and place her at his nose "so that your heart may live." Maat the goddess was the favorite daughter of the creator, the one who brought her father joy. *Maat* as a concept was the ordering and governing principle of the created world.[14] The opposite of *maat* was *isfet* (chaos, disorder) or *gereg* (wrongdoing, evil). The creator and all his/her creations were to live on and through *maat*. All Egyptian rulers, and those who helped them to govern, were supposed to establish the state of *maat* on earth, "as it was in the First Time."

A series of cosmic events was part of the First Time. Shu and Tefnut separated from their father and came together in the first sexual union of male and female. Tefnut then gave birth to another pair of deities, a son Geb, who was associated with the earth, and a daughter Nut, who was associated with the sky. Geb and Nut embraced each other so ardently that there was no room between them for anything to exist. Nut conceived children but could not or would not give birth to them. Geb and Nut seemed to want to become one, reversing the movement toward diversity. If creation was to continue, another separation was necessary.

In his new manifestation of giver of life, Shu separated his children Geb and Nut. According to Coffin Texts spell 76, Shu lifted up his daughter Nut and set his son Geb under his feet. This image was first portrayed in detail on coffins and funerary papyri at the end of the New Kingdom. Geb is shown sprawling at the bottom of the picture, sometimes still in a state of sexual arousal. Shu stands with his arms raised supporting the arched body of Nut (see Figure 42). This arm position was the hieroglyphic symbol that wrote the word *ka* (life force or vital essence), which helps to emphasize that Shu is making life possible. Many other beings, including the entities known as the Heh gods, can be shown assisting Shu to support the sky above the earth.

Shu created a space between earth and sky in which creatures could breathe the air that gives life. In this space, the sun could rise for the first time and drive away the primeval darkness. This first sunrise is "the perfect moment" celebrated in numerous Egyptian texts and images. From this moment the creator was chiefly manifest in the world as the sun god Ra. The boundaries of the physical world became fixed, though the upper sky (Nut), the atmosphere (Shu), and the earth (Geb) were still encircled by the dark primeval waters. As part of establishing the divine order, Shu and Tefnut also become two different types of time. "Shu is Eternal Recurrence and Tefnut is Eternal Sameness."[15] This began a great cycle in which everything had to change to survive and yet everything remained fundamentally the same.

The separation of Nut and Geb made it possible for their children to be born. These were the gods Osiris, Seth, and Horus "the Two-Eyed" and the goddesses Isis and Nephthys. Some sources leave out Horus. A tradition as old as the Pyramid Texts had Seth break violently out of his mother's womb. Seth was a god whose nature linked him with chaos, so the birthday of Seth was said to be the day on which disorder and strife first entered the world.

Osiris, Seth, Isis, and Nephthys, together with Geb and Nut, Shu and Tefnut, and Ra-Atum, made up the four-generational group of deities known as the Ennead of Heliopolis or the Great Ennead. Horus, the sky falcon whose two eyes were the sun and the moon, was probably left out of the nine because he was usually thought of as a manifestation of the creator sun god. The number nine was sometimes used by the Egyptians to indicate "many," so the establishment of the Ennead can stand for the creation of the whole pantheon of deities. Other deities were said to come into existence through words spoken by the creator or from substances exuded from his/her body, such as saliva, sweat, or blood.

Now that a world existed, it could be inhabited by the whole range of beings conceived of by the creator. These included all manner of animals, birds, fish, and reptiles "which are on the back of Geb." In addition to these, there was "god's herd"—humanity.

The Creation of Humanity.   The creation of humanity does not occupy a central position in Egyptian myth. Some creation accounts omit humans altogether. They are only mentioned in passing in the Memphite Theology, listed between gods and cattle (a term covering all animals). The Egyptians sometimes divided sentient beings into four types: gods, kings, the spirits of the dead, and living people.

The Pyramid Texts of the Old Kingdom concentrate on the afterlife of the king and have little to say about living people, so it is not surprising that they contain no allusions to myths about the creation of humanity. Such myths seem to have been well established by the time of the Middle Kingdom. Several spells in the Coffin Texts include speeches referring to the creation of humanity. In Coffin Texts spell 1130, the Lord of All says that he created deities from his sweat and "people from the tears of my eye." Everything that came from a god's body was deemed to be divine and capable of creative power. As with the sneezing and spitting that produced Shu and Tefnut, wordplay is involved. The Egyptian words for *people* and for *tears* were homophones; they sounded similar although they would have been written differently. Most such mythical wordplay was ephemeral or relatively insignificant, but the association of people with divine tears was a popular theme for over 2,000 years.

Several different traditions about the tears of the creator are discernible even in Middle Kingdom writings. In Coffin Texts spell 80, these tears belong to the period of pre-creation. Humanity, it says, came forth from the Sole Eye, which was sent out while the creator Atum was still alone and inert in the primeval waters. The cause of the Eye's weeping is not stated, but it may be from loneliness as it searches for other beings. The potential to produce humans is contained in the Eye, but they cannot come into existence until the world has been created. This is described later in the text, when Shu separates the earth and sky and gives the breath of life to all creatures on earth, including people, "in accordance with the command of Atum." So Atum wills the creation of humanity, but another deity carries it out.

In Coffin Texts spell 714, humanity is said to have sprung from tears wept by the creator because of the anger against him, tears that caused a temporary state of blindness. This may be a reference to the rage of the Sole Eye when she discovers that the creator has grown a new eye in her absence. The creator's blindness implies a temporary loss of his power of creative insight or perception (Sia). Humanity is the imperfect product of rage and misery: a genesis suited to the rebellious role humanity plays in mythical history.

One hymn to the creator states that humanity came forth from the two divine eyes, which are the sun and the moon.[16] In the account of creation in the Bremner-Rhind Papyrus, people originate in the tears wept by the creator on the return of Shu and Tefnut. It is not clear whether these are tears of joy at the reunion with his children or tears of sorrow at the angry reaction of the solar eye. In the cosmogony of Neith, the sun god Ra is said to weep when he is first born because he finds himself alone and unable to see his mother. It is these tears of sorrow and loneliness that produce humanity. In contrast, deities arise as a byproduct of Ra's joy when his mother, Neith, returns. So, most versions of the tears myth provide an explanation for the perpetually sorrowful and imperfect state of humanity.

In spite of this imperfection, the creator was said to have done many things to help humanity. In Coffin Texts 1130, the Lord of All describes his four good deeds. These were to create the four winds to give the breath of life to every body, to make the annual Nile flood so that everyone would get enough food, to create everyone with equal potential, and to make every person's heart "remember the West." This last deed implies that from the beginning humans were destined for an eternal life in the Beautiful West, the realm of the dead. A Middle Kingdom text set in the turbulent First Intermediate Period compares humanity with a flock and the (unnamed) creator with the good shepherd who cares for them. "For their sakes He made heaven and earth, and drove away the rapacity of the waters. So that their nostrils should live He made the winds. They are images of Him, come forth from His flesh. For their sakes He rises in heaven. For them He made plants and flocks. . . ."[17]

New Kingdom hymns to the creator god Amun also refer to god making people "in his own image" but are vague about how this was done. In a hymn to Ptah this god is said to have "crafted people" as well as fashioning the physical forms of the gods. The bodies of deities were usually said to be made of precious metals and stones, but those of people were made from mud or clay. These were the materials used by the creator god Khnum, who "formed all on his potter's wheel."

Khnum did not perform this task just once during the First Time. His wheel was said to turn every day. He appears to be a god of continuous creation, working to make the bodies of all creatures destined to live on earth. Khnum shapes a body for each individual before they are born and a double for their *ka* or vital force. Hymns in the temple of Esna elaborate on this idea. They list all the parts of the human body created by Khnum and the functions they are to perform, such as the tongue for speaking and the legs for walking. The list includes both male and female body parts.

The Egyptian word for *people* used in creation texts was normally written with pictures of a man and a woman following the phonetic part of the word. Humanity seems to have been divided into two genders from the beginning. This is in contrast to other ancient mythologies that made woman an afterthought or an offshoot of the male body. One surviving text may suggest the existence of a myth of this type. This is the New Kingdom story known as the Two Brothers (see "Mythology in Literature" under "New Kingdom and Third Intermediate Period " in "Introduction").

After being falsely accused of trying to rape his brother's wife, Bata goes to live in a remote valley. There he meets the Ennead of Heliopolis. These nine gods decide to give Bata a wife to relieve his loneliness. Khnum shapes a woman with a body more beautiful than any other, and the divine exhalations of the Ennead give her life. This "perfect woman" soon leaves Bata to marry the king of Egypt and subsequently murders her husband in several of his incarnations. In this story, women seem to be regarded as intrinsically flawed.[18] Much the same could be said, however, of most categories of being in the Egyptian universe. Even the creator was not always all-powerful or all-knowing.

Period of Direct Rule by the Creator Sun God

Summary: The creator sun god, usually identified as Ra, ruled the earth for a long period. There was no separation between gods and people during this era. Some deities defied the authority of the sun god when he began to age. The goddess Isis plotted to make her unborn son the heir of Ra. The Eye of Ra quarreled with her father but was persuaded to return to defend him. When humanity rebelled against his rule, Ra sent his Eye to destroy the evildoers and withdrew to live in the sky.

Most Egyptian chronologies start with a mythical period when Egypt and the rest of the world were ruled directly by creator gods. The creator was thought of as living in a palace in Egypt, the most favored part of his creation. Many cultures have a myth of a lost golden age, when gods or semidivine rulers presided over a world without pain or conflict. The Egyptian material only partly fits this pattern.

In the reign of Ra, the gods, including Maat, live on earth, and the creator cares for his creation in person. Everything should be in harmony with the divine order, but two things prevent this age from remaining one of perfect peace and joy. First, the sun god gradually grows old; second, there are plots and rebellions against his authority. Peace and joy do not generate interesting stories, so it is hardly surprising that the only myths set in this era deal with the decline and end of the sun god's reign.

The aging of the sun god is described in a story known in modern times as Isis and Ra or the True Name of Ra. Its ancient title places it among "the spells for warding off poison from the First Time," and the narrator is the scorpion goddess Serqet. Her monologue forms part of a healing spell, but it is composed in an excellent literary style.[19] As the story occurs in few sources, it cannot be seen as a very important part of the mythical cycle, but the names of the sun god recorded in the story reflect the kind of theological speculation found in New Kingdom hymns to the creator. Gaining power over a supernatural being by discovering its secret "true name" is a constant theme of Egyptian magical and funerary texts and a common motif in the folktales of many cultures.

The True Name of Ra.   The story begins with a statement by Serqet that the creator "made heaven, earth, the waters, the breath of life, gods, people, small and large cattle, reptiles, birds, and fishes." Deities and people were both ruled by the creator in his identity of Ra. He appeared in many forms and was known by many names, but none of these was his true name. This name was concealed in his stomach to prevent any hostile force from using it against him.

Only one deity dared to challenge Ra's authority; that was his "daughter" Isis. She was "cleverer than millions of gods." She knew everything in heaven and earth except the name of Ra. So she "plotted in her heart how to discover the name of this noble god." Isis's opportunity comes when Ra starts to show symptoms of old age, such as a drooping mouth and a tendency to drool. Isis finds some of Ra's saliva on the ground. She mixes it with earth and shapes it into a snake. When the snake comes to life, she leaves it at a crossroads where Ra passes every day.

When Ra next walks this road to view his creation, he is bitten by the unseen snake. The poison burns like fire, and Ra gives a terrible scream that disturbs all the gods. As the snake has come from the body of Ra just like the Eye goddess, it presumably has the same terrible fiery poison as that goddess's snake form. At first, Ra is unable to speak because his lips are trembling and his limbs are shaking. "The poison had overwhelmed his body like the inundation overwhelms everything in its path." Then the sun god takes courage and explains to his followers that he has been stung by an unknown creature, not created by him. He summons his "children," the other gods, to see if any of them can help him.

The gods are distraught at the catastrophe that has overtaken Ra. Isis pretends to be as bewildered and upset as the rest. She asks Ra if one of his own creations has rebelled against him and promises to destroy the attacker with her powerful magic. Ra then tells again how he was stung while walking through the Two Lands (Egypt) because "my heart longed to see what I have created." He gives a vivid de-

Figure 13. Votive bronze statuette of Isis with her son, Horus the Child. (Cleveland Museum of Art, Bequest of Harley C. Lee and Elizabeth K. Lee, 1993. 110)

scription of the symptoms of snake bite. He feels colder than water and hotter than fire; he is drenched with sweat and has lost his sight.

Isis claims that she can help if Ra will tell her his name. Ra describes himself by many phrases that define his role as creator. He is the one who created the physical world, he "made the bull for the cow so sex came into being." He is the one who causes the Nile to flood. He is the one who divided the year into seasons and the day into hours. He ends by proclaiming that he is called Khepri in the morning, Ra at noon, and Atum in the evening, but none of these is his true name; so the pain continues.

Isis insists that she cannot heal him without knowing his true name. When the pain gets worse, Ra gives in and whispers his name to Isis. The actual true name is not given in the story.[20] Ra tells Isis that when the time comes, she can pass on the secret to Horus, the son who will be born to her. Then Isis recites magical words that drive the poison out of Ra and destroy it. The mention of Horus at the end of the narrative provides a justification for the behavior of Isis. By gaining knowledge of the secret name to pass on to her son, she is ensuring that Horus will become the ruler of Egypt. The Egyptian audience for this story would know that her marvelous child, Horus, is himself destined to be poisoned in a similar way by a close relative and only cured through the secret knowledge of one of the gods.

Isis was not the only goddess to act against her "father," the creator sun god. Isis acted in a secret manner, but the goddess known as the Eye of Ra openly defied his authority. The story of the quarrel between the solar eye and her father and its eventual resolution is sometimes known as the myth of the Distant Goddess.

The Distant Goddess.   As described earlier, the Sole Eye was a separable active force even when the creator was still inert in the primeval waters. The Eye was sometimes treated as a female form of the sun god, but she was also called the "daughter of Ra." Various important goddesses were associated with this role, most commonly Bastet, Hathor, Mut, Sekhmet, Tefnut, and Wadjyt. For reasons that are rarely stated, the Eye goddess becomes angry and uncontrollable and refuses to stay with her father, Ra. Originally, this may only have been thought to happen when the Eye returned with Shu and Tefnut. Later versions of the myth seem to relate to the period when the world and humanity were well established.

In these versions, the Eye goes to a distant realm, sometimes identified with the Nubian or Libyan deserts. There she rages in her terrible leonine form, destroying everything she meets. Ra is left vulnerable to his enemies, so he sends out one or more of the gods to persuade his daughter to return. This is a dangerous undertaking because the fiery power of the solar eye is stronger than all other deities.

In some versions the chosen divine messenger is Onuris (Inhur). Onuris was a hunter god whose name means "the one who brings back the distant one." The Onuris myth is only known from scattered allusions. It seems that as the most powerful and cunning of hunters, Onuris is able to track down and subdue the solar lioness. He brings her back to Egypt and is rewarded with marriage to the lion goddess.

Figure 14. A dwarf god celebrating the return of the Distant Goddess. A relief in a temple which originally stood on the island of Philae. (Courtesy of Geraldine Pinch)

Other texts name Shu as the one who goes to persuade his sister-consort Tefnut to return. A reference to Shu in Coffin Texts spell 75 as having "pacified her who is in the middle of her rage" may allude to this mythical role. Thoth sometimes accompanies Shu or undertakes the mission on his own.[21] As "the heart and tongue" of the gods, Thoth uses wise words to appease the dangerous goddess.

Several versions of an elaborate literary treatment of this myth were current in the late first millennium BCE. In the longest of these, Hathor-Tefnut is roaming the distant southern desert in the form of a "Nubian cat." Thoth disguises himself as a dog-faced baboon to approach the angry goddess. He alternately harangues and cajoles her. Thoth lectures her about her duty and dignity as the daughter of Ra. He tells her about the desolate and gloomy state that Egypt has fallen into without her bright presence. He paints word pictures of the delicious food offerings and the singing and dancing she will receive in the temples of Egypt if she returns. Thoth also tells her a series of entertaining animal fables on the theme of cosmic justice.

The best known of these is the story of the lion and the mouse.[22] It tells of a mighty lion who (like the Distant Goddess) inspired fear wherever he went. One day, in the remote mountains where the lion lived, he met a panther suffering horrible wounds. The lion asked the panther who had pulled out his fur and ripped his skin. The panther replied that it was "Man." The lion did not know what men were, but he resolved to find Man and punish him.

On his journey he encountered chained horses, donkeys, cows, and oxen. The lion asked them who had imprisoned them, and they all replied "Man." Then the lion found a bear and another lion who had both been tricked and tortured by Man. The lion vowed that he would make Man suffer the same pain he had inflicted on all these animals.

As the lion searched for Man, a tiny mouse ran under his paw. The mouse begged the lion not to crush him. He pointed out that he was too small to satisfy the lion's appetite. The mouse promised that if the lion gave him his life, he would one day save the lion in return. The lion laughed at this, because he thought that no one was powerful enough to endanger him, but he let the mouse go anyway.

The lion did not realize how cunning Man was. A hunter had set a net over a hidden pit. The lion fell into the trap and was caught in the meshes of the net and bound with leather straps. He struggled for hours but could not free himself. In the middle of the night, the little mouse came and told the lion that he had come to repay him for the gift of life, because "it is beautiful to do good." The mouse gnawed through the straps and ropes until the lion was free. Then the mouse climbed into the lion's mane, and they went back to the mountains together.

The implication of this and the other fables is that if the destructive anger of the solar eye is not balanced by the justice and truth personified by Maat, the world will slide into chaos. The volatile goddess is not easy to persuade. One vivid passage describes how she becomes angry with Thoth and transforms from a cat into the terrible solar lioness whose eyes and nostrils spurt flame. Then "Thoth jumped like a frog, he quivered like a grasshopper."

Eventually, Thoth lures the goddess back toward Egypt. On the borders she is greeted with music and dancing that help to transform her into the "beautiful of face." This is the first of a series of benevolent forms of the Eye goddess.[23] An obscure passage deals with an attack on the goddess while she is sleeping. Thoth wakes her in time, and the forces of chaos are defeated. Eventually the goddess reaches Memphis, the capital of Egypt, where she is transformed into Hathor of the Southern Sycamore and joyfully reunited with her father. She is needed to defend the creator sun god from his enemies. Chief among these, as in the fable of the lion and the mouse, is "Man."

In many mythologies, the gods make several attempts at creating people before they are satisfied. Such myths usually involve the destruction of the unsatisfactory part of humanity. As early as the Middle Kingdom, there are references to the creator deciding to destroy humanity and abandon the earth.[24] The fullest version of this myth is given in a text known as the Book of the Heavenly Cow, which is inscribed in five royal tombs of the New Kingdom. The earliest copy is on one of the large golden shrines surrounding the coffins of King Tutankhamun.[25]

The Destruction of Humanity.   After Ra had become the ruler of both gods and men,

> Humanity plotted against him, while his majesty, may he live, may he prosper, may he be healthy, had grown old. His bones became silver, his flesh became gold, his hair true lapis-lazuli. When his majesty saw how humanity was plotting against him, his majesty said to his followers "Summon for me, my Eye, Shu, Tefnut, Geb, Nut and the father and mothers who were with me when I was in the primeval waters, as well as the god Nun.[26] Let him bring his followers with him, but bring them secretly in case the humans see and their hearts escape.

The gods and goddesses all came and asked Ra to speak. He told them, "Humanity, which came into being from my Eye, is plotting against me. Advise me what you would do about it." Nun and the other deities advise Ra to send his Eye against the rebels. "No Eye is more able to smite them. Let it go down as Hathor."

The guilty ones among humanity flee into the desert through fear of Ra, but Hathor slaughters them and wades in their blood. When she returns to Ra, she tells him that she has "overpowered humanity and it was sweet to my heart." Ra replies, "I shall have power over them as king by culling them." Thus, says the text, "the Powerful One came into being."[27]

The goddess intends to continue her slaughter the next day, but for reasons that are not explained, Ra has changed his mind. He summons messengers who can travel as fast as shadows and sends them to fetch a large quantity of a red mineral. Then he orders the Side-Lock Wearer in Heliopolis, a title of the high priest of Ra, to grind up the mineral while his maid servants mash barley to make beer. They make 7,000 jars of beer and add the red mineral to it to make the beer look like blood. Ra has the beer taken to the place where the goddess plans to destroy humanity. Before dawn Ra pours the red beer out until the fields are flooded to a depth of "three palms."[28] When the goddess arrives at dawn, she sees her own beautiful reflection in the flood. "She drank and it delighted her heart. She came back drunk without having noticed humanity." Ra welcomed her back and from that day on alcohol was drunk during the festivals of Hathor.[29]

It is not clear whether Ra took pity on humanity after the first day's slaughter or whether he only wanted to save the portion of humanity that he regarded as innocent. The latter is probably implied by the fact that the people killed on the first day have fled to the desert, part of the realm of chaos. These people become Enemies of Ra, a group that is shown in the Underworld Books being horribly tortured in the afterlife. The second day's slaughter is to take place in fields, presumably in the agricultural land of the Nile valley, usually associated with the realm of order.

The goddess Maat was sometimes said to have been sent down to live among humanity. She would stay with a virtuous person even after their death, but in times of general disorder and strife she would withdraw. Humanity was sometimes divided into the Followers of Horus (good) and the Followers of Seth (bad). This division appears to justify the ruthless destruction of many humans by the gods. A ritual drama inscribed on the walls of the temple of Horus of Edfu describes a rebellion by the people of Nubia in the 363rd year of Ra's reign. The rebels are tricked into killing each other, and their leader, Seth, is beheaded. A myth in Papyrus Jumilhac tells how the goddess Isis transforms herself into a form of Hathor, slaughters all the Followers of Seth with fire, and wades in their blood. This might seem to be a direct borrowing from the Book of the Heavenly Cow, but it should probably be seen as an example of a repeating pattern of events.

In the Book of the Heavenly Cow, even though the rebels have been defeated, the world can never be the same again. Ra announces that he is sick and weary, and he cannot bear to remain on earth. Nun, the god of the primeval waters, orders Shu and Nut to help Ra. Nut is transformed into a cow, and Ra rides away on her back. As the earth darkens, some of humanity beg Ra to stay, and they shoot at his enemies. This, says the text, was how death came into being. From this point on, humanity has to fight and die to maintain the divine order.

Nut carries Ra up into the heavens, and the single creator god transforms himself into many heavenly bodies. He creates the fields of paradise for the spirits of the dead. Nut "began to tremble because of the height," so Ra creates the Heh gods who live in twilight. Shu and the Heh gods support the body of Nut. Then Ra tells Geb to warn the powerful serpents that live under the earth not to abuse their magic because he will still look down on them. Ra puts Osiris in charge of humanity and calls "the moon of Thoth" into being, so that Thoth can rule the night sky as his deputy. This begins the era when the world was ruled by a series of lesser gods.

Period of Rule by Other Gods

Summary: After the creator had withdrawn, the earth was ruled by a series of gods. Violent struggles sometimes accompanied the transfer of power from one generation to the next. Osiris, son of Geb, was chosen as king of Egypt and ruled with his sister, Isis. Their ideal reign was brought to an end by the jealousy of their brother, Seth. This god and his followers murdered Osiris and mutilated his body. With the aid of magic, Isis was able to revive the body of Osiris long enough for her to conceive a son. Isis fled to the marshes where she gave birth to Horus.

Both the child Horus and the body of Osiris were frequently attacked by Seth and his followers. Horus survived to challenge Seth's right to rule Egypt. The two gods fought each other in many different ways. The Eye of Horus was damaged by Seth, and the testicles of Seth were damaged by Horus. Thoth restored the damaged Eye, and eventually Horus prevailed. He became king of Egypt and was reconciled with Seth. Horus performed rites that helped Osiris to rise again as king of the Underworld. In time, Horus was succeeded as king of Egypt by a series of gods and demigods.

The Reigns of Shu, Geb, and Osiris.   Egyptian king lists trace the ancestry of historical kings back into a mythical age. According to Manetho's history of Egypt, this age lasted for over 11,000 years.[30] The order of the rulers in this divine dynasty was not fixed. Creator deities such as Ptah or Ra sometimes begin the list of divine ancestors, but either Shu or Geb may be named as the first god-kings of Egypt. Other sources treat Osiris or his son Horus as the first Egyptian kings. In stories such as Astarte and the Sea (see "Astarte" in "Deities, Themes, and Concepts") and the Two Brothers, the Great Ennead seem to rule as a group. The idea that each generation of the Ennead must have ruled in turn is probably a later rationalization of mythical history to fit an established pattern of royal succession.

Hymns to Shu in the Harris Magical Papyrus hail this god as the eldest son and heir of Ra and the king of Upper and Lower Egypt. The myth of Shu's separation of his children Geb and Nut to create the cosmos seems at some point to have been reinterpreted in more human terms of sexual jealousy and father-son rivalry. The latent hostility between Shu and his son, Geb, is made explicit in a text of the fourth century BCE.[31] Like Ra before him, Shu has to contend with the forces of chaos and with rebels against the divine order. Geb challenges Shu's leadership, which causes the latter to withdraw from the world. Geb either rapes his mother, Tefnut, or takes her as his chief queen; thus he separates Shu from his sister-wife, as Shu had previously separated Geb from his sister-

Figure 15. A ruler of the fourth century BCE worships Osiris Wenenefer (center), shown as an idealized king of Egypt. Relief in the temple of Behbeit el-Hagar. (Courtesy of Geraldine Pinch)

wife. That Geb's claim to the throne is disputed is clear from an episode in which he tries to put on his father's headdress and is burned by its serpent guardian. Eventually, Geb is accepted as ruler and has to rally his forces to defend Egypt against the "children of Apophis."

More usually, Geb was regarded as the legitimate ruler of everything on earth. In the Book of the Heavenly Cow, Geb seems to be the chosen heir of the departing sun god. The warnings in this text about the need to control "the snakes who are in the earth and the water" suggest that Geb's reign was not thought of as a peaceful one. In the fragmentary tale of Astarte and the Sea, a sea monster opposes the gods and exacts tribute from Geb and Nut. A few scattered references allude to a myth in which Osiris tries to seize power from his father, Geb.[32]

When Geb passed on the throne to his eldest son, Osiris, it might be logical to assume that he withdrew under the earth as Ra and Shu had withdrawn to the sky. There is, however, no clear account of this happening. After the reign of Osiris, Geb takes on the role of judge in the Divine Tribunal of the gods. This Tribunal usually seems to meet in Egypt itself rather than in the underworld.

In most Egyptian sources, the reign of Osiris is only described in the vaguest terms. Osiris is the good king, and Isis is his queen and chief protector. The oldest references to Osiris link him with the astral or the funerary spheres. By the end of the Old Kingdom it became customary for all kings to be regarded as a form of Osiris after they died. The idea that Osiris had once reigned on earth as these kings did probably postdates this development.

When Greek writers began to take an interest in the myths of Osiris, they recreated Osiris and Isis as the great "culture heroes" who taught agriculture and crafts to the peoples of the world and established law and religion. Plutarch claimed that Osiris had civilized the whole world, a way of acknowledging the cultural debt that the Greeks felt they owed to Egypt. For the Egyptians, "culture heroes" were largely unnecessary, since most aspects of civilization were already implicit in the creator's establishment of *maat*.

The Murder of Osiris.   The death of Osiris is one of the most important events in Egyptian myth and one of the most obscure. There are no detailed accounts of the murder until the late first millennium BCE, and even these occur in descriptions of Egyptian religion by foreigners. In the Pyramid Texts, Seth is named as the attacker of Osiris and, by implication, as his killer. In Pyramid Texts spell 477, Seth claims to be taking revenge for a kick that Osiris had given him. Later tales loosely based on the Osiris myth make sexual jealousy a motive for the falling out between the two brothers. Some Egyptologists have argued that Osiris was originally a god of the dead rather than a god who died,[33] but once the concept of Osiris's death was established, a slayer had to be identified.

Many Egyptian texts imply that Seth took the form of a dangerous animal, such as a wild bull, a wild ass, or a crocodile, to kill his brother in a lonely place. The Pyramid Texts and the Coffin Texts allude to Osiris being cast down or trampled and his body thrown in the Nile. In later times it was often stated that Osiris died by drowning. Being a god, Osiris probably had to be killed in several different ways to render him permanently dead.

A belief developed that the attack on Osiris was a unique and terrible crime, carried out on the "night of the great storm." Yet in theological terms, his was a necessary death. By dying, Osiris becomes ruler of the underworld and a source of life for others. A remarkable dialogue in Book of the Dead spell 175 has Osiris complain about his sad fate to Atum. The creator god replies that Osiris has been favored beyond all others. He has been granted an eternal kingdom in the "land of silence," whereas his son will be the perpetual ruler in the land of the living. Many Egyptian thinkers tried to make sense of death by making something positive out of the death of Osiris, but it is the loneliness and despair of Osiris that is the most memorable element in this dialogue.

Early allusions to the death of Osiris all imply that it took place in a remote spot with no witnesses. Classical writers change this into a public assassination. Diodorus Siculus (whose visit to Egypt is described in "Introduction") says that Osiris was butchered by "his brother Typhon" (Seth). Typhon divided the body into twenty-six pieces and gave one piece to each of his followers to keep.

Plutarch relates that in the twenty-eighth year of Osiris's reign, Typhon (Seth) and his followers plotted against him. Typhon secretly obtained the exact measurements of his brother's body and had a beautiful chest made to fit it.[34] Typhon displayed the chest at a feast and promised to give it to whoever could fit inside it. Seth's seventy-two followers all tried the chest, but it did not fit any of them. Finally Osiris lay down in the chest. As soon as he did so, the conspirators bolted on the lid and sealed the chest with molten lead. Then they threw it into a branch of the Nile, which carried the chest out into the Mediterranean sea.

Isis was away in the city of Coptos, but she heard a terrible lament from the deities of the northern marshes and knew that Osiris was dead. She searched Egypt for the body and followed sightings of the chest all the way to Byblos in the Lebanon.[35] There the chest had grown into a marvelous tree that the king of Byblos had felled and made into a pillar in his palace. Isis stayed in the palace for a while in disguise before declaring herself and demanding the pillar containing her husband's coffin. She brought the coffin back to the Delta, but one night Typhon found it. He tore the body into fourteen parts and scattered them throughout Egypt. Isis searched for the parts and buried each in the place where she found it. The penis of Osiris had been eaten by fish, so she had to replace this with a model.[36] Some parts of Plutarch's narrative have few parallels in Egyptian sources, but from the Pyramid Texts onward, Isis is presented as a grieving wife searching the country for her murdered husband.

Isis is usually helped by her sister, Nephthys, and both goddesses may take bird form to carry out the search. When Isis finds the body or its parts, she restores them to wholeness. This originally seems to have meant that Isis was able to reverse the putrefaction of the flesh so feared by the Egyptians.

By the end of the second millennium BCE, the idea of the mutilation of the body by Seth was firmly established. This concept was greatly elaborated in the Ptolemaic and Roman Periods. Lists on temple walls mention fourteen or sixteen parts of the body of Osiris buried at various sacred sites. This was sometimes increased to forty-two parts, one for each district of Egypt.

The vigil of Isis and Nephthys as they watch over and lament the body of Osiris is one of the keynote images of Egyptian culture. It is unusual in showing deities experiencing strong emotion, even though this emotion is conveyed by formalized gestures of mourning, such as beating the brow.

Isis already knows that she is destined to bear a child who will be king. In order to bring this about, she has to revive the sexual powers of Osiris, just as the Hand Goddess aroused the penis of the creator to create the first life. A relief at Abydos shows the all-important moment when Isis in bird form uses her wings to fan the breath of life into Osiris. Hymns celebrate the exaltation of Isis when she knows that she has conceived the child who "is king even in the egg." Summoned by her cry of triumph, other deities acknowledge and bow down to the unborn Horus.

At some point, the myth of the death of Osiris and the restoration of his body by Isis was combined with the cult of Anubis as protector of the dead and overseer of funerary rites. All aspects of an Egyptian funeral were given mythical precedents in the mummification, entombment, and revivification of Osiris. A number of myths, particularly in Papyrus Jumilhac, deal with attempts by Seth and his followers to destroy or despoil the body of Osiris. The corpse is successfully protected by the magic of Thoth and by the ferocity of Anubis in his role as guardian of the tomb.

The Birth and Childhood of Horus.   After a pregnancy of ten months, Isis gives birth to a son called Horus. This god was often referred to as Horus, son of Isis, to distinguish him from Horus the Elder, the sky god whom some traditions made a brother of Osiris and Seth. These two gods had distinct mythologies but were often treated as aspects of the same deity.

The place of Horus's birth is said to be in the Delta, usually in the region of Chemmis. To evade his enemies, the divine child was hidden inside a papyrus thicket or on a floating island. This "nest of Horus" is one of the few mythical places that is commonly shown in Egyptian art. Temple wall scenes depict kings in the role of the Horus child in the marshes being washed or suckled by a cow. This cow can be identified with a number of goddesses but most often with Hathor, whose name literally means Mansion of Horus. She seems to have been regarded as the mother of Horus the Elder and the wet nurse or foster mother of Horus the Younger.[37] Many other deities were imagined as protecting the divine child whenever Isis was forced to be absent.

In literary spells these deities can be changed into the humble human inhabitants of the marsh. The theme of the poisoning of the infant Horus was a common one in magical texts (see "Horus the Child" and "Serqet" in "Deities, Themes, and Concepts"). Several spells start with Isis lamenting because her child has been poisoned. The source of the poison is usually the bite of an earth-dwelling snake.

Since destroying your enemies by sending a dangerous animal after them was a standard Egyptian curse, Seth should probably be regarded as the instigator of the attack. In one spell, Isis appeals to her mother, Nut, and her father, Geb, the controller of the earth snakes. In others she challenges the creator sun god to heal her innocent child. The creator sends one of his manifestations or attendant deities to drive the poison out of Horus, to the great joy of Isis.

The Metternich Stela and other magical stelae of this type show Horus as a naked child triumphing over all kinds of dangerous creatures. Some of these creatures, such as the oryx (a species of desert-dwelling antelope), were particularly associated with Seth. In a few magical texts it is the foolishness or greed of the young Horus that is to blame for his plight. In one spell, the young god suffers from a terrible stomachache after naughtily eating a sacred fish and has to appeal to his mother for help.[38] Horus is still an impetuous youth when he takes up the struggle to avenge the death of his father and gain the crown of Egypt.

The Struggles of Horus and Seth.
Some sources give Seth a reign of hundreds of years; others imply an interregnum, during which Seth and Horus struggle to establish who is fit to rule Egypt. Seth is consis-

Figure 16. Cippus (magical stela) with a central figure of Horus the Child overcoming evil animals and reptiles. (Chicago Oriental Institute Museum)

tently portrayed as sexually abusing the young Horus. This may be implied in the Pyramid Texts by the frequent references to the mutilation of the eye of Horus and the testicles of Seth.[39] The injury to Seth is sometimes interpreted as castration and sometimes merely as losing the "seed" from his testicles.

In the Middle Kingdom Kahun Papyrus, Horus complains to Isis that Seth has been admiring his buttocks and wants to sleep with him. Isis advises her son to tell Seth that he dares not sleep with him unless Seth shares some of his magical strength. When Seth has agreed to make Horus stronger, Horus must pretend to let Seth have his way but take care to catch all Seth's semen in his fingers.

The Middle Kingdom text breaks off at this point, but a version of the story is found in the New Kingdom Contendings of Horus and Seth. In this text, Horus catches Seth's semen in his hand and brings it to his mother. Isis cuts off the polluted hand and throws it in the river (see "Sobek" in "Deities, Themes, and Concepts"). After making Horus a new hand, she uses her own hand to give Horus an erection and catches his semen in a pot. In this episode Isis is appropriately playing the role of the Hand Goddess who combines with the penis of the creator to make the first life.

Isis spreads the semen of Horus on the leaves of some lettuces in Seth's garden. When Seth eats the lettuces he becomes pregnant by Horus and gives birth to a radiant disk through the top of his head. Thoth takes the disk and places it on the brow of Horus as a sign that he is the true heir of the creator sun god.[40]

A cluster of myths deal with the mutilation of the eye or eyes of Horus (see "Eyes of Horus" in "Deities, Themes, and Concepts"). In Horus's sky falcon form, his eyes could be regarded as the sun and the moon or as the morning and evening stars. References in the Pyramid Texts to the eye of Horus being made small by the finger of Seth may relate to lunar phenomena (see "The Egyptian Year" under "Cyclical Time" later in this chapter). Later texts, such as Book of the Dead spell 17, imply that the eye was torn out and swallowed or broken into pieces by Seth.

In some versions, both eyes of Horus are blinded or torn out. Although Seth is the aggressor, he is sometimes said to be punishing Horus for mutilating or raping his mother, Isis.[41] In the Contendings of Horus and Seth, Horus becomes angry with his mother for helping Seth and cuts off her head. One myth has Thoth heal Isis by giving her a cow's head to replace the head that Horus has taken away.[42] The Ennead decrees that Horus should be punished. Seth rips out the eyes of Horus and buries them on a mountainside, where they grow into lotuses. In this story, the eyes of Horus are restored by his foster mother, Hathor. In other versions he is healed by Isis or Thoth. The latter is particularly associated with finding the eye of Horus when it is lost or putting it back together when it has been torn into many pieces. This myth mirrors the mutilation and reunion of the body of Osiris.

Many references to the contests between the Two Fighters imply that Horus and Seth were gods of equal strength. These probably reflect the tradition that Horus and Seth were brothers. Other versions adapt to the concept of Seth fighting with his younger and weaker nephew by making Horus win through guile. In the Contendings of Horus and Seth, the two gods compete by turning themselves into hippopotami and seeing who can stay under water longer. Later Horus challenges Seth to a race in stone boats. Horus's boat is only wood painted to look like stone. Seth tries to make a real stone boat that sinks as soon as it is launched.

The combat between the two gods was reenacted on temple lakes. By the first millennium BCE, the duel had become a battle between opposing sides with the Followers of Horus fighting the Followers of Seth. In the sacred play the Triumph of Horus, Horus pursues Seth by boat and attacks him with harpoons.

The Triumph of Horus.   The Two Fighters disturbed the whole cosmos with their quarrel. The case needed to be brought before a Divine Tribunal so that right could be established and a peace made. This Divine Tribunal is usually headed by Geb, though the ultimate authority is the creator sun god. The Tribunal is said to assemble in various places, but most often in Heliopolis.

Myths deal with two different trials. In what is probably the older tradition, it is Osiris who is the plaintiff against Seth. Sometimes the body of Osiris is said to be present in court supported by Isis and Nephthys. Seth tries to justify his violence toward his brother but fails. Osiris is vindicated as "one true of voice," a term that came to be applied to all the virtuous dead. Only then, some sources imply, could Osiris complete his metamorphosis into the ruler of the underworld. Osiris is not resurrected in the sense of returning to life as an individual on earth. He enters into a new kind of existence in a separate realm that most beings can only reach by dying.

In some accounts Seth is punished by being forced to carry the body of Osiris to its final resting place. While performing this humiliating task, Seth can be envisaged as a boat, a carrying chair, a bull, or an ox. Even after Osiris became ruler of the dead, his corpse was preserved in a tomb, where it remained a source of great power.

In a parallel tradition, the disputants are Horus and Seth. Various deities put the case for each side. Osiris is sometimes represented as sending messages from the underworld to support his son's case. Osiris ominously reminds the other gods that only he can create the crops that feed them. Seth's claim rests chiefly on his being the strongest of the gods, whereas Horus stresses the legitimacy of his place in the royal succession. This argument between might and right must have seemed topical at many crisis points in Egyptian history.

It would be natural to assume that this crucial myth would always have the same ending, but many variations on the divine verdict are recorded. These variations are due to the fluctuating status of Seth as a national god and to the different contexts in which the myth might be used. The strength of Seth was needed to defend the gods from their enemies, so it was necessary to reintegrate the loser into the community of the gods.

In order to reconcile the Two Fighters and turn them into the Two Lords, the Divine Tribunal divided the land between Horus and Seth. Horus got Lower Egypt and Seth Upper Egypt, or Horus the Black Land of the Nile valley and Seth the Red Land of the deserts. The image of Horus and Seth uniting the Two Lands to support the ruling king was a popular one in royal art up to the end of the New Kingdom (see Figure 46).

In the Memphite Theology and other texts, however, this division of the kingdom is subsequently challenged, and Horus is given all of Egypt. The tale of the Contendings of Horus and Seth, written down at a time when the cult of Seth was particularly popular, has Seth summoned to live with Ra in the sky as god of storms. This fits with Seth's traditional role as a powerful protector of Ra in his sun boat.

In versions of the myth that occur in hymns or rituals concerning Osiris, Seth is driven out of Egypt rather than being compensated with any kind of divine realm. He may even be given over to Horus and Isis to be punished or executed. This is his fate in most temple texts of the first millennium BCE. At Edfu, the triumph of Horus over Seth was celebrated with the cutting up of a hippopotamus—the final act in the sequence of mutilations that began with the dismemberment of Osiris (see Figure 32).

Hymns and literary accounts of the Horus and Seth conflict usually end with a chorus of praise for the newly crowned Horus. Royal rituals and funerary texts that are structured by episodes from the Osiris myth have a different focus. Before or during his own coronation, Horus is represented as carrying out a series of rituals for his father, Osiris, including the Opening of the Mouth and the raising of a symbolic pillar (see "*Djed* Pillar" in "Deities, Themes, and Concepts"). These acts correspond with stages in the royal funerary ritual performed by the heir of the deceased king to ensure that king's survival in the afterlife. These rites validated the royal succession by confirming Osiris in his new role as king of the dead and Horus in his role as king of the living.

In these contexts, Osiris is represented as too weak or passive to achieve the transformation to ruler of the underworld without his heir's help. Here he seems to embody the vulnerability of the Egyptian state in dangerous transitional periods. Other sources, such as hymns to Osiris, portray the god as having been created by Atum to be a powerful and terrifying force, the underworld equivalent of the sun god.[43] The "inertness" of Osiris is then comparable to that of the creator before the First Time.

The "time of Horus" was made the prototype for the reign of every king. Hymns refer to it as a time of peace and prosperity when evil and crime were unknown. In most Egyptian king lists, the reign of Horus is followed by periods of rule by other deities, such as Thoth and Maat. Then come nine *akhu* (spirits), associated with Hierakonpolis, Buto, and Heliopolis; towns that are known to have been important in the early history of Egypt. With these kings, and with a series of kings of lesser status known as the Followers of Horus, myth blends imperceptibly into history.

Period of Rule by Kings

Summary: Dynasties of gods and demigods were succeeded by dynasties of human kings who acted as intermediaries between humanity and the gods. This period corresponds with the time span of Pharaonic history. Gods and goddesses mainly communicated with people through temple rituals, oracles, or dreams, though deities might still be encountered beyond the boundaries of the Black Land. Most humans could only enter the divine realm by dying, but stories were told of priest-magicians who had the power to pass between the worlds of the living and the dead.

The king was responsible for upholding the divine order in the world of the living. Failure to obey the laws of *maat* could lead to periods of chaos. These only ended when a new royal champion of *maat* arose. The gods might intervene in history by fathering such hero-kings.

Once the gods had withdrawn, humanity had to play an active role, through ritual and ethical behavior, in keeping any kind of divine presence on earth. Regular offerings and elaborate rites ensured that deities were present in statues or sacred animals kept in temples, but their true forms were thought to be in the divine realm.

On temple walls, kings are shown perpetually interacting with the gods, but specific communications from a deity to an individual king are usually described as coming in the form of a dream or a portent. The best known example is King Thutmose IV's dream encounter with the deity manifest in the Great Sphinx at Giza (see "Sphinx" in "Deities, Themes, and Concepts"). Similar dreams were occasionally recorded by private individuals of the elite class. It was probably the **ba** of a person that was thought to be able to enter the divine realm in sleep and converse with gods and spirits. Ordinary Egyptians did not expect to meet their deities until after they had died.

Strange Encounters.   Encounters between people and deities are described in stories that use mythological themes, but these usually take place beyond the Nile valley. In the story of the Two Brothers, it is only after the hero, Bata, leaves Egypt for the remote Valley of the Pine that he meets the Ennead. In the tale known as the Shipwrecked Sailor, an Egyptian survives a shipwreck in the Red Sea and is washed ashore on a paradise island. When he makes an offering to the gods to thank them for the food he finds on the island, a giant human-headed serpent appears.

The sailor is terrified, but the serpent promises that no harm will come to him and that he will be reunited with his family. The serpent reveals that there were once seventy-five snakes on the island, suggesting that he may be the creator sun god who traditionally had seventy-five forms. The serpent eventually sends the sailor back to Egypt laden with treasure but warns him that he will never find the "island of the spirit" again.

The hero of this tale does not behave heroically in the sense of being particularly strong, brave, or selfless. All the sailor does is show the proper attitude for humans by giving thanks to the gods even in adversity and by believing the serpent's message of hope. In most Egyptian tales, intelligence and natural eloquence or book learning are more admired than feats of arms or willingness to die with honor. The main characters are often priest-magicians (see "Imhotep" and "Magicians" in "Deities, Themes, and Concepts") who deal with threats from ghosts, demons, and foreign sorcerers by using spells, amulets, and rituals. The ability to communicate with supernatural beings is the basis of their power. Some stories feature magicians who are able to see the true forms of the gods or enter the *Duat* while still alive, but Egyptian literature is full of warnings about the misuse of such powers by the magicians or their royal patrons.

Magical tales were often set in the time of famous kings, such as Djoser (c. 2667–2648 BCE) or Rameses II (1279–1213 BCE), whose reigns were sufficiently far in the past to be imagined as an age of marvels. Nearly all Egyptian tales feature some royal characters, who are not always shown in a favorable light. In literature, kings and princes may be fallible or even cruel and lustful. In most royal inscriptions, by contrast, kings are presented as heroes on a cosmic stage.

Kings and Gods.   Each king fulfilled the creator's plan and the judgment of the Divine Tribunal: that Horus, son of Osiris, should always rule. Ideally, every new king (Horus) had to succeed his father (Osiris), even if history had to be reedited to accomplish this so that intervening reigns or lack of blood relationships were ignored.

Many kings claimed that they, like Horus, had been chosen to rule "while still in the egg." In practice, it was the inauguration rituals that turned the chosen heir into "the living Horus." Since the office of kingship was so vital to the stability of Egyptian society, interruptions in the royal succession had to be explained as direct interventions by deities. The accession of individual kings might be validated by giving them a divine parent. One such royal birth myth is found in the inauguration inscriptions of King Horemheb (c. 1319–1307 BCE).[44]

Horemheb was a soldier who served under Akhenaten and Tutankhamun, but the inscription presents his career in mythological terms. He is called the son of Horus, Lord of Hnes: the form of the Horus worshipped in Horemheb's native town. Horemheb claims that his exceptional qualities were evident as soon as he was born and that Horus of Hnes always intended that he should be king. To bring this about, Horus takes Horemheb to Thebes and presents him to the god Amun-Ra at Karnak and Luxor temples. Horemheb is accepted by Amun-Ra and by his daughter, the Eye goddess, and acclaimed by a gathering of all the gods. Horemheb is then able to restore the country and its institutions to the way things were "in the time of Ra."

This inscription can be interpreted as a factual account of Horemheb's inauguration at Thebes during the Opet Festival in the presence of statues of the gods, but it elevates these events to the divine realm. A historical event of the fourteenth century BCE becomes part of the repeating cycle of the acceptance of the rightful heir by the Divine Tribunal and his restoration of harmony to Egypt.

In the Egyptian worldview, each reign was supposed to be a successful battle by the leader of the forces of order (the king or a prince representing him) against the forces of chaos (rebels, foreigners, and dangerous creatures or natural forces). Such victories were routinely attributed to the reigning king whether or not they had actually taken place, so that much Egyptian history is mythical in the modern sense of not being factually true.

Rameses II, for example, presented himself as a hero-king even though his greatest achievement was probably the peace treaty he negotiated with the rival Hittite empire. Scenes of his famous battle against the Hittites at Qadesh decorate the walls of many of the temples that he built. Conforming to the mythical prototype of the champion of order, Rameses is shown as a gigantic figure triumphing over chaotic crowds of enemies. A poem that accompanies the reliefs stresses the vulnerability of the king, however, and claims that disaster was only averted through the intervention of the god Amun.[45]

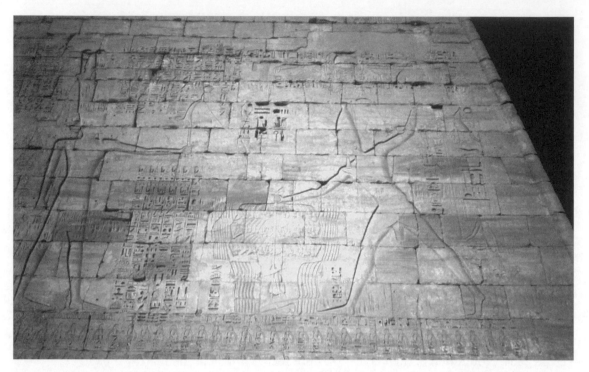

Figure 17. King Rameses II smites the enemies of Egypt and the divine order while Amun-Ra looks on. Relief in Karnak temple. (Courtesy of Geraldine Pinch)

Royal, religious, and literary texts all admit the possibility that if humans fail to obey the laws of *maat*, chaos can get the upper hand. Specific acts, such as desecrating the tombs of the dead or failing to build proper homes for the gods, are sometimes blamed for these periods of national disaster. At such times, the gods withdraw even further from humanity, and "their sanctuaries are empty."

Some texts, such as the Middle Kingdom Words of Neferti or the Roman Period Potter's Oracle, project graphic descriptions of "a land in calamity" into the future. The prophecy of Neferti describes a period of turmoil and misery but ends with a vision of "a king from the south" who will overcome rebels and foreign enemies so that "Truth will return to its proper place, with Chaos driven outside."[46] This future was the recent past for the author of the prophecy, as the "king from the south" was Amenemhet I, a commoner who founded the Twelfth Dynasty.

This alternation between order and chaos was seen as the pattern of human history, but a few writings allowed the possibility that one day the slide into chaos would not be stopped by a royal hero, humanity would be totally destroyed, and the world would end.

Return to Chaos

Summary: The end of the world will come about because of quarrels among deities or rebellions by humanity. The creator will become weary, and the world will return into the dark primeval waters from which it came.

In Book of the Dead spell 175, Atum complains to Thoth about "the children of Nut," a term that can refer to the fourth generation of the Great Ennead or to the gods in general. The children of Nut are accused of making rebellion, war, and carnage and of dividing up the wholeness of creation. Thoth, who was in charge of fixing the length of all creatures' lives, decrees that their years will be cut short.

In the Tale of the Shipwrecked Sailor, the serpent deities are suddenly destroyed by fire. Only the great serpent (the creator) and his little daughter (the Eye goddess/Maat) survive the holocaust. The serpent god warns the sailor that when he leaves, the "island of the spirit" will sink beneath the sea. This evokes an image of the Primeval Mound, the place of creation, being covered by the *nun* again.

In Coffin Texts spell 1130, after the creator has described the gifts he has given to humanity, he goes on to say that after millions of years he will become one with Osiris. When this happens, there will no longer be a division between life and death, and everything on earth will go through a period of catastrophic change. In Book of the Dead spell 175, Atum declares that after millions of years he will destroy everything that he has made "and the land will return into the Deep, into the Flood, as it was before (creation)." A spell in the Harris Magical Papyrus has the magician claim that he can, like the creator, cause the earth to go down into the primeval waters and the south to become north.

This strain of thought seems to be reflected in the Roman Period Hermetic text known as the Asclepius. In this dialogue, Hermes Trismegistus warns that in the "old age of the world" the gods will go back to heaven, Egypt will be deserted, and "all the people will die."[47] References to an absolutely final destruction are rare in Egyptian or Egyptian-based texts. Even the Asclepius promises that the supreme god will remake the world. The **eschatology** of Egypt is most truly represented by the cycles of destruction and renewal expounded in the New Kingdom Underworld Books. Many of the events from this linear time line recur in cyclical time.

CYCLICAL TIME

The Egyptian universe remained eternally the same only through constant change in the form of cycles of decay, death, and rebirth. The Ouroboros, a snake

Figure 18. The sun child inside the Ouroboros snake supported by the sky cow and the lions of yesterday and tomorrow. Vignette from the funerary papyrus of Herweben. (British Museum)

swallowing its own tail, was an Egyptian image adopted by many other cultures as a symbol of eternity. It signified the capacity of the universe to perpetually renew itself, so that every end could also be a beginning.

The Egyptian Year

The great events of Egyptian myth could be treated either as things that happened once in the remote past or as things that needed to happen over and over again. The inauguration of a king, which ideally took place at New Year, reenacted the creation of the world and the reign of the sun god as well as the establishment of "the living Horus" on the throne of his father.[48] Each year of a king's reign was seen as mirroring the great cycle of the creation, decay, and renewal of the cosmos. An annual renewal of kingship ceremony at Thebes seems to have involved a reenactment of a vital stage in the process of creation: the union between the creator and the Hand goddess.[49] After thirty years, the length of a generation, the king had to undergo a much more elaborate renewal process to identify himself once again with the life-giving youthful forms of the creator and the sun god.[50]

The last month of the year was feared as a time when the gods seemed to be punishing humanity as they had after the rebellion against the sun god (see "Sekhmet" in "Deities, Themes, and Concepts"). The new year began with the coming of the inundation. By the Ptolemaic Period, the first Nile flood was said to have been caused by the return of the Distant Goddess from Nubia. Every year, the fearsome goddess had to be persuaded to return home and take on a benevolent form as she reached the southern border of Egypt. Kiosk-shrines built on the water's edge were decorated with comical figures of dwarfs or ani-

mals dancing and playing musical instruments to pacify the goddess and welcome the inundation (see Figure 14).

Alternatively, the Nile flood could be seen as the tears that Isis wept every
year for her murdered husband or as the efflux from the decaying body of Osiris
(see "Osiris" in "Deities, Themes, and Concepts"). During the flood season,
Egypt resembled the *nun* again. When the floods began to recede, the land appeared to rise up like the Primeval Mound, and the fields could be planted. The
growth cycle of food crops (particularly wheat and barley) was linked to the
myth of Osiris. The scything down of the grain and its trampling and winnow-
ing were equated with the murder and dismemberment of the "good god." The
sprouting of the seed that began the next agricultural cycle was celebrated as a
resurrection for Osiris. There were annual festivals in which corn mummies—
miniature figures of Osiris filled with mud and seeds—were planted in sacred
areas and watered till they sprouted.[51] These ceremonies were not just a re-
membrance of long-ago events; the death and renewal of Osiris were seen as
archetypal acts that maintained the cosmos.

The mutilation and dismemberment of Osiris could also be linked to the
lunar calendar (see under "Moon" in "Deities, Themes, and Concepts"). The
full moon could represent both the complete body of Osiris and the complete
eye of his son, Horus. Each month as the moon waned, the body of Osiris and
the Eye of Horus were divided. Evil seemed to triumph, until the waxing of the
moon "completed" these two symbols of beneficent power again. Periodic
eclipses of the moon were explained by myths such as that of Seth taking the
form of a black boar to swallow the eye of Horus and being forced to expel it
again. Regular astronomical events such as the appearance of the morning star
or the heliacal rising of Sirius also feature in Egyptian myth (see "Stars and
Planets" in "Deities, Themes, and Concepts"), but by far the most significant
heavenly phenomenon was the daily rising and setting of the sun.

The Solar Cycle

The apparent movement of the sun across the sky was seen both as a life cycle
and as a journey. The daily life cycle of the sun was more an extended metaphor
than a narrative. The sun was said to be born each morning from the womb of
the sky goddess, Nut. At dawn the sun was a child—a daily repetition of the
emergence of the sun child during the First Time. At noon, the sun reached the
peak of his strength and could be portrayed as a triumphant falcon. By evening
he was an old man, virtually the only god to be shown as old. The common

Figure 19. Symbolic image of the solar cycle painted on a coffin. Two baboon deities adore the ram-headed god inside the solar disk. (Courtesy of Geraldine Pinch)

identification of the evening sun as Atum linked it with the myth of the creator growing weary and letting the world sink back into the *nun*. Sunset was equivalent to death, and the sun's flesh and soul passed into the underworld. After moving through the underworld reviving its inhabitants with his light, the sun would be reborn. Each sunrise was a new beginning for the cosmos.

In early times, this cycle could be described in more brutal terms.[52] In the evening, the sun god died by being eaten by his mother, the sky goddess, and was replaced by a multitude of stars. In the morning, the reborn sun god ate all the star gods, staining the sky with their blood (the redness of dawn) and absorbing their power. The one god became many and the many gods became one, so life came out of death.

Other sources envisaged the sun god in an eternal voyage across the skies above and below the earth. At sunset, the Day Boat of the sun left the upper sky to be replaced by the barques for the moon and the stars (see "Boats" in "Deities, Themes, and Concepts"). The Night Boat carrying the sun god was towed on water and over sand through the twelve regions of the underworld.

Just as the creator had to overcome darkness and chaos to create the world, the sun and his defenders had to subdue the monsters that embodied darkness and chaos. Just as the creator made deities and people in the First Time and gave them life, the Night Sun gave new life to all the beings in the *Duat*. In the fourth hour of the night, the sleeping dead were revived by the sun god and experienced a lifetime in his presence. Thus the reign of the sun god, the lost golden age of Egyptian myth, was reenacted every night. The fate of the human dead was locked into the solar cycle.

The Journey of the Soul

Egyptian concepts of the afterlife are strikingly diverse.[53] The Beautiful West could be seen as a place of joyful reunions or as a state of terrifying isolation. Death was regarded both as a unique event and as part of the continuous process of decay and renewal. There was no promise of eternal peace for the Egyptian dead. The afterlife was full of dangers and difficulties to be overcome, a belief that probably reflected the experience of life of the average Ancient Egyptian.

After death each individual faced a journey through the underworld to reach the presence of one of the gods who could grant eternal life. The deceased would find themselves in an eerie landscape of rivers, deserts, and lakes of fire, inhabited by demons and monsters. The adventures of the soul in this landscape are similar to the fairy tales of other cultures, but the prize to be won was not a precious object or the hand of a princess, but eternal life. Some deities were helpful to the dead, but others were hostile unless approached in the right way. The soul of the deceased had to act like a magician and overcome threats by knowing protective spells and the true names of the beings he or she would encounter.

Armed with these powers, the soul would eventually reach a divine domain. The last ordeal might be the judgment of the heart in the presence of Osiris and the assessors of the underworld. The goal of the journey was to be transformed into an *akh*, an "effective" or "transfigured" spirit. Those who failed to justify their existence in the divine court faced a second death in the jaws of the Eater of Souls. The fortunate spirits could take their place among the stars or among the followers of Osiris, Ra, Thoth, or Hathor, but they could not escape the cycles of destruction and renewal.

The soul might experience life in the **Field of Reeds**, a paradise similar to Egypt, but this was not a permanent state. When the night sun passed on, darkness and death returned. The star-spirits were destroyed at dawn and reborn each night. Even the evil dead, the Enemies of Ra, continuously came back to life like Apophis so that they could be tortured and killed again.

As the Western Souls, the justified dead formed part of the crew of the embattled **Boat of Millions**. They might be thought of as rowing or towing the sun boat or even defending it against the forces of chaos. The vignette to Book of the Dead spell 39 shows a dead person taking on Seth's role of spearing the Apophis serpent. In death, everyone could be a cosmic hero in the perpetual struggle that was the central feature of Egyptian myth.

NOTES

1. The translation is by James P. Allen from his *Genesis in Egypt: The Philosophy of Ancient Egyptian Creation Accounts*, 2d ed., Yale Egyptological Studies 2 (San Antonio, TX, 1995). For other important surveys of Egyptian creation myths, see S. Bickel, *La cosmogonie égyptienne avant le Nouvel Empire*, Orbis Biblicus et Orientalis 134 (Freiburg and Göttingen, 1994); and M. Bilolo, *Les Cosmo-Théologies Philosophiques D'Heliopolis et Hermopolis*, The Thought of Ancient Egypt and Nubia, vol. 2 (Kinshasa and Munich, 1986).

2. Unattributed quotations are the author's translations from Egyptian texts listed in "Appendix: Primary Sources."

3. Such a temporal framework is seen, for instance, in the account of the creation of the world in seven days described in the book of Genesis. For ancient creation myths in general, see the chapter "Chaos and Cosmogony" in M. R. Wright, *Cosmology in Antiquity* (London and New York, 1995).

4. This is one of the reasons why Ptah precedes Ra in some lists of gods who ruled the world. Although the imagery of the Primeval Mound is drawn from the inundation, the land is said to rise rather than the waters to fall. The rising of the mound was also seen in sexual terms as the life-bringing erection of the earth god.

5. The parts of Egyptian temples decorated with marsh foliage may represent this stage of the *nun* when chaos had been subdued by the creator to realize its potential. The mounds, which were places of life, had their evil counterparts in the shifting sandbanks, which were a danger to anyone traveling by water.

6. The question of whether this means that Egyptian religion developed into a form of monotheism is explored in Siegfried Morenz, *Egyptian Religion* (London and Ithaca, 1973); and in Erik Hornung, *Conceptions of God in Ancient Egypt: The One and the Many*, trans. John Baines (Ithaca, 1982) (see "Egyptian Myth: Annotated Print and Nonprint Resources").

7. The main purpose of this ritual was to allow the *ka* (vital force) of the being depicted to enter and "inhabit" the statue. When performed on mummies, the ritual was thought to restore the senses of the deceased, so that they could breathe, speak, eat, hear, see, and smell again in the afterlife.

8. For the creator as an androgynous deity, see J. Zandee, "The Birth-Giving Creator-God in Ancient Egypt," in *Studies in Pharaonic Religion and Society in Honour of J. Gwyn Griffiths,* ed. A. B. Lloyd (London, 1992), 169–185; and K. Mysliwiec, "La mère, la femme, la fille et la variante feminine du dieu Atoum," *Etudes et Travaux* 13 (1983): 297–304.

9. Two different terms for spitting that sound like the names Shu and Tefnut are used in this text. The Egyptians were fond of etymological explanations for the nature of deities. These explanations are often false in linguistic terms, but they can provide information on religious ideas.

10. Writers on Egyptian myth refer to the Eye of Ra as the Eye Goddess or as the solar eye (the sun disk) in distinction to the lunar eye (the moon disk).

11. For this interpretation, see chapter IIIC in Allen, *Genesis in Egypt.*

12. In representations of solar deities, this cobra is shown in front of or coiled round the sun disk. The *uraeus* cobra formed part of many Egyptian royal headdresses.

13. Confusingly, in spite of the story of the Sole Eye searching for Shu and Tefnut, the Eye is quite often identified as Tefnut. The role of a deity is often defined by the pair or group of which he or she forms a part. When Tefnut is paired with Maat, they usually play the contrasting roles of the fierce and gentle daughters of the creator.

14. For a comprehensive discussion of the place of *maat* in Egyptian culture, see the chapter "The Concept of Maat" in Erik Hornung, *Idea into Image: Essays on Ancient Egyptian Thought,* trans. Elizabeth Bredeck (Princeton, 1992); or J. Assmann, *Ma'at: Gerechtigkeit und Unsterblichkeit im alten Ägypten,* (Munich, 1990).

15. The translation is that of Allen, *Genesis in Egypt,* 25–26. For other translations of the Egyptian terms *neheh* and *djet,* see 'Time and Eternity' in Hornung, *Idea into Image.* These two forms of time are occasionally shown as deities supporting the sky.

16. The hymn, from Papyrus Cairo 58032, is translated in John L. Foster, *Hymns, Prayers, and Songs: An Anthology of Ancient Egyptian Lyric Poetry,* ed. Susan Tower Hollis (Atlanta, GA, 1995), IV.32.

17. Richard B. Parkinson's translation of a passage from "The Teaching for King Merikare," in Parkinson, *The Tale of Sinuhe and Other Ancient Egyptian Poems, 1940–1640 BC* (Oxford, 1997), 226.

18. It has been suggested that the negative attitude toward women displayed in this story was part of an adverse reaction to the reigns of several powerful queens. See L. H. Lesko, "Three Late Egyptian Stories Reconsidered" in *Egyptological Studies in Honor of Richard A. Parker* (Hanover, NH, 1986), 98–103.

19. The language used in this text suggests that it may have been based on a Middle Kingdom original. The words of the spell were to be declaimed over images of deities drawn on the patient's skin or on a piece of linen applied to the patient's throat. A healing herb to be drunk in wine or beer is also mentioned. The whole spell is said to have proved effective against poison on countless occasions.

20. The name itself would have been the type of "secret knowledge" that was only passed on to the initiated. Some of the Pyramid Texts, which were for the eyes of the king, do claim to give the true name of the creator. New Kingdom hymns threaten that any unauthorized person who speaks the true name of god will die instantly.

21. Thoth may not originally have been linked to this myth, but the Egyptian sense of symmetry demanded that as Thoth restored the lost and wounded lunar eye of Horus, he should also bring back the solar eye of Ra. The various stages in the development of the myth cycle of the solar eye were first studied by H. Junker in *Der Auszug der Hathor-Tefnut aus Nubien* (Berlin, 1911); and by W. Spiegelberg in *Der Ägyptische Mythus vom Sonnenauge* (Strasbourg, 1918).

22. For a full translation, see Miriam Lichtheim, *Ancient Egyptian Literature*, vol. 3: *The Late Period* (Berkeley, Los Angeles, and London,1980), 156–159.

23. This section of the myth is probably based on a list of names, epithets, and festivals of goddesses. By the Greco-Roman Period, and probably earlier, the myth of the Distant Goddess was linked with the winter solstice and the annual return of the inundation from the far south. The flood took some weeks to spread northward, so the priests of each major temple would greet it in turn. For the wild celebrations that marked the return of the wandering goddess, see J. C. Darnell, "Hathor Returns to Medamud," *Studien zur Altägyptischen Kultur* 22 (1995): 47–94.

24. These references are chiefly in the texts known as the Teaching for King Merikare and the Words of Neferti; see Parkinson, *The Tale of Sinuhe*, 138, 226. In another work of this period, the Dialogue of Ipuur, the protagonist expresses the opinion that it would have been better if the sun god had realized the true nature of humanity "in the first generation" and struck them all down. See Parkinson, *The Tale of Sinuhe*, 185, 197.

25. The best translation of and commentary on this text are to be found in Erik Hornung, *Der ägyptische Mythos von der Himmelskuh*, 2d ed., Orbis Biblicus et Orientalis 46 (Freiburg and Göttingen, 1997). For a recent discussion, see A. Spalinger, "The Destruction of Mankind: A Transitional Literary Text," *Studien zur Altägyptischen Kultur* 28 (2000): 257–282.

26. These cosmic beings are treated here as courtiers attending the king of the gods. It is a characteristic of Egyptian deities that they can manifest themselves in different forms and different locations at the same time.

27. "(Female) Powerful One" is the meaning of the name of the lion goddess Sekhmet. Egyptian myths are full of wordplay of this kind.

28. This would be a depth of about 9 inches / 22.5 centimeters. The mineral used to dye the beer was probably either ocher or hematite.

29. One of Hathor's epithets was Lady of Drunkenness. A calendar for the temple of Mut at Karnak records the serving of special red beer at a festival celebrating the pacification of the solar eye. See A. Spalinger, "A Religious Calendar Year," *Revue d'Egyptologie* 44 (1993): 161–184.

30. *Manetho, Aegyptiaca*, trans. and ed. W. G. Wadell (London, 1940).

31. See "Appendix: Primary Sources" under "Ismailia naos." Some Egyptologists believe that this unusual text was influenced by the Greek myth of Zeus's overthrow of Chronos. This may be so, but the fact that the story was inscribed on a shrine in the holiest part of a temple shows that the designers of the temple considered it important and meaningful.

32. According to Papyrus Salt 825, Osiris was slain by Geb and then brought back to life.

33. E. Otto, for example, wrote that Osiris "is from the beginning a dead god to whom poetic thought later attributes a past life." See *Egyptian Art and the Cults of Osiris and Amon*, trans. K. Bosse-Griffiths (London, 1968), 28.

34. "He who was put in the chest" is a traditional epithet of Osiris, but it refers to being encoffined after mummification. Plutarch's story may be an imaginative attempt to explain the coffins in the form of the body of Osiris that were popular at many periods.

35. Cedar of Lebanon was the favored wood for royal and elite coffins and for the barque-shrines used to carry statues of deities.

36. The only partial parallel to this incident in an Egyptian text is an episode in the tale of the Two Brothers in which Bata cuts off his own penis after being accused of adultery by his brother. He throws it in the river where it is eaten by a catfish. Bata's name links him with Seth, however, rather than with Osiris. It may be that a myth about Osiris's losing his penis was created to balance the ancient myth about Seth losing his testicles.

37. This is a role that could be of great significance in Egyptian culture, particularly among royalty, who were often raised by foster mothers. Many writers have noted parallels between the myth of Horus in Chemmis and the story of Moses being hidden in a floating basket among the rushes and then given to his own mother to wet nurse.

38. The sacred fish was probably the one that helped to guide the sun barque through the rivers of the underworld. For a translation of this spell, see Number 49 in J. F. Borghouts, *Ancient Egyptian Magical Texts* (Leiden, 1978).

39. H. te Velde argues in *Seth, God of Confusion* (Leiden, 1977) that the Eye of Horus was damaged because of sexual activity between Horus and Seth but that through the intervention of other deities, even this unorthodox union resulted in new life.

40. In this story the disk seems to be the solar disk, but in other versions it is a lunar aspect of Thoth, who is born from the "union" of Horus and Seth.

41. A spell from the Harris Magical Papyrus (BM 10042) refers to Isis weeping on the riverbank after Horus has had sex with her. This myth may have arisen through the common identification of Horus with the fertility god Min, "the bull of his mother" (See "Min" in "Deities, Themes, and Concepts.")

42. The myth is in the New Kingdom Papyrus Sallier IX. This seems to be the earliest example of a myth devised to explain the animal-headed divine forms common in Egyptian art. Plutarch angrily dismisses the story that Horus beheaded his mother as a ridiculous lie.

43. See the hymns to Osiris translated by M. Lichtheim in *Maat in Egyptian Autobiographies and Related Studies*, Orbis Biblicus et Orientalis 120 (Freiburg and Göttingen, 1992).

44. For a recent translation of these inscriptions, see William J. Murnane, *Texts from the Amarna Period in Egypt* (Atlanta, GA, 1995), 230–233.

45. See B. G. Ockinga, "On the Interpretation of the Kadesh Record," *Chronique d'Egypte* 62 (1987), 38–48; or C. Broadhurst, "Religious Considerations at Qadesh, and the Consequences for the Artistic Depiction of the Battle," in Lloyd , *Studies in Pharaonic Religion*, 77–81. Both sides suffered heavy losses at Qadesh.

46. The translation is by Parkinson, *The Tale of Sinuhe*, 139.

47. The translation of the text is by Brian P. Copenhaver in *Hermetica* (Cambridge, 1992), 81–82.

48. See D. O'Connor, "The Dendereh Chapel of Nebhepetre Mentuhotep: A New Perspective," in *Studies on Ancient Egypt in Honour of H. S. Smith*, ed. A. Leahy and W. J. Tait (London, 1999), 215–220.

49. See L. Bell, "Luxor Temple and the Cult of the Royal Ka," *Journal of Near Eastern Studies* 44 (1985): 251–294.

50. For this interpretation of the Sed Festival, see Hornung, *Idea into Image*, 53–54.

51. Or the corn mummies were left in a desert wadi until a flash flood brought the seeds to life. The best account of these objects is M. J. Raven's "Corn-mummies" in *Oudheidkundige Mededlingen het Rijksmuseum van Oudheden te Leiden* 63 (1980): 7–38. For the Osiris myth as part of the agricultural cycle, see Henri Frankfort, *Kingship and the Gods: A Study of Ancient Near Eastern Religion as the Integration of Society and Nature* (Chicago, 1948),181–197.

52. This myth has been reconstructed by Katja Goebs in her forthcoming study, *Crowns in Egyptian Funerary Literature—Symbols of Royalty, Rebirth and Destruction.*

53. For a survey of the full range of beliefs, see John H. Taylor, *Death and the Afterlife in Ancient Egypt* (London, 2001).

3

DEITIES, THEMES, AND CONCEPTS

DEITIES, NAMES, AND DATES

A complete list of the deities named in Ancient Egyptian texts would need several hundred entries. This selection concentrates on the gods and goddesses who are prominent in myth.

The forms of divine names given in this book are those that have been most commonly used by Egyptologists. Some are the Greek versions of the original Egyptian names. Many of these, such as Osiris (for Wsjr) or Thoth (for Djhwtj), are too well known to change. Alternative spellings of divine names that may be found in other books are given in brackets. These alternatives are due to the fact that the exact vowel sounds were not usually indicated in Egyptian scripts.

For the dates of the various periods mentioned in the entries (for example, Old Kingdom) see the Chronology on page ix.

PRIMARY SOURCES

Each entry is followed by a selection of primary sources cited in abbreviated form. An alphabetical list of these abbreviations is given in "Appendix: Primary Sources."

AKER
Aker was an earth god who guarded the eastern and western horizons. He took the form of a pair of conjoined sphinxes facing away from each other (see Figure 45).
    See also Sphinx

AKHET
The horizon, a place of transition for gods and the dead, was known as Akhet. The Double Horizon consisted of the Western Horizon where the sun god died at sunset and the Eastern Horizon where he was reborn at sunrise. The standard

Figure 20. Amun-Ra visits a queen to sire a divine child. The couple are supported by the goddesses Serqet (left)and Neith (right). Line drawing of a relief in Luxor temple. (Art Resource)

image of the horizon was a sun disk between two mountain peaks. Two shining trees grew on these mountains, and the Double Horizon was guarded by a double sphinx or twin lions.

See under Feline Deities; Ra; Shu and Tefnut

AMMUT

Ammut was a monstrous goddess who devoured the hearts of the evil dead.

See also Hippopotamus Goddesses

AMUN
(AMON, AMMON, AMEN)

Amun was the mysterious creator god whose name meant Hidden One. He was most commonly shown as a bearded man in the prime of life wearing a headdress surmounted by a double plume. His origins are obscure, but Amun and his female counterpart Amunet (Amaunet) were listed among the divine protectors of the king in the Pyramid Texts. Amun and Amunet were part of the group of eight primeval deities who came to be known as the Ogdoad of Hermopolis. During the Middle Kingdom, Amun gradually became the chief god of the Theban area, where he acquired a new consort, Mut, and a son, Khonsu. In the New Kingdom, the cult of Amun was combined with that of the creator sun god Ra. Amun-Ra was worshipped as the King of the Gods and creator of the world and its inhabitants.

In his chief cult temple at Karnak in Thebes, Amun, Lord of the Thrones of the Two Lands, ruled as a divine pharaoh. Unlike other important deities, Amun does not seem to have been thought of as living in some distant celestial realm. His presence was everywhere, unseen but felt like the wind. His **oracles** communicated the divine will to humanity. Amun was said to come swiftly to help Egyptian kings on the battlefield or to aid the poor and friendless. When he was manifest in his cult statues, Amun periodically visited the **necropolis** of Thebes to unite with its goddess, Hathor, and bring new life to the dead.

Amun tended to be the subject of speculative theology rather than mythical narratives, but he did play a role in the creation myths of Hermopolis. One of his incarnations was as the Great Shrieker, a primeval goose whose victory shout was the first sound. In some accounts this primeval goose laid the "world egg;" in others, Amun fertilized or created this egg in his ram-headed serpent form known as Kematef ("He who has completed his moment"). The temple of Medinet Habu in western Thebes was sometimes identified as the location of this primal event. A cult statue of the Amun of Karnak regularly visited this temple to renew the process of creation.

By the end of the New Kingdom, Amun was often depicted as a virile ram with curved horns or as a ram-headed sphinx. It was in these forms that he was primarily worshipped in Nubia and Libya. As early as the Middle Kingdom, Amun had been linked with the god Min to become the embodiment of male sexual power. Amun-Min, the "bull of his mother," was an **ithyphallic** self-generating god. Amun-Ra was the mysterious originator of all life, the "one who made himself into millions." In the temples of Thebes he was given a partner in the form of a royal priestess known as the "god's wife" or "god's hand." One of her duties seems to have been to physically arouse the god so that he would continue the ongoing work of creation by generating life.

Like the ram-god Banebdjedet, Amun was said to mystically unite with the queen of Egypt to sire the heir to the throne. This royal-birth myth was depicted in several Theban temples (see Figure 20). The idea persisted as late as the Greco-Roman Period, when legends were told about how the world-conquering Macedonian king, Alexander the Great, was sired by Amun. Alexander seems to have been acknowledged as the god's son when he made a pilgrimage to the remote temple of Amun at Siwa Oasis. According to some Classical writers, Alexander and his companions were in danger of dying in the desert when two serpents appeared to lead them safely to Siwa. The oracle of Amun at Siwa was believed to be infallible. The Greeks wove it into their own mythology, claiming that the heroes Perseus and Heracles had consulted Amun/Zeus there.

See also Aten; Atum; Birds; Boats; Khepri; Min; Mut; Ogdoad of Hermopolis; Ra

References and further reading:

J. Assmann. *Egyptian Solar Religion in the New Kingdom: Re, Amun, and the Crisis of Polytheism.* Translated by Anthony Alcock. London and New York: 1995.

G. Hart. "Amun." In *A Dictionary of Egyptian Gods and Goddesses.* London and Boston: 1986, 4–17.

V. A. Tobin. "Amun and Amun-Re." In *The Oxford Encyclopaedia of Ancient Egypt I,* edited by D. B. Redford. Oxford and New York: 2001, 82–85.
Primary sources:
PT 301; Leiden hymns; P. Boulaq XVII; Amun prayers; Qadesh inscriptions; Khonsu Cosmogony; Arrian Book 3; Alexander Romance

ANAT (ANATH, ANTA)

Anat was a Near Eastern warrior goddess worshipped in Egypt from the late Middle Kingdom onward. In the mythology of the Canaanites of Ugarit, Anat was the sister, lover, and avenger of the storm god Baal. In Egypt she was regarded as a daughter of Ra and a consort of the storm god Seth. She was a formidable defender of the sun god and protected kings on the battlefield.

In Egyptian art, Anat was usually represented as a woman carrying a shield, a spear, and an axe. One spell refers to Anat fighting alongside Ra against a troop of wild donkeys who embodied the forces of chaos. So fierce was this contest that Anat gathered the blood of the wounded sun god in fifteen metal bowls. King Rameses III claimed that Anat had been his shield in the equally desperate struggle against the invading Sea Peoples.

In Canaanite mythology, Anat and Baal mated in the forms of cow and bull; in Egypt, Anat was called the "great cow of Seth." In a myth used in several spells, Seth sees the Seed Goddess bathing and has sex with her. Only the creator sun god is allowed to mate with the Seed Goddess, so this sacrilegious act poisons Seth. Anat, "the woman who acts like a warrior," hastens to her father Ra to demand help for Seth. Perhaps out of fear of his warrior daughter, Ra has Isis cure Seth with her magic.

See also Astarte; Eye of Ra; Hathor; Seth

References and further reading:
J. van Dijk. "Anat, Seth and the Seed of Pre." In *Scripta signa vocis,* edited by H. L. J. Vanstiphout et al. Groningen, Netherlands: 1986, 31–52.
J. Goodnick Westenholz. "Goddesses of the Ancient Near East 3000–1000 BC." In *Ancient Goddesses: The Myths and the Evidence,* edited by L. Goodison and C. Morris. London: 1998, 63–82.
Primary sources:
P. Chester Beatty VII; HMP; P. Leiden I 343–345.6; H&S

ANDJETY (ANEDJETI)

Andjety was the local god of Busiris whose attributes were the crook and the flail.

See also Osiris

ANTI (ANTY)

An Upper Egyptian falcon god who was brutally punished for crimes against the gods, Anti was closely associated with both Horus and Seth. He was usually depicted as a falcon in a boat, but he could be shown as a griffin or as a man with the distinctive head of the Seth animal. Anti sometimes embodies the bad qualities of Horus, but in Coffin Texts spell 942 he is a manifestation of Seth who is shaved or skinned by a goddess in revenge for "turning the land upside down."

A myth in Papyrus Jumilhac explains why the cult statue of Anti is made of silver rather than the usual gold. Anti was condemned for some terrible crime that he had committed, probably the decapitation of a cow goddess. His skin and his flesh were flayed off his bones as a punishment and hung on a pole. Like all gods, Anti's flesh was made of gold and his bones of silver, so only the silver was left. When Anti was forgiven, the cow goddess restored his flesh with her healing milk.

Anti seems to be identical with Nemty, another divine falcon who was punished by the gods. In a New Kingdom story the Divine Tribunal retires to an island to consider whether to award the crown of Egypt to Horus or Seth. The deities who make up the Tribunal do not want to be disturbed by Isis, the mother of Horus. They order Nemty, the divine ferryman, not to take any woman who looks like Isis to the island. Isis disguises herself as an old hag and bribes Nemty with a gold ring to ferry her to the island. After she makes a fool of Seth, he demands that Nemty be punished. The Divine Tribunal orders all Nemty's toes (or claws) to be chopped off. Nemty vows that gold shall be taboo in his town forever, providing another explanation for the use of silver in his temples.

This was not the end of Nemty's misfortunes. A spell recounts how Horus and a god who is probably Nemty travel together in a golden boat. When Nemty is bitten and poisoned, he begs Horus to heal him. Horus offers to help in exchange for Nemty's true name. Nemty tries to fool him by giving the grandiose names of other deities, but in the end he has to tell the truth. Horus cures him and gains lasting power over Nemty.

See also Anubis; Bes and Beset; Horus; Seth

References and further reading:

J. F. Borghouts. "The Edition of Magical Papyri in Turin: a Progress Report." In *La Magia in Egitto*, edited by A. Roccati and A. Siliotti. Milan: 1987, 257–270.

G. Hart. "Anti." In *A Dictionary of Egyptian Gods and Goddesses*. London and Boston: 1986, 19–21.

Primary sources:

CT 942; H&S; Cairo calendar; PJ

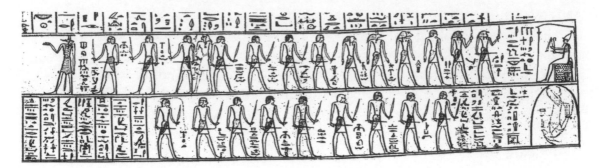

Figure 21. Anubis (far left), the Sons of Horus, and other deities defeat and imprison Seth. In this page from Papyrus Jumilhac, Seth (far right) is shown upsidedown below the throne of Osiris. (Art Resource)

ANUBIS (ANPU, INPW)

Anubis was the terrifying canine god who presided over the mummification of bodies and guarded burials. He was usually shown as a seated black jackal or as a man with the head of a jackal or wild dog. Anubis helped to judge the dead, and he and his army of messengers were charged with punishing those who violated tombs or offended the gods.

The jackals and wild dogs who lived on the edge of the desert were carrion eaters who might dig up shallowly buried corpses. To avert this horrible end for their dead, the early Egyptians tried to placate Anubis, "the dog who swallows millions." Most of the epithets of Anubis link him with death and burial. He was "the one who is in the place of embalming," "the Lord of the Sacred Land" (the desert cemeteries), and "the Foremost of the Westerners," that is, the leader of the dead. Anubis had a female counterpart, Anput, who is also shown as a jackal.

For most of the Old Kingdom, Anubis was the most important funerary deity. His figure was carved in tomb entrances to warn off grave robbers at a time when no other deities could be shown in nonroyal tombs. By the end of the third millennium BCE, Osiris had become the King of the Dead. Anubis was incorporated into the Osiris myth as the god who invented mummification to preserve the corpse of Osiris. He became the chief guardian of the mummy of Osiris and a supporter of Isis and her son, Horus. Anubis came to be regarded as a son of Osiris, but the darker side of his character was remembered in the epithet "the one who eats his father."

Anubis's title, Master of Secrets, chiefly referred to the gruesome secrets of the embalming tent. He was particularly associated with the bandaging of mummies and with the ceremony known as the Opening of the Mouth Ritual. This was performed to give the mummy back the senses it had enjoyed in life.

In the Book of the Dead, Anubis is shown in the throne room of Osiris supervising the weighing of the hearts of the dead. Among his duties was to fetch the hearts of the Followers of Seth.

A story recorded in the first millennium BCE tells how the wicked god Seth disguised himself as a leopard to approach the body of Osiris. He was seized by Anubis and branded all over with a hot iron. This, according to Egyptian myth, is how the leopard got its spots. Anubis then flayed Seth and wore his bloody skin as a warning to evildoers. By this era, Anubis was said to command an army of demon messengers who inflicted suffering and death.

Anubis remained an important funerary god in the Roman Period, but his cult was singled out for abuse by Roman writers. This may have been partly because of his popularity with **necromancers**. Demotic spells explain how to summon Anubis, the Keeper of the Keys to the Underworld, by methods such as drawing his image in the blood of a black dog. When he appeared, Anubis was used as a go-between to fetch gods and spirits from the underworld to answer the magician's questions. Anubis also acted as an enforcer of curses; a role he plays to this day in horror films.

See also Nephthys; Osiris; Seth; Thoth; Wepwawet

References and further reading:

D. M. Doxey. "Anubis." In *The Oxford Encyclopaedia of Ancient Egypt I*, edited by D. B. Redford. Oxford and New York: 2001, 97–98.

S. T. Hollis. "Anubis's Mortuary Functions in 'The Tale of the Two Brothers.'" In *Hermes Aegypticus*, edited by T. DuQuesne. Oxford: 1995, 87–100.

Primary Sources:

PT 437; CT 825, 936; BD 175; PJ; I&O; PDM XIV.1–92, 395–427; PDM Supp.101–30

ANUKET (ANUKIS)

Anuket was a goddess worshipped on Egypt's southern border.

See also Satet and Anuket

APIS

Apis was a bull kept at Memphis who was the most important of all sacred animals. In life, the Apis bull was honored as the physical manifestation of Ptah; in death he was worshipped as a form of Osiris. A festival called the Running of the Apis Bull is recorded as early as the First Dynasty. By the Late Period the Apis bull had become a kind of national mascot.

When an Apis bull died, he was mourned as if he were Osiris himself and given an extravagant funeral. Priests searched Egypt for a calf with the right markings to be recognized as the new Apis. The mother of the chosen calf was given a name (such as "the one of Bastet") and honored as a manifestation of

Isis. The new bull was crowned at full moon by the high priest of Ptah. Then he and his mother were installed in palatial quarters in the grounds of the temple of Ptah. The actions of the Apis bull were carefully watched because they were believed to predict the future.

The Apis bull came to be closely linked to the myth of the repeated death and regeneration of Osiris. Diodorus Siculus was told that when Osiris died, his soul had passed into the first Apis bull and was then preserved in each new bull. According to Plutarch, each Apis bull was believed to be miraculously generated by the light of the moon. Herodotus, on the other hand, recorded that each Apis was conceived when a lightning bolt hit his mother.

Herodotus also related that an Apis bull of the sixth century BCE was stabbed to death by the invading Persian king, Cambyses. The king is said to have been driven mad as a punishment for this sacrilegious act. Plutarch also referred to a legend about the slaughter of the Apis bull by Cambyses. He says that after the bull was killed, its corpse was thrown out of the temple. No carrion eaters would come near the holy animal, except dogs. By devouring the body of the Apis bull, dogs lost their place of honor in Egyptian religion and became "unclean" animals.

> ***See also*** Cattle; Ptah; Sokar
>
> ***References and further reading:***
>
> H. S . Smith. *A Visit to Ancient Egypt. Life at Memphis and Saqqara (ca 500–30 BC)*. Warminster, England: 1974.
>
> D. J. Thompson. "Apis and Other Cults." In *Memphis under the Ptolemies.* Princeton: 1988, 190–211.
>
> ***Primary sources:***
>
> Diodorus I.84–85; Herodotus H III.27–30; I&O 20, 44; P. Vindob

APOPHIS (APEP)

Apophis was the most dangerous of the chaos monsters who constantly threatened the divine order. He was sometimes described as a huge crocodile but was usually shown as a giant snake. Every night Apophis attacked the boat of the sun god as it passed through the underworld. He was beaten back and slaughtered, but however many times he was killed he always came back to life again.

In Egyptian myth, snakes can be divine protectors or symbols of renewal, but the Apophis snake seems to be an entirely destructive force. He was the negative counterpart of the snake form of the creator god. Apophis was first mentioned in the twenty-first century BCE. A much later creation myth explained that Apophis sprang from the saliva of the goddess Neith when she was still in the primeval waters. Her spit became a snake 120 yards long. He

Figure 22. A form of the sun god known as the Great Tom Cat slays Apophis under the ished *tree at Heliopolis. From a painting in a tomb at Deir el-Medina. (Courtesy of Geraldine Pinch)*

was "the Great Rebel," the "Evil One" who led the forces of chaos against the sun god Ra.

The idea of the Apophis snake may have come from the African python, which can open its mouth wide enough to swallow a person. Apophis is probably the unnamed snake demon who tried to swallow the *nun*, the primeval waters, but was forced to cough them up again. The eyes of Apophis seem to have been particularly feared, and he was said to make a terrible roaring sound. The movement of his body could cause earthquakes, and he was associated with the hidden sandbanks that were a danger to boats on the Nile. It has been suggested that a combination of the snake and crocodile forms of Apophis may be the origin of the dragons of medieval legend.

In Egyptian accounts of the nightly journey of the sun through the underworld, Apophis usually attacks in the seventh and the twelfth hours of the night. Powerful deities stand in the prow of the solar **barque** to protect the sun god against Apophis. Seth, the strongest of the gods, can be shown clubbing or spearing the Apophis snake. The fight between Seth and Apophis has sometimes been interpreted as a myth to explain thunderstorms. Another myth, of which no detailed version survives, told how the Great Tom Cat, a form of Ra, cut off the head of Apophis under the sacred *ished* tree "on the night of making war and driving off the rebels."

The spirits of the dead were expected to join in the struggle against Apophis, and rituals were performed in temples to ensure his defeat. In the Book of Overthrowing Apophis, the most terrifying deities in the Egyptian pantheon were evoked to combat the chaos serpent and destroy all the aspects of his being, such as his body, his name, his shadow, and his magic. Priests acted out this unending war by drawing pictures or making models of Apophis. These were cursed and then destroyed by stabbing, trampling, and burning.

> **See also** Atum; Boats; Crocodiles; Feline Deities; Ra; Seth; Snakes
> **References and further reading:**
> J. F. Borghouts. "The Evil Eye of Apophis." *Journal of Egyptian Archaeology* 59 (1973): 114–150.
> E. Hornung. "The Triumph of Magic: The Sun God's Victory over Apophis." In *The Valley of the Kings: Horizon of Eternity.* London and New York: 1990, 103–113.
> **Primary sources:**
> CT 414; BD 17, 39, 108; Ad; BOD; BOG; BRP

ARSAPHES

> *See* Heryshef

ASH

Ash was the god of the western desert and its oases. Later identified with Seth.

ASTARTE (ASHTARTE)

Astarte was a Near Eastern war goddess who was introduced into Egypt during the Second Intermediate Period. In Egyptian myth she became the daughter of Ra or Ptah and a consort of Seth. She is probably the same goddess worshipped by the Philistines as Ashtoreth and the Canaanites as Ashera. She also had much in common with the important Mesopotamian goddess Ishtar (Ashtar), the Lady of Battle. In Egyptian art, Astarte was usually shown naked, brandishing weapons and riding on horseback or driving a chariot. This made her a very alien figure. Egyptian goddesses were not usually shown naked, and Egyptian women never rode horses.

The lion was one of Astarte's sacred animals, and Astarte was sometimes given a lion's head. This identified her with the Eye of the Sun: the solar lioness who protected her father Ra. Like other goddesses who play this role, Astarte could also appear as a beautiful seductive woman.

In a New Kingdom story, Seth is offered the goddesses Astarte and Anat as compensation for losing the throne to Horus. A spell refers to Astarte and

Anat's becoming pregnant but not giving birth, possibly because of Seth's association with abortion. Astarte is also linked with Seth in a fragmentary New Kingdom tale known as Astarte and the Sea. This story is very similar to a myth from Ugarit in northern Syria in which the god Baal overcomes the sea monster Yam.

The tale begins with an account of the separation of the earth and sky and the creation of the world. The rule of the creator is challenged by Yam (the Sea), who embodies the chaotic aspect of the primeval ocean. Yam demands the tribute due to an overlord. The harvest goddess, Renenutet, delivers boxes of treasure, but it is not enough. Renenutet sends a bird messenger to Astarte's house to wake the goddess and tell her to take more tribute to Yam. Astarte weeps at the message, but she goes to the shore and sings and dances to attract the sea monster. Yam then wants her for his bride. Astarte is welcomed by the **Ennead**, who give up some of their most precious possessions to form her dowry.

Yam threatens to flood the whole earth if he does not get what he wants. When Yam comes to collect the treasure, he is challenged by Seth. In the Ugaritic myth, Baal kills the sea monster, scatters the pieces of its body, and declares himself king. The damaged Egyptian version probably ended with Seth defeating Yam and claiming Astarte as his prize.

See also Anat; Eye of Ra; Renenutet; Seth

References and further reading:

A. L. Perlman. *Asherah and Astarte in the Old Testament and in Ugaritic Literature.* Berkeley: 1978.

J. B. Pritchard. *Palestinian Figurines in Relation to Certain Goddesses Known through Literature.* New Haven: 1943.

Primary Sources:

H&S; Astarte and the Sea; P. Leiden I 343–345.4; HMP

ATEN (ATON)

Aten was a form of the sun god promoted by King Amenhotep IV in the fourteenth century BCE. This king changed his name to Akhenaten, which probably means "one effective on behalf of Aten." He built huge roofless temples to Aten, at first in Thebes and then in a new capital city, Akhetaten (Horizon of Aten). Aten was shown as a disk or sphere with rays ending in human hands holding the symbol of life. In Akhetaten (modern Tell el-Amarna), Aten was worshipped as the "sole god without equal." He was the god of light who had made the world and sustained it every day.

Surviving hymns to Aten stress his role as benevolent creator. There is no long sequence of events leading up to creation. Aten is simply said to have "made everything according to his heart" when he was alone. This act of creation was renewed every morning at sunrise. The hymns list the creatures given life by Aten in loving detail. "The flowers live because of your rays, the seeds sprout from the soil when you shine. Refreshed by your sight all flocks of animals frisk. Birds in the nest fly up joyfully, beating their wings in praise of the living Aten, their creator." It is emphasized that Aten created all the foreign countries and their peoples, not just Egypt and the Egyptians. The only category of beings who are missing are the numerous gods and goddesses who would come first in more traditional accounts of creation.

The worship of Aten as the solar disk had been prominent from the beginning of the New Kingdom. In the early years of Akhenaten's reign, Aten was identified with various manifestations of the creator sun god such as Ra-Horakhty and Shu. Later these references to other deities were purged, and Aten was redefined as "the light which comes from the solar disk." This could not really be depicted, so the disk-and-rays image of Aten may be no more than an elaborate hieroglyphic writing of the god's name. The rays only hold out life to the king and the female members of the royal family. Everyone else was expected to receive life from Akhenaten and his chief queen, Nefertiti, in return for absolute loyalty.

The worship of the most popular creator god, Amun-Ra, was banned, and the cults of other deities were neglected or ignored. Akhenaten tried to abolish most of the complex mythology that had grown up around the solar cycle. There was to be no nightly struggle against the forces of chaos. Akhenaten's theology produced no explanation for the presence of evil or sorrow in the world. When the Aten was absent at night, all creatures "sleep as though dead." The actual dead were no longer thought to pass into another world. They could only expect to spend eternity adoring Aten in his temples, woken every morning by his light.

Akhenaten's ideas never seem to have gained popular acceptance. A few years after his death, his policies were reversed. Amun-Ra became the chief deity of the state again, and Aten went back to being an aspect of the sun god. Speculation continued, however, about whether all deities were simply transient manifestations of the one creator.

See also Amun; Ra; Shu and Tefnut

References and further reading:

R. E. Freed et al. *Pharaohs of the Sun: Akhenaten. Nefertiti. Tutankhamun.* Boston: 1999.

E. Hornung. *Akhenaten and the Religion of Light.* Translated by D. Lorton. Ithaca and London: 1999.

Primary sources:

Aten hymns

ATUM (ATEM)

A creator deity who began and ended the world, Atum was the senior deity of the group of nine gods known as the Ennead of Heliopolis. When Atum became aware of his loneliness, he masturbated and impregnated himself with his own semen to produce the divine siblings Shu and Tefnut. Atum and Ra were often regarded as the primordial and solar aspects of the creator. The joint deity Ra-Atum (or Atum-Ra) wore the **Double Crown** of Upper and Lower Egypt to indicate his position as King of the Gods. Within the daily solar cycle, Atum was the setting sun "who becomes old every evening."

At the beginning and end of each of the great cycles of existence, Atum took form in the

Figure 23. Atum adored by King Rameses II on an obelisk moved to Tanis. (Courtesy of Geraldine Pinch)

primeval waters as a snake or an eel. Atum and the Apophis serpent have been interpreted by some Egyptologists as the positive and negative forces within chaos. The name Atum comes from a word meaning completeness or totality. The potential for all life was contained within Atum. When the Primeval Mound came into existence, Atum had a place to begin creation. He conceived and gave birth to the first two-gendered deities. As the "father and mother" of the gods, Atum was the ultimate divine and royal ancestor.

In the act of creation, Atum was shown in human form holding or sucking his erect penis. From the New Kingdom onward, the Hand of Atum was personified as a goddess, usually Hathor Nebet-hetepet or Iusaas. The image of the hand and the penis coming together to create life could be replaced by the concept of a divine union between the male and female principles inherent in the creator. A Hand of Atum is also mentioned in magical texts as a powerful talisman to drive away evil. In Egyptian symbolism, beings and images often had dual sexual and **apotropaic** meanings.

Another part of Atum with an independent existence was his eye. The coalescence of Atum with Ra is expressed in the myth in which Atum sends out his eye to bring light to the primeval darkness. This eye was also a goddess who was both the daughter and the consort of the creator. The Eye goddess was mainly referred to as the Eye of Ra, but occasionally as the Eye of Atum. These terms could be used to express a contrast between the headstrong and dangerous aspect of this goddess (the Eye of Ra) and her more amenable, protective aspect (the Eye of Atum). Sometimes, however, the Eye of Ra was the sun and the Eye of Atum was the moon.

At a later stage in mythical history, Ra-Atum and his warrior daughter fought a great battle against the forces of chaos. The key event was the slaughter of the chaos monster Apophis under the *ished* tree. This was a sacred tree growing in Heliopolis that was linked to the destiny of all beings. During this battle, Ra-Atum took the form of a cat, a mongoose, or an ichneumon, all predators that kill snakes (see Figure 22).

In solar mythology Atum was often paired with Khepri. They were complementary opposites, the setting and rising sun. In some Underworld Books, Atum is shown as an elderly man leaning on a stick. This is a rare phenomenon in Egyptian art, but it reflects the literary tradition that the sun god aged and became vulnerable to rebellions by deities and people. Such rebellions led to great changes in the nature of the world, such as the creator sun god's departure from earth to live in the heavens or the dissolution of the whole cosmos. In Book of the Dead spell 175, Atum warns Osiris that after millions of years he will destroy everything that he has made.

See also Bastet; Eye of Ra; Khepri; Ra; Shu and Tefnut

References and further reading:

K. Mysliwiec. "Atum." In *The Oxford Encyclopaedia of Ancient Egypt I,* edited by D. Redford. Oxford and New York: 2001, 158–160.

J. Zandee. "The Birth-giving Creator-god in Ancient Egypt." In *Studies in Pharaonic Religion and Society,* edited by A. B. Lloyd. London: 1992, 169–185.

Primary sources:

PT 527, 600, 606; CT 76, 80; BD 17, 175; Ad; BOG Hours 2, 3, 7; HMP; Magical statue texts; MT; BRP

BAAL

Baal was a Syrian storm and sky god often identified with Seth.

See also Anat; Seth

BABI (BABA)

Babi was a fierce and virile baboon god.

See also Baboons

Figure 24. A deceased woman and a baboon adoring the sun. Vignette from a copy of the Book of the Dead. (Courtesy of Geraldine Pinch)

BABOONS

The "dog-faced" baboon (*Papio cynocephalus*) was an important sacred animal. The male baboon was particularly associated with ferocious gods and lunar deities. Baboons in a group were often dawn gods who helped the sun to rise.

Statues and figurines of baboons were placed in temples and tombs from the Protodynastic Period onward. A god called Babi seems to have been endowed with the aggressive virility of a dominant male baboon. This deity lived on the entrails of the dead but could be persuaded to help deceased men to enjoy the pleasures of sex in the afterlife. Another early baboon deity was known simply as the Great White One. He seems to have been a personification of the royal ancestors, but his name suggests that he had a lunar aspect.

The lunar gods Khonsu and Thoth both had baboon forms. Colossal statues of baboons flanked the entrance to Thoth's greatest temple at Hermopolis. Initially this baboon form may only have been associated with Thoth's lunar aspect. Later it was prominent whenever Thoth was honored as the god of scribes and writing, perhaps because a baboon's dexterous hands resemble those of people. In a tale from the Greco-Roman Period, a magician makes two wax baboons come to life and write down thirty-five good stories and thirty-five bad stories.

A baboon was often shown sitting on top of the scales in which the hearts of the dead were weighed against the feather symbol of truth. This baboon was sometimes identified with Thoth, the recorder of divine judgments, and sometimes with Khonsu, "who eats the hearts of the dead." Four baboons with scorching breath guarded the Lake of Fire in the underworld, where they judged the rich and the poor alike. It was in the form of a baboon that Thoth traveled through the Nubian desert in search of the fiery daughter of the sun god.

The eight baboons of the horizon were associated with solar worship. These baboons (sometimes reduced to four or two) were shown standing on their hind legs and raising their front paws to greet the rising sun. "The baboons, the souls of the east, praise you when they call out to you at the appearance of your sun disk." The baboons were sometimes equated with the eight Heh gods who held up the sky. The separation of earth and sky so that the first sunrise could take place was one of the most important episodes in the Egyptian creation story. This cosmic event was repeated each dawn.

Wild baboons do stretch and chatter when waking up and moving off at first light. This was interpreted as singing and dancing for the sun god Ra, so baboons were thought to be the first creatures to pay proper religious observances. Baboons were kept as sacred animals in several Egyptian temples. There was a belief reported by some Classical writers that the most learned Egyptian priests understood the secret language of baboons. This was thought to be the natural language of true religion.

> ***See also*** Eye of Ra; Khepri; Khonsu; Moon; Ogdoad of Hermopolis; Ra; Thoth
> ***References and further reading:***
> H. te Velde. "Some Remarks on the Mysterious Language of the Baboons." In *Funerary Symbols and Religion*, edited by J. H. Kamistra et al. Kampen, Netherlands: 1988, 129–137.
> ***Primary sources:***
> BD 15, 100, 126; Ad 1st hour; KASP; Solar hymns; Petese; EofS

BANEBDJEDET (BANEBDJED)

A ram god associated with the town of Mendes (Djedet), Banebdjedet was the northern equivalent of the god Khnum. His sacred animal was a ram or a goat. His consort was a fish or dolphin goddess called Hatmehyt (Foremost of the Fishes), who seems to have been the original local deity of Mendes.

As the word for ram (*ba*) and the word for soul or manifestation sounded the same in Egyptian, ram gods were often regarded as manifestations of other deities. Banebdjedet could be shown with four rams' heads representing the four *bas* of the creator sun god. This linked Banebdjedet with Osiris, who was often named as a *ba* of the sun god. The Book of the Heavenly Cow states that "the *ba* of Osiris is the ram of Mendes." Passages in the Coffin Texts suggest that the soul of Osiris took refuge in Mendes when his body was killed by Seth. Banebdjedet could also be identified with the first four gods to rule Egypt: Ra-Atum, Shu, Geb, and Osiris. Huge granite shrines for these four deities were set up in the sanctuary at Mendes.

Banebdjedet was not always treated as a form of Osiris. In a New Kingdom story, he is consulted by the Divine Tribunal. When they order the ram god to judge between Horus and Seth, he diplomatically suggests that they ask the goddess Neith instead. When that fails to settle matters, Banebdjedet proposes that the throne be given to Seth because he is older than Horus.

Ram gods were particularly renowned for their virility, and one of Banebdjedet's epithets was Lord of Sexual Pleasure. A stela from a chapel in the Ramesseum complex records that the god Ptah took the form of Banebdjedet to sleep with a mortal woman. The son that resulted was the future pharaoh, Rameses II. Greek writers reported that a male goat was honored as a fertility god at Mendes and identified with the Greek god Pan. A Persian king of the fourth century BCE is alleged to have gone mad after sacking the temple and eating the sacred goat. The sexual aspect of the cult at Mendes made it particularly disliked by early Christians. Banebdjedet's form as a ram or goat-headed man was reinterpreted as a devil figure who entered Western tradition as the horned King of the Witches.

> **See also** Heryshef; Imhotep; Khnum; Osiris
> **References and further reading:**
> H. de Meulenaere. "Cults and Priesthoods of the Mendesian Nome." In H. de Meulenaere and P. MacKay. *Mendes II.* Warminster, England: 1976,174–177.
> G. Hart. "Banebdjedet." In *A Dictionary of Egyptian Gods and Goddesses.* London and Boston: 1986, 52–53.
> **Primary sources:**
> CT 60; H&S; RBM; Mendes stela; Hibis texts; Herodotus H II.46; Diodorus I.84

BASTET (BAST, BOUBASTIS, PASHT)

Bastet was a feline goddess who mothered the king and destroyed his enemies. Her name probably means She of the Ointment Jar. Her main cult center was at Bubastis in the eastern Delta. As "the Eye of Ra who protects her father Ra," she was a manifestation of the solar eye. Bastet was regarded as both the daughter and the consort of Atum-Ra. Their son, Mahes (Mihos), was a lion deity. Bastet herself was generally shown as a lion-headed woman until the end of the second millennium BCE, when her cat and cat-headed forms became prominent.

From the Pyramid Texts onward, Bastet has a double aspect of nurturing mother and terrifying avenger. It is the demonic aspect that mainly features in the Coffin Texts and the Book of the Dead and in medical spells. The "slaughterers of Bastet" were said to inflict plague and other disasters on humanity. One spell advises pretending to be the "son of Bastet" in order to avoid catching the plague. Bastet may be the poisoned cat who is cured by Ra in a myth alluded to in another healing spell.

Figure 25. Block showing Bastet in the ruins of her temple at Bubastis. (Courtesy of Geraldine Pinch)

A Twelfth Dynasty text compares an Egyptian king to Sekhmet when he smites wrongdoers and to Bastet when he protects his loyal subjects. The contrast between these two goddesses came to be expressed visually by their lioness and cat forms. Bastet was one of the goddesses associated with the story of the Distant Goddess, the daughter of Ra who quarrels with her father and retreats into the desert. She was particularly identified with the form of this goddess known as the "Nubian cat," who could be shown with the body of a spotted cat and the head of a Nubian woman. A god, usually Thoth or Shu, persuades the wandering cat to return to Egypt, where she is transformed into a compliant and fertile divine consort.

Some scholars have interpreted this as a myth about the taming of female sexuality. According to the Greek writer Herodotus, however, women were freed from all constraints during an annual festival at Bubastis. They celebrated the festival of the goddess by drinking, dancing, making music, and displaying their genitals.

The erotic reputation of the followers of Bastet is reflected in a story about Prince Setna composed in the later first millennium BCE. Setna encounters Taboubu, the beautiful daughter of a priest of Bastet, and instantly falls in love with her. Taboubu agrees to meet Setna in the house of Bastet in Memphis. Before she will sleep with him, Taboubu makes the infatuated Setna sign a deed giving her all his possessions. He even lets her kill his own children and feed their bodies to cats and dogs. Setna is about to embrace Taboubu when he finds himself alone and naked on the public highway. It has all been an illusion to punish Setna for stealing a magical book from a tomb. In this story, the irresistible Taboubu may be a manifestation of Bastet herself, playing her traditional role of punisher of humans who have offended the gods.

See also Eye of Ra; Feline Deities; Magicians; Moon; Mut; Sekhmet

References and further reading:

J. Malek. *The Cat in Ancient Egypt.* London: 1993, 94–111, 126–127.

G. Pinch. "The Nicholson Museum Hathor Capital." In *Egyptian Art in the Nicholson Museum,* edited by B. Ockingo and K. Sowado. Sidney: In press.

Primary sources:

PT 508; Loyalist Instruction; Sekhmet litany; BRP; Setna cycle

BAT

Bat was a primeval cow goddess worshipped in the Mansion of the Sistrum.

See also Cattle; Hathor

BATA

Bata was a bull god regarded as a form of Seth.

See also Cattle

BENU BIRD (PHOENIX)

In some Egyptian creation myths the *benu* bird is the oldest living creature. When the first land rose out of the dark waters of chaos, the shining *benu* bird alighted on this primeval mound. Its cry was the first sound ever heard. The earliest references to the *benu* bird seem to describe it as a yellow wagtail, but it was later shown as a type of heron (see Figure 11).

The word *benu* probably comes from an Egyptian verb meaning to rise and shine. The *benu* bird may originally have been identified with Venus as the morning star, making it the forerunner of the renewal of creation each dawn. The cry of the *benu* bird was the point at which time began. It was also the *benu* bird who would announce the end of time and the return of the world to chaos.

From the Pyramid Texts onward, the *benu* bird was closely associated with the creator sun god. In Heliopolis, the center of solar worship, the *benu* bird was said to perch on the **benben** stone, a kind of primitive **obelisk**, or in the branches of a sacred willow tree. When Egyptian kings had reigned for thirty years, they asked the *benu* bird to renew their strength and vitality.

Both Ra and Osiris could be identified with the *benu* bird, an expression of the "secret knowledge" that these two gods were one. As a manifestation of Osiris, the *benu* bird led the spirits of the dead through the dangers of the underworld. Some spells in the Book of the Dead aim to assist the dead to transform themselves into *benu* birds, so that they can travel freely between worlds.

The *benu* bird seems to have been the prototype for the Classical myth of the phoenix, a creature of which there was never more than one at a time. In the fifth century BC, the Greek writer Herodotus claimed to have visited Heliopolis and been told about a marvelous red-gold bird known as a phoenix. This bird was said to visit the temple of the sun at Heliopolis every 500 years carrying the ashes of its parent inside an egg of myrrh. It was presumably from this egg that the next phoenix would eventually hatch.

See also Atum; Birds; Primeval Mound; Ra

References and further reading:

R. T. Rundle Clark. "The Phoenix." In *Myth and Symbol in Ancient Egypt.* London: 1959, 245–249.

S. Quirke. "*Benu* Bird of Ra, the 'Phoenix' of Egypt." In *The Cult of Ra Sun-worship in Ancient Egypt.* London: 2001, 27–30.

Primary sources:

PT 600; CT 76, 335; BD 13, 17, 29b, 83; Herodotus H II.73

BES AND BESET

Bes and Beset were protective dwarf deities closely associated with childbirth and rebirth. A number of dwarf deities are known from Egyptian art under the names of Aha, Hity (Haty), or Bes. They often appear in groups—strangling snakes, waving knives, or playing musical instruments. Aha, whose name means Fighter, attacked and overcame the forces of evil such as demons, chaos serpents, and foreign sorcerers. Hity was a kind of divine exorcist who drove away evil by stamping, dancing, and banging a drum or a tambourine. Bes, and the female counterpart whom Egyptologists call Beset, performed similar functions.

By the end of the second millennium BCE, Bes and Beset were sometimes identified with the divine siblings, Shu and Tefnut. Paradoxically, Bes became a giant dwarf whose body reached from the underworld to the heavens. He could also be regarded as a special embryonic form of the creator sun god. It may be in this role that Bes can be shown as an androgynous being suckling or cuddling baby Bes figures, monkeys, or kittens. In the first millennium BCE, the joint deity Horus-Bes figured in magic as a divine healer and protector.

Egyptian "old wives" probably told stories about the antics of Bes, but they do not survive in the written record. The evidence for dwarf deities is mainly pictorial. They appear on magical objects, bedroom furniture, and items used to contain or apply makeup. Bes amulets and figurines were popular for over 2,000 years. Some women even decorated their bodies with Bes tattoos to improve their sex life or fertility.

The masklike face of Bes has wide eyes, a flat nose, and a projecting tongue. It is framed by hair that sometimes looks like a lion's mane. Originally Bes may have been a dwarf wearing the entire skin of a lion or a leopard. By the later second millennium BCE he is usually a half-human, half-animal creature, with a furry body, a long tail, and a face as ugly as an "old monkey." The spotted pelt of some Bes and Beset figures may relate to the myth in which the flayed skin of Anti or Seth becomes a protective garment for the champions of order. The ugliness of Bes and the way in which he often displays oversized genitals added to his effectiveness as an apotropaic deity.

Beset had the same lion-mask features as Bes. She was sometimes shown as a dwarf and sometimes with a body of normal proportions. Beset is unusual in being portrayed naked. In Egyptian myth, goddesses seem to undress for one of two reasons: to overcome some hostile force by their sexual power or to give birth. Some figurines of Beset may show her pregnant. As a "divine mother," Beset could be a form of Isis or Hathor.

Complex Bes and Beset figurines of the Third Intermediate Period include visual allusions to the myth of the Distant Goddess Hathor-Tefnut. She wandered as a cat in the Nubian or Libyan deserts until she was persuaded to return by Shu and Thoth, who had taken the form of apes or monkeys. Dwarf deities such as Bes and Hity are shown in temples of the Greco-Roman Period capering like monkeys and making music to pacify the returning goddess (see Figure 14).

During the New Kingdom, Bes was usually paired with the fearsome hippopotamus goddess Taweret rather than with Beset. The two deities appear in scenes celebrating the births of kings and commoners. Bes and Taweret were also the guardians of the divine infants worshiped in the Birth Houses of temples of the first millennium BCE. Temple and magical texts give Bes or Bes-Shu the role of opening the womb to allow a child to be born.

The symbolism of birth was reproduced in tombs to help the dead to new life. Some royal tombs and **sarcophagi** show Bes with hippopotamus-faced demons protecting the lion-shaped bed on which the deceased hoped to be reborn. A painted statue of Bes dominates a tomb chamber in the recently discovered Valley of the Golden Mummies.

See also Eye of Ra; Feline Deities; Hathor; Hippopotamus Goddesses; Horus the Child; Shu and Tefnut

References and further reading:

M. Malaise. "Bes." In *The Oxford Encyclopaedia of Ancient Egypt I*, edited by D. Redford. Oxford and New York: 2001, 179–181.

J. F. Romano. "The Origin of the Bes Image." *Bulletin of the Egyptology Seminar* 2 (1980): 39–56.

Primary sources:

RBM; HMP; Medamud hymn; Edfu calendar

BIRDS

Egypt was very rich in bird life. The river Nile and the marshes teemed with water birds, carrion eaters and birds of prey soared above the deserts, and huge flocks of migratory birds passed overhead or wintered in the south of the country. Many Egyptian deities had bird forms, but flocks of birds were used as a symbol of chaos. In some Egyptian creation myths, a bird was the first living being. The heavens could be imagined as a cosmic hawk. Many spells claimed to bestow the power to fly to the celestial realm or between the worlds of the living and the dead. The *ba*, the Egyptian concept that is closest to Western ideas about the soul, could be shown as a human-headed bird.

Birds were traditionally hunted with throw sticks or nets. There was a Birdcatcher God, who was the son of the Marsh Goddess. Migrating birds were probably seen as foreign invaders, and large flocks could strip fields and orchards bare. This may be why the common sparrow was used as a symbol in words denoting evil things. In temples of the Greco-Roman Period, gods are shown assisting the king to pull a clap net tight on a chaotic mass of birds. At Kom Ombo temple, bound foreign prisoners are pictured among the struggling birds, emphasizing that the bird-catching ritual is part of the eternal war between order and chaos.

As the divine order was created out of the swamps of chaos, water birds such as the goose, the heron, or the ibis were associated with the first stages of creation. A primeval goose, named Gengen or Negeg, shrieked or cackled as it laid the world egg. One of the tasks of the virtuous dead was to guard this egg. The remains of the primeval egg were said to be preserved in the temple of the ibis god, Thoth. In the temple of Horus at Edfu, the first bird was said to be a hawk who alighted on a mat of vegetation floating on the primeval waters.

Many other gods and a few goddesses had a hawk form, including Anti, Montu, Sokar, Sopdu, Hathor, Nephthys, and Isis. Horus was able to manifest himself as a sky falcon 1,000 **cubits** long. Egyptian kings were revered as earthly manifestations of Horus. When they died, they were said to fly to the horizon in the form of a falcon to unite with the sun disk. The sun disk itself was often shown with wings. Texts at Edfu claim that this was to commemorate Horus assuming this form to blind the enemies of the sun god.

Horus could also appear as a griffin, a monster combining the powers of a hawk, a lion, and a snake. By the Greco-Roman Period, the griffin was seen as a symbol of divine retribution. In one of the parables told by the god Thoth to the Distant Goddess, two vultures who represent sight and hearing learn that even the mighty lion can be slaughtered by the griffin if he disobeys the laws of Ra. Another of these parables concerns a vulture and a cat who are both punished for breaking an oath sworn by Ra. The vulture in this parable is fiercely maternal, which reflects the fact that one of the Egyptian words for vulture (*mwt*) sounded the same as the word for mother. The vulture goddess Nekhbet was a mythical mother to every Egyptian king. Queens traditionally wore headdresses in the form of a vulture.

The goddesses Isis and Nephthys could take the form of kites, small birds of prey that also ate carrion, to watch over the body of Osiris. One episode in the New Kingdom story the Contendings of Horus and Seth tells how Isis tricked Seth into admitting that Horus was in the right. She then turned into a kite and flew up into a tree to mock Seth from the safety of its branches.

Isis and Nephthys, and other goddesses such as Maat, could also be shown as winged beings. Their outspread wings offered protection and shade, like those of the vulture goddess Nekhbet. In her bird form, Isis used her wings to fan the breath of life back into her murdered husband. The ostrich feather worn by the god Shu was also associated with the breath of life.

After death the personality survived as a *ba*. This had the power to leave the mummy and travel through the Egyptian cosmos, though only the virtuous soul would find a safe place to alight. From the New Kingdom onward the *bas* of the dead were shown as part bird, part human. The bird body could be that of a stork, a vulture, or a hawk. A sequence of spells in the Book of the Dead allows the *ba* to transform itself into a falcon, a heron, a swallow, or the legendary *benu* bird (phoenix).

The dead also aspired to join the "imperishable stars" of the northern sky, which were sometimes pictured as swallows. In one myth, Ra devours all the other deities. He vomits them out again as fish, but they change into birds and fly up to the heavens to become stars.

> **See also** Amun; Anti; *Benu* Bird; Eye of Horus; Horus; Isis; Primeval Mound;
>   Sokar; Sopdu; Thoth; Two Ladies
> **References and further reading:**
> E. Hornung. "Body and Soul." In *Idea into Image: Essays on Ancient Egyptian
>   Thought.* Translated by Elizabeth Bredeck. Princeton: 1992, 167–184.
> P. F. Houlihan. *The Birds of Ancient Egypt.* Warminster, England: 1986.
> **Primary sources:**
> BD 77–78, 83–86, 110; BofNut; H&S; Cairo calendar; LWD; Edfu cosmology; EofS.

BOATS

Boats were one of the most important forms of transport in Ancient Egypt, especially during the **inundation** season, so it is natural that they are prominent Egyptian myth. From a very early period the divine realm was thought of as a watery region high above the earth consisting of rivers, islands, and marshes. The **Duat**, the Egyptian underworld, also contained rivers, lakes, and marshy areas. Therefore, deities and the spirits of the dead were often shown or described as traveling by boat. In actual cult practice, when divine statues left their sanctuaries they were transported in boat-shaped shrines.

In the Pyramid Texts, the deceased king voyages to the horizon on a raft or skiff made from reeds. Groups of full-size timber boats were buried near royal tombs for most of the third millennium BCE. Scenes on some tomb walls from this era show the mummies of important people being taken by boat on a posthumous pilgrimage to Busiris or Abydos, the holy towns of Osiris, the god of the underworld.

In many passages in the Coffin Texts and the Book of the Dead, the deceased soul has to persuade a divine ferryman to help him or her across the rivers of the underworld. To succeed, it was necessary to know the names of the ferryman and every part of his boat. The deceased could also be shown sailing their own boats with the help of the goddess of the sweet north wind. Other funerary spells were intended to assist the dead to join the crew of the solar barque. This was the boat in which the sun god traveled across the sky and through the underworld.

The solar barque was called the Boat of Millions because all the gods and all the souls of the blessed dead might be needed in its crew. The crew is sometimes referred to as rowing the solar barque, but this is never shown. Instead, a number of deities, often in the form of jackals or cobras, can be depicted towing the boat along (see Figure 43). In some Underworld Books there are two solar barques, the Day Boat (Mandjet) and the Night Boat (Mesektet). It is possible that the two huge cedar-wood boats buried beside the Great Pyramid of Khufu (Cheops) represented these barques.

The sun god can be shown alone in the Day Boat, but in the Night Boat other deities usually stand on deck ready to defend the vulnerable nocturnal form of the sun. The dangers included submerged sandbanks and attacks by hostile crocodiles, turtles, and snakes. The worst of these enemies was the monstrous chaos serpent Apophis. Sometimes the solar barque was surrounded or followed by a whole fleet of small boats carrying various protective deities and emblems. The prow and stern posts of these boats terminate in crowns, snakes, or human or animal heads.

The moon god and many star deities were also pictured traveling the heavens in boats. As early as the First Dynasty, the celestial falcon, Horus, had been shown in a boat. Several episodes in the prolonged conflict between the Two Lords, Horus and Seth, took place in boats. In one text, Horus challenges Seth to a race in stone boats. In the Greco-Roman Period temple at Edfu, texts and reliefs tell the story of the triumph of Horus over the forces of Seth. With the help of various deities, Horus repeatedly harpoons the Seth-hippopotamus who attacks his boat. The boat of Horus seems to be presented as an earthly counterpart of the beleaguered solar barque. This whole drama was probably acted out from real boats on the temple lake each year.

At Abydos a model boat representing the *neshmet* barque, "the warship of the gods," took part in a reenactment of the myth of the death and revival of Osiris. The priests who carried such boat-shrines played the role of the crew of the divine barques. The small boat-shrines were sometimes transported between temples on actual boats. The most famous of these was the "great noble boat" image used as the main cult of Amun-Ra at Karnak. A story dating to the early first millennium BCE tells how a priest called Wenamun was sent to Lebanon to buy logs of cedar to make a new boat for Amun-Ra. He suffered many trials and adventures, including losing all the gold and silver that was meant to pay for the timber. The ending is missing, but the story probably concluded with Wenamun's triumphant return to Thebes with the precious cedar.

See also Apophis; Horus; Osiris; Ra; Sokar

References and further reading:

E. Hornung. *The Valley of the Kings: Horizon of Eternity.* New York: 1990, chaps. 5 to 6.

K. A. Kitchen. "Barke." In *Lexikon der Ägyptologie I.* Wiesbaden: 1975, 619–625 (in English).

Primary sources:

CT 398; BD 99–102, 136; Ad; BOG; BOD; H&S; Triumph of Horus; Wenamun

CATTLE

The nomadic ancestors of the Ancient Egyptians were dependent on their herds for survival. There is evidence that cattle were treated as sacred animals as early as the sixth millennium BCE. Cattle cults remained a central part of Egyptian religion and mythology during the whole span of Pharaonic culture. Human beings were said to be "God's cattle." Bulls were revered as symbols of masculine strength and virility. Many gods had a bull form, and sacred bulls were kept at some temples. A sky goddess who took the form of a cow was among the earliest of Egyptian deities. The cow goddess under all her names represented the loving and nurturing aspect of the divine. The king, and later humanity in general, played the role of the calf of the divine cow.

From early times the king of Egypt was compared with the leading bull of a herd, able to defeat all challengers. Bulls as fighters were particularly associated with the war god Montu, who was manifest on earth as the Buchis bull. The white bull of Min embodied male sexuality. The mysterious process of heredity was celebrated in the concept of kings and gods being "the bulls of their mothers." The Mnevis bull was the messenger of the creator sun god, Ra-Atum, who

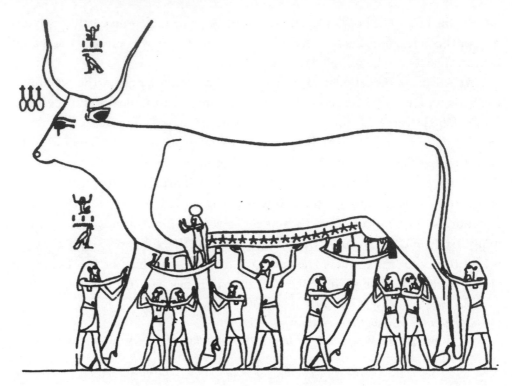

Figure 26. The sky goddess in cow form from the Book of the Heavenly Cow. She is supported by Shu and the eight Heh gods. Heavenly bodies sail in boats along her starry belly. (Art Resource)

engendered all life. The Apis bull was an earthly manifestation of the creator god Ptah. The moon could be thought of as a virile young bull when it was waxing and as an old ox when it was waning.

Bull imagery was not entirely positive. Wild bulls were ritually hunted and killed as symbols of the forces of chaos. In some accounts, Seth took bull form to trample his brother Osiris to death. This Seth-bull was castrated by Anubis and forced to carry the coffin of Osiris to burial. In the New Kingdom story the Two Brothers, one of the brothers is called Bata, a name of Seth in his bull form. This Bata transforms himself into a magnificent bull to visit the wife who has deserted him to marry the king of Egypt. The queen persuades her husband to sacrifice this bull in the hope of getting rid of Bata. He then transforms himself into two beautiful trees that the Queen has cut down. She accidentally swallows a sliver of the wood and falls pregnant. The child turns out to be Bata reborn. Bata has become "the bull of his mother" and has fathered himself.

In the Pyramid Texts, "the great wild cow of the marshes" is the king's mother or wet nurse in the afterlife. In Pyramid Texts spell 485a, the dead king is described as "the golden calf" of the milk goddess Hesat (Hezat). Two parallel cow and calf myths developed. In one, the cow goddess Mehet-Weret (the Great Flood) gave birth to the sun child in the primeval marsh at the dawn of time. The great creator goddesses Hathor and Neith could both be identified with the Mehet-Weret cow. Neith was said to have carried the infant sun god the length of Egypt seated between her horns. In the second myth, the Ihet cow gave birth to and suckled the infant god Horus in the marshes of Chemmis. The Ihet cow was most commonly identified with Isis or Hathor. One of Seth's many crimes was stealing milk from the cow who suckled Horus.

Royal birth scenes show a pair of cow-headed goddesses suckling the newborn king and his *ka.* Life, stability, and power were said to enter the king with the milk of the divine cow. From the Middle Kingdom onward, kings identified with Horus in Chemmis by depicting themselves being suckled by a divine cow hidden inside a papyrus thicket. Nonroyal people eventually became part of this mythical archetype by showing themselves sheltering beneath the head of the divine cow.

An Upper Egyptian deity called Bat ("female soul") may have been the earliest cow goddess to be associated with sky. Her cult was later absorbed into that of Hathor. Both Hathor and the sky goddess Nut could be imagined as a gigantic cow whose body was patterned with stars. The Book of the Heavenly Cow describes how Nut first lifted the sun god into the heavens between her horns. A red or gold solar disk is nearly always shown between the horns of cow goddesses.

In graphic myths, the sun god sails along the belly of the cow each day. At night he traveled through the inner sky along an underworld river that was sometimes identified with Mehet-Weret.

The horned head of the sky cow acted as a symbol for the whole daily cycle of the death and regeneration of the sun. The sky cow was the mother of the cosmos, who gave birth to the diurnal and nocturnal forms of the sun.

A further elaboration of this idea turned the chest in which Osiris was regenerated into the body of a cow goddess called Shentayet. The ordinary dead could hope to be welcomed into the underworld by other forms of the divine cow. A bull, who may be Osiris, Lord of the Cows, and seven cows with names such as the One of Chemmis and the One Who Is Great of Love feature in a spell for "staying alive forever."

See also Apis; Hathor; Horus; Isis; Mehet-Weret; Min; Montu; Moon; Neith; Nut; Seth; Two Ladies

References and further reading:

F. A. Hassan. "Primeval Goddess to Divine King: The Mythogenesis of Power in the Early Egyptian State." In *The Followers of Horus,* edited by R. Friedman and B. Adams. Oxford: 1992, 307–321.

Figure 27. Mummified sacred crocodiles stored in the temple of Sobek and Horus at Kom Ombo. (Courtesy of Richard Pinch)

D. Kessler. "Bull Gods." In *The Oxford Encyclopaedia of Ancient Egypt I,* edited by D. Redford. Oxford and New York: 2001, 209–213.

G. Pinch. "Cows." In *Votive Offerings to Hathor.* Oxford: 1993, 160–183.

Primary sources:

PT 271, 485a; BD 141, 148; BHC; RBM; TB; PJ

CROCODILES

The Nile crocodile is one of the world's largest reptiles. It was honored in some regions of Ancient Egypt and despised in others. The best-known crocodile deity was Sobek, but a number of gods and demons had awe-inspiring crocodile forms. In some traditions, a crocodile was the first creature to emerge from the primeval waters. Crocodiles could be symbols of the life-giving power of the primeval waters or of the forces of chaos who tried to swallow up and destroy life.

Death by crocodile was particularly dreaded because the body would be devoured. Epithets for crocodiles include "mouth of terror" and "the one who seizes." When they seized people, crocodiles were thought to be carrying out the vengeance of the gods or the decrees of fate. Diodorus Siculus claimed that crocodiles were revered in Egypt because one had saved King Menas (Menes) when he was chased into Lake Moeris by his own dogs. This is very similar to an incident in the New Kingdom Tale of the Doomed Prince, in which the prince has to jump into a lake when his trusted dog attacks him. The "crocodile who was his fate" offers to save him in return for help against a water demon.

King Menas is said to have founded the city of Krokodilopolis in the Fayum in gratitude for his escape. The Roman Period Book of the Fayum lists and illustrates many of the crocodile cults of this region (see Figure 44). In the Fayum there was a taboo against hunting crocodiles because "the *ba* (manifestation) of Sobek is crocodiles." Crocodiles were kept as sacred animals in some temples and mummified after death.

At Athribis, the local crocodile god Khenty-Khety came to be regarded as a form of Horus. Yet on magical stelae, Horus the Savior was asked to "drive away all the crocodiles of the river." At Edfu, crocodiles were reviled as Followers of Seth. A crocodile son of Seth called Maga was a fearsome opponent for Horus, son of Osiris. In temple texts at Edfu, the king promises to kill all crocodiles and crush their eggs.

In the afterlife, the souls of the dead had to evade the Crocodiles of the Four Directions, who were enemies of the four *bas* of the sun god. In enigmatic scenes in New Kingdom royal tombs, the nocturnal sun has to pass through the body of the crocodile Penwenti, who symbolizes the primeval waters, in order to be reborn. Greek and Roman writers recorded a bizarre Egyptian belief that ichneumons (a type of mongoose) killed crocodiles by running down their throats and gnawing their way out through the bowels. This may be a misunderstanding of the mythical conflict between the sun god Ra in the form of an ichneumon and Apophis in the form of a crocodile or a snake.

> ***See also*** Apophis; Horus the Child; Magicians; Neith; Onuris; Seth; Sobek
> ***References and further reading:***
> C. Eyre. "Fate, Crocodiles, and the Judgement of the Dead. Some Mythological Allusions in Egyptian Literature." *Studien zur Altägyptischen Kultur* 4 (1976): 103–114.
> P. Wilson. "Slaughtering the Crocodile at Edfu and Dendera." In *The Temple in Ancient Egypt,* edited by S. Quirke. London: 1997, 179–203.
> ***Primary sources:***
> BD 31–32; DP; BOE; HMP; Herodotus H II.68–69; Diodorus I.34, 89; Strabo G XVII.44, 47; BOF

DJED PILLAR

The **djed** was one of the most common of Egyptian symbols. It was used in the **hieroglyphic** script to write a word that means "stability" or "immutability." The original *djed* may have been a pillar made from reeds or sheaves of corn, but in time it came to be thought of as the backbone of the murdered god Osiris. The *djed* was sometimes personified as a separate god known as "the august *djed*."

Some early uses of the *djed* symbol imply that it could be thought of as a pillar holding the sky above the earth. Once a year the reigning king joined in a ceremony at Memphis to raise a tall *djed* column by pulling on ropes. Ptah, the chief god of Memphis, carried a scepter that combines the *djed* with an **ankh,** the symbol of life. Life, stability, and power were the three qualities that gods traditionally bestowed on kings. Raising the *djed* column was also part of the **Heb Sed** (jubilee festival) through which an aging king's powers were renewed. On some occasions the raising of the *djed* was preceded by a mock combat between people representing the opposing forces of order and chaos.

By the New Kingdom, the *djed* was closely associated with the mythology of Osiris. The taboo subject of the murder of Osiris could be alluded to by saying that Seth had "laid the *djed* on its side." Scenes in temples or royal tombs show the god Horus (or the king playing the role of Horus) raising the *djed* column to help his father Osiris to rise from the dead. The Book of the Dead contains a spell to be spoken over a gold *djed* amulet hung round the neck of a mummy. This spell promises that the dead person will get back the use of his or her spine and be able to sit up again like Osiris. A *djed* column was sometimes painted on the bottom of coffins for the same reason. Model *djed* columns became one of the amulets most commonly placed on mummies.

> ***See also*** Horus; Osiris; Ptah; Sokar
> ***References and further reading:***
> R. T. Rundle Clarke. *Myth and Symbol in Ancient Egypt.* London: 1959, 235–238.
> R. H. Wilkinson. *Reading Egyptian Art.* London: 1992, 164–165.
> ***Primary sources:***
> RDP; BD 142, 155

ENNEAD OF HELIOPOLIS

The first four generations of deities in the creation myth of Heliopolis were referred to as the Ennead of Heliopolis.

> ***See also*** Atum; Geb; Isis; Nephthys; Nut; Osiris; Seth; Shu and Tefnut

EYE OF RA

The Ancient Egyptian word for eye (*irt*) sounded like a word for "doing" or "acting." This may be why the eyes of a deity are associated with divine power at its most interventional. Since the word *irt* was feminine in gender, divine eyes were personified as goddesses. In different contexts, the eyes of the creator were identified with various celestial bodies, such as the disk of the sun, the full moon, the morning star, and Sopdet (Sirius). These celestial eyes could all be shown as the part-hawk, part-human eye known as the *wedjat* eye (see Figure 12). The Eye of Ra was regarded as Ra's daughter and protector. This Eye goddess was associated with both fire and water. Her fiery glance destroyed the enemies of the divine order while her tears created life.

After the primordial creator god Atum had produced Shu and Tefnut, they became lost in the watery darkness of the *nun*. Atum sent his Eye to find them "and gave light to darkness." This act was sometimes interpreted as the first sunrise and the moment when Atum was united with Ra to become the creator sun god. In the earliest versions of the myth, the Eye that was sent forth may have been thought of as the morning star that precedes the sunrise.

The Eye returned with Shu and Tefnut, but wept with rage when she saw that Ra-Atum had grown a new solar eye: the Glorious One. Human beings were created from the tears of the angry Eye or from the tears of joy shed by Ra-Atum's new eye (see "The Creation of Humanity" under "Linear Time" in "Mythical Time Lines"). Ra-

Figure 28. A king is given power over foreign lands by Sekhmet, one of the goddesses who could be known as the Eye of Ra. Relief in the temple of Seti I at Abydos. (Courtesy of Richard Pinch)

Atum placated the angry Eye by placing her on his forehead as the uraeus. Shown as a cobra coiled around the sun disk, she was more powerful than all other deities.

Important goddesses such as Hathor, Bastet, and Mut can be called both the Eye of Atum and the Eye of Ra. Other Egyptian texts refer to these two eyes as if they were separate entities. This may be to distinguish between the creative and destructive aspect of the Eye goddess. The pupil of the Eye could be thought of as a womb in which gods and other beings were formed. A child or a dwarf can be shown inside the Eye, representing the sun that will be born in the red sky of dawn.

The unblinking gaze of the Eye of Ra could embody the dangerous aspects of the sun's heat. The rays of the sun were compared with arrows shot by a divine archer to destroy the wicked. They could dry up the water of life and turn fertile land into desert. A myth with many variants deals with a quarrel between Ra and his daughter, the Eye goddess. She goes off into the deserts to the south or west of Egypt and lives as a savage lion or a wild cat (see "The Distant Goddess" under "Linear Time" in "Mythical Time Lines"). The sudden disappearance of the Eye of Ra has been interpreted by some Egyptologists as a solar eclipse.

Ra misses his daughter and needs his Eye to defend himself against the forces of chaos and the rebels among humanity. He sends one or more of the gods on a dangerous mission to retrieve the wandering goddess. The ferocious goddess is pacified by Thoth, Shu, or Onuris and persuaded to return to Egypt. In the Greco-Roman Period, the return of the Eye goddess was linked with the heliacal rising of Sirius that signaled the coming of the dangerous but life-giving Nile flood.

The goddess is given an ecstatic welcome by all creation and is reconciled with her father. She then becomes his consort and the mother of a divine child who will be the new form of the sun god. In some places a pair of goddesses was worshipped as the aggressive and pacified forms of the Eye of Ra, such as Satet and Anuket at Aswan and Ayet and Nehemetawy at Herakleopolis.

On many occasions the Eye goddess fought on behalf of her father, Ra. When part of humanity rebelled against the aging sun god, the Eye was sent down as Sekhmet, the raging lioness, to destroy the rebels (see "The Destruction of Humanity" under "Linear Time" in "Mythical Time Lines"). Such was her ferocity that she had to be tricked into returning to her father to prevent her from devouring all of humanity. In the fight against the Apophis monster, the Eye of Ra fought him under many names such as Bastet, lady of terror; Wadjyt, the Devouring Flame; Sekhmet, the Glorious Eye; and Wosret, the Great One.

The feline Eye goddess also represented royal power at its most brutal. Kings were described as striking down their enemies as Sekhmet had destroyed the enemies of Ra. Satirical cartoons that showed valiant mice winning a war against cats may have been a coded way of expressing the hope that ordinary Egyptians could overcome royal tyranny.

See also Apophis; Atum; Bastet; Hathor; Mut; Onuris; Ra; Satet and Anuket; Sekhmet; Snakes; Stars and Planets; Thoth

References and further reading:

J. C. Darnell. "The Apotropaic Goddess in the Eye." *Studien zur Altägyptischen Kultur* 24 (1997): 35–48.

H. te Velde. "Mut, the Eye of Re." *Studien zur Altägyptischen Kultur* Beiheft 3 (1988): 395–403.

Primary sources:

CT 76, 80, 1000; BD 17; Crossword hymn; BHC; Mut ritual; BRP; Sekhmet litany; Kom Ombo texts; EofS

EYES OF HORUS

The Horus eye combines a human eye and eyebrow with some of the facial markings of a falcon (see Figure 12). Such eyes are used for the animal forms of various deities associated with the sky. When Horus was imagined as a celestial falcon, his right eye was the sun and his left eye was the moon. In Ancient Egyptian, the word for eye is a feminine noun, so the eyes of male deities could be personified as goddesses. The temporary loss or mutilation of one or both of the eyes of Horus was a common theme in Egyptian myth. The aggressor was usually named as Seth, and the attack put the whole cosmos in danger. Horus was sometimes said to have rescued his own eye, but the idea that it was restored by another deity was more common. This "whole" or "completed" eye was known as the **wedjat** (**udjat**). The *wedjat* eye could represent almost any aspect of the divine order, including kingship and the offerings made to the gods and the dead. It also became one of the most popular of all Egyptian amulets.

Two versions of Horus are known: with eyes (Khenty-irty) and without eyes (Khenty-en-irty). They could be represented by an ichneumon, an animal noted for its keen sight, and a type of eyeless shrew. The vengeful Horus Khenty-en-irty was one of the gods who perpetually tortured the evil dead. Horus the Elder was said to have one green eye and a "lesser" white eye. Green was sometimes equivalent to red in Egyptian symbolism, so this was the solar eye. The white (or silver) eye was the moon. The red and white crowns of Egyptian kings could be equated with the solar and lunar eyes. From the Old Kingdom onward, pairs of *wedjat* eyes were painted on coffins for the deceased to look out through. The glare of these celestial eyes also had apotropaic force to protect the deceased.

As with the murder of Osiris, the wounding of the lunar eye is never very clearly described. Some passages in the Pyramid Texts speak of Seth devouring or trampling the "lesser eye." Others imply that Seth gouged out the pupil of the eye of Horus with his finger or caused it to bleed or weep. A later tradition had Seth in the form of a black boar swallowing the eye or causing it to go blind with rage.

When Horus is treated as the vulnerable son of Isis rather than as the cosmic falcon, the narratives are more explicit. In the Contendings of Horus and Seth, Seth tears out both the eyes of Horus to punish him for beheading his mother in a fit of rage. Seth buries the eyes on a mountainside where they grow into lotus flowers. Meanwhile, the goddess Hathor heals Horus with gazelle milk and restores his eyes. A similar story in Papyrus Jumilhac has Anubis bury boxes containing the eyes of Horus on a mountainside. Isis waters the eyes to bring them back to life, creating the first grape vines in the process. This myth reenforces the common ritual identification of the Eye of Horus with the wine, food, and perfumes offered to the gods in temples. The growth of useful plants from the buried eyes of Horus is a parallel to the growth of barley and wheat from the body of his father, Osiris.

Myths that involve a single lunar Eye of Horus often name Thoth as the god who rescued it from under the earth or under water. At some point, the eye must have been torn apart like the body of Osiris, since Thoth is said to have put the pieces together again. The six parts of the *wedjat* eye (pupil, brow, and so on) were used in the hieroglyphic script to write the fractions that made up the standard grain measure. Rituals of counting and completing the Eye of Horus were performed in temples every month, linking it to the lunar cycle.

Once the eye was restored to Horus, he used it to revive his murdered father, Osiris. In commemoration of this event, a *wedjat* eye was often placed over the evisceration wound on a mummy to make the body whole again. Horus the Physician and Thoth, the Physician of the Eye of Horus, were asked to heal all kinds of ailments. Drugs used in Egyptian medicine were prescribed in measurements based on the *wedjat* eye. An abbreviated version of the Eye of Horus is still used by pharmacists as a symbol of their profession.

> ***See also*** Eye of Ra; Feline Deities; Horus; Moon; Onuris; Seth; Thoth
> ***References and further reading:***
> J. G .Griffiths. "Remarks on the Mythology of the Eyes of Horus." *Chronique d'É-gypte* 33 (1958): 182–193.
> G. Rudnitsky. *Die Aussage über das Auge des Horus.* Copenhagen: 1956.
> ***Primary sources:***
> PT 111, 145, 160, 587; CT 249, 157, 934–936; RDP; Ad 10th hour; BD 17, 112; PBM 10059; H&S; PJ

FELINE DEITIES

Many Egyptian deities were represented by predators of the cat family (*felidae*). There were North African and Near Eastern species of lions, and leopards and cheetahs were found to the south of Egypt. Smaller cat species, such as servals, inhabited the deserts or marshes. One of these species, *felis silvestris libyca*, seems to have been domesticated by the Egyptians by around 2000 BCE. Cats were chiefly prized for their ability to kill pests such as rats, mice, and snakes. Similar predators, such as mongooses and genets, seem to have been regarded as

Figure 29. A king appeasing a lion-goddess who is too dangerous to be looked at directly. A Ptolemaic relief in the temple of Horus at Edfu. (Courtesy of Geraldine Pinch)

members of the cat family by the Egyptians. The characteristics of several feline species were sometimes combined in a single image.

Lion gods were not as important as lion goddesses, but the lion was an ancient symbol of royal power. Male leopards and panthers (black leopards) were associated with the uncontrollable rage of the god Seth, whereas female leopards played a protective role. Leonine goddesses usually have a short mane or ruff like that of a lynx or an adolescent male lion. Since they function as a manifestation of the wrath of the sun god, their gender is ambiguous. The lion was a component of Egyptian monsters such as Bes and Taweret, the sphinx and the griffin. These mythical creatures were invoked as magical guardians of people and places. There are many mentions in the Pyramid Texts of the deity Ruty (Double Lion) who guarded the horizon, the place of regeneration for deities and kings. This deity may derive from earlier images of a pair of leopards or panthers who seem to represent the sky. By the New Kingdom, the spotted leopard-lions of the horizon were identified with the first divine couple, Shu and Tefnut. An alternative representation of the place of the sun's birth was a pair of striped cats flanking a lotus flower.

Many other feline deities acted as ferocious guardians. According to a temple ritual, the body of Osiris was guarded by four lion goddesses: Wadjyt, Sekhmet, Bastet, and Shesmetet (Smithis). In the Pyramid Texts the goddess Mafdet helps the dead king by clawing out the eyes of evil snakes. Her sacred animal may originally have been some kind of mongoose, but she was later depicted as a cheetah or a lynx. As the divine executioner, Mafdet served justice by running down and slaughtering the "enemies of Ra." Her symbol was a harpoon fixed to a block.

The Coffin Texts mention Pakhet the Great who hunts by night as a lioness or a panther. Her name means "the one who scratches." The claw amulets worn by Egyptian queens and princesses may evoke the protective might of this goddess. The lion-headed Barque of Pakhet provided an escort for the solar barque. Like other feline deities, she could also take the form of the fire-spitting cobra who protected the sun god's heirs.

Unnamed lions, lionesses, panthers, and cats are shown on magical objects fighting the traditional enemies of the divine order (see, for example, Figure 30). The images of lions and cats tearing out the throats of foreign captives may allude to the myth of the Eye of Ra being sent down in her lion form (Sekhmet) to destroy the humans who had rebelled against the sun god. Other goddesses who could be identified with the lion form of the creator's eye included Bastet, Hathor, Mehit, Mut, Tefnut, and Wadjyt.

When the eye who was the first-born daughter of Ra became alienated from her father, she wandered the deserts in the form of a lion or a cat (see "The Distant Goddess" under "Linear Time" in "Mythical Time Lines"). A relief in the temple of el-Dakka in Nubia showed this goddess with the full mane of a lion and the swollen teats of a nursing lioness. In this form she was dangerous even to other deities. Those she devoured would be annihilated forever, with no hope of rebirth. In her cat form she was a fierce fighter but a force for good. The myth of Thoth and Shu luring the Distant Goddess back to Egypt with promises of food and comfort mirrors the way the Egyptians had transformed wild cats into pets.

It was in cat form that the daughter of Ra assisted her father in an epic battle against the chaos monster Apophis. One terrible night Ra himself took the form of the Great Tom Cat and fought the Apophis serpent under the *ished* tree at Heliopolis. He sliced up Apophis with his knife and split the *ished* tree in two, creating the twin trees of the horizon (see Figure 22).

In her pacified form, the feline daughter of Ra united with the creator sun god to produce a divine child. At Bubastis, the lion god Mahes (Mihos, Myusis) was the cub of Bastet and Atum-Ra. In the first millennium BCE, Bastet was increasingly represented as a fertile mother, suckling or surrounded by many kittens. Her dangerous leonine form was played down but not forgotten. An Instruction Text of the Greco-Roman Period warns Egyptian men that women are like a friendly cat when you can give them what they want and like a raging lioness when you cannot.

> *See also* Bastet; Eye of Ra; Hathor; Mut; Onuris; Ra; Sekhmet; Shu and Tefnut; Sphinx
>
> *References and further reading:*
>
> L. Delvaux and E. Warmenbol (eds.). *Les Divins Chats D'Égypte.* Leuven, Belgium: 1991.
>
> J. Malek. *The Cat in Ancient Egypt.* London: 1993.
>
> *Primary sources:*
>
> PT 295, 297–8, 519; CT 335, 470; BD 17, 125; LofR; Mut ritual; EofS; Ankhsheshonq.

GEB

Geb was the chief earth god and the mate of the sky goddess Nut. They were the children of Shu and Tefnut, the first divine couple. Geb and Nut formed the third generation in the group of nine gods who made up the Ennead of Heliopolis. In the early stages of creation, the earth god and the sky goddess were locked in a passionate embrace. The forcible separation of Geb and Nut by their father Shu was one of the most important cosmic events in Egyptian myth.

Geb was nearly always shown in human form. His skin could be painted green, probably to symbolize the plants that "come forth from the body of Geb." Living creatures were said to "crawl on the back of Geb." None of these life-forms could come into being until Shu separated Geb and Nut so that air and light could exist between them. After their separation, Geb and Nut became the parents of five divine children: Osiris, Horus the Elder, Seth, Isis, and Nephthys. As a sky goddess, Nut was also considered to be the mother of all heavenly bodies, so Geb was sometimes called the "father" of the sun god Ra. In the Book of Nut, Geb is said to be appalled by Nut's habit of eating her children. He is rebuked by the sun god, who explains that Nut's behavior is a necessary part of the cycle of death and rebirth.

Geb himself was said to swallow up the dead, and he was in charge of the dangerous snakes who lived under the earth. Like other **chthonic deities**, Geb could be a terrifying god, responsible for destructive earthquakes. The ceremony of "hacking the ground" was said to honor Geb but may in origin have been a rite to subdue the dangerous earth god. A myth found only in an inscription of the fourth century BCE tells how Geb violently rebelled against his parents. He seized the throne from Shu and forced Tefnut to be his queen. Geb assumed most of the divine regalia of Ra but was bitten by the fiery serpent who guarded the sun god and all legitimate rulers.

It was more common to regard Geb as the appointed "heir of the gods" and the leader of the Great Ennead. He was seen as the chief of the inhabitants of earth. Egyptian kings were said to sit on "the throne of Geb." Geb was usually the main judge in the great dispute between the rival gods Horus and Seth. Geb continued this role as a judge of the dead in the afterlife. Those found guilty of being "enemies of Ra" were tied to the "stakes of Geb" to be executed. As the father of Osiris, Geb could be invoked to provide fatherly help to all dead persons who were ritually identified with Osiris.

See also Horus; Nut; Osiris; Shu and Tefnut

References and further reading:

F. T. Miosi. "Some Aspects of Geb in the Pyramid Texts." *Bulletin of the Egyptology Seminar* 10 (1989/90): 101–107.

H. te Velde. "Geb." In *Lexikon der Ägyptologie II.* Wiesbaden: 1977, 427–429 (in English).

Primary sources:

PT 356, 592; CT 80, 515; BD 181, 185; BHC; BOE; BofNut; Ismailia Naos

HAND OF ATUM

The female element or partner of the creator deity, often identified as the goddesses Iusaas or Hathor Nebet-hetepet, was referred to as the Hand of Atum.

See also Atum; Hathor

HAPY (HAPI)

A deity or group of deities who embodied the life-giving power of the inundation, Hapy was usually depicted as a very fat man with pendulous breasts and blue or green skin. Though Egypt was totally dependent on the annual Nile flood, the inundation god was not a high-ranking deity.

The river Nile was thought of as flowing out of the primeval waters (the *nun*) that continued to encircle the world. Hymns and spells credit the creator with making the Nile rise each year so that the fields of Egypt could be irrigated. The flood was said to come from two caverns that were imprints of the creator's sandals. The god Khnum was in charge of these "secret caverns of Hapy."

The potentially destructive aspect of the flood could be embodied by the solar lioness known as the Distant Goddess. The powers of the flood to irrigate and fertilize the Nile valley were represented by Hapy. For this reason, Hapy has been called a "fecundity figure" rather than a Nile god. Some Egyptologists interpret Hapy as an androgynous deity, whereas others see his peculiar body shape as signifying abundance. Hapy can appear as a single deity but is most often shown in pairs or groups. Temples were often decorated with rows of fecundity figures carrying the produce of each district of Egypt.

Hymns to Hapy point out that every aspect of Egyptian life was dependent on the food that he brought. All creatures are said to rejoice at his arrival: frogs croak, bulls bellow, and crocodiles roar. Hapy is called the Lord of Fishes, the one "who greens the Two Banks," and "the maker of barley and wheat." Hapy's life-giving waters were also credited with a role in reviving the murdered god Osiris, who came back each year with the barley.

See also Heqet; Khnum; Nun; Osiris; Sons of Horus

References and further reading:

J. Baines. *Fecundity Figures.* Warminster, England: 1985.

J. Lindsay. *Men and Gods on the Roman Nile.* London: 1968, chaps. 3, 6, 17.

Primary sources:

CT 317–321; Hapy hymns; Famine stela

HATHOR (ḤWT-ḤR)

Hathor was the golden goddess who helped women to give birth, the dead to be reborn, and the cosmos to be renewed. This complex deity could function as the mother, consort, and daughter of the creator sun god. Many lesser goddesses came to be regarded as "names" of Hathor in her contrasting benevolent and destructive aspects. She was most commonly shown as a beautiful woman wearing a red solar disk between a pair of cow's horns.

Hathor's name means "domain (or mansion) of Horus," which may make her the original mother of the celestial falcon. In the Pyramid Texts, the domain of Horus was a special part of the sky where the dead king would be rejuvenated. As Lady of the Stars, Hathor was associated with the nocturnal sky. As the Eye of Ra, she could be identified with the solar disk or the morning or evening star (Venus). By the Greco-Roman Period, Hathor was honored as a moon deity. She was the goddess of all precious metals, gemstones, and materials that shared the radiant qualities of celestial bodies, such as gold, silver, copper, turquoise, lapis-lazuli, and faience.

In Pyramid Texts spell 406, the Eye of Ra (here the solar disk) is "upon the horns of Hathor." This seems to be an early reference to the myth of the sun god being lifted up into the heavens on the head of the celestial cow. Another divine cow, Mehet-Weret, who was often regarded as a primeval form of Hathor, had given birth to the sun god and lifted him above the primeval waters. Hathor could also be identified with the alternative image of the primeval lotus from which the sun child emerged in the first dawn. She could be worshipped as the "mother" of all child gods, such as Nefertem, Ihy, and Harsomatus, whose birth was a celebration of the ability of the cosmos to renew itself. Horus performed a similar function for kingship, and Hathor was often shown as a cow maternally protecting the youthful Horus-king inside a papyrus thicket. The power to rule entered Horus with the milk of Hathor.

By giving birth to the sun child, Hathor became her own mother (or grandmother) since she traditionally came into being as the Eye of Ra, the adult form of the sun god. The Eye of Ra was often described as "the Daughter of Ra who protects her father." Hathor was called the Foremost One in the Barque of Millions because she stood in the prow of the solar barque leading its defense against the chaos serpent Apophis. Ra sent his Eye to punish the rebellious descendants of the humans who had been created from the tears of the Eye (see "The Creation of Humanity" and "The Destruction of Humanity" under "Linear Time" in "Mythical Time Lines"). In her savage lion form, the Eye had to be rendered drunk before she could return to the heavens as beautiful, gracious Hathor.

The Distant Goddess who abandoned Ra to live in feline form in the deserts beyond Egypt could also be named as Hathor. This identification came relatively late, but Hathor had long been regarded as the goddess of foreign lands and their products. When the Distant Goddess returned, she brought the inundation with her, but she had to be pacified with music, dancing, feasting, and drunkenness. This was the mythical justification for the wild, ecstatic elements in Hathor's cult. It was proper for the whole of creation to rejoice when Hathor appeared again in all her radiant beauty and joined forces with her father.

The union of Hathor and the creator could be thought of in sexual terms or, more abstractly, as a merging of the creator with his own active power. Hathor was the goddess who personified both the hand that made Atum ejaculate and the divine "seed" itself. As the female creative principle, she could be the most seductive and alluring of deities. This erotic side of her nature made Hathor the patroness of lovers in Egyptian poetry and justified the Greeks in identifying her with Aphrodite.

In the Contendings of Horus and Seth, the sun god Pre (Ra) becomes angry when he is insulted by the baboon god Babi and lies down on his back. This implies that the creator sun god was sinking back into the inert state that would mean the end of the world. Hathor, Lady of the Southern Sycamore, visits her father Pre and shows him her genitals. He immediately laughs, gets up, and goes back to administering *maat* (justice). Hathor has aroused the sun god and driven away his evil mood.

The Underworld Books present Ra and his daughter in less human terms. As the goddess of the West, Hathor welcomes the setting sun into her outstretched arms. For both gods and people, Hathor eased the transition from death to new life. The time and manner of a person's death was decreed by a sevenfold form of Hathor. As Lady of the Necropolis, she opened the gates of the underworld. As a tree goddess, she revived the newly dead with shade, air, water, and food. The spirits of the dead could imbibe eternal life from the milk of the seven Hathor cows.

The Coffin Texts and the Book of the Dead have spells to help the deceased live forever as a follower of Hathor. In a Late Period story, Hathor rules the underworld, emerging to punish those who behave unjustly on earth. By the Greco-Roman Period, dead women in the afterlife identified themselves with Hathor instead of Osiris. It was only after Isis took over many of her attributes that Hathor lost her place as the most important of Egyptian goddesses.

See also Cattle; Eye of Ra; Eyes of Horus; Feline Deities; Hippopotamus Goddesses; Horus; Horus the Child; Lotus; Mehet-Weret; Sekhmet; Shu and Tefnut; Snakes

References and further reading:
P. Derchain. *Hathor Quadrifons.* Istanbul: 1972.
B. Lesko. "Hathor, Goddess of Love." In *The Great Goddesses of Egypt.* Norman, OK: 1999, 81–129.
G. Pinch. *Votive Offerings to Hathor.* Oxford: 1994.
Primary sources:
PT 303, 534, 705; CT 334, 482–484, 497–500, 588; BD 39, 103, 170; Ad; BHC; H&S; PV; Edfu calendar; Dendara calendar; P. Carlsberg 180

HATMEHYT

Hatmehyt was a Delta goddess shown as a woman with a dolphin or a *schilbe* fish on her head.

See also Banebdjedet

HEH GODS

The Heh gods were the gods of twilight who helped Shu to support the sky. A single Heh god was the hieroglyphic sign for "millions of years" or infinity.

See also Baboons; Ogdoad of Hermopolis; Shu and Tefnut

HEKA (HIKA)

Heka was the god of magic as a creative force.

See also Sia and Hu

HEQET (HEQAT, HEKAT)

Heqet was a frog goddess who helped women to give birth and the dead to be reborn. The knife-wielding frogs shown on ivory wands are probably Heqet in her role as defender of women and children. Heqet, Mistress of Joy, was among the

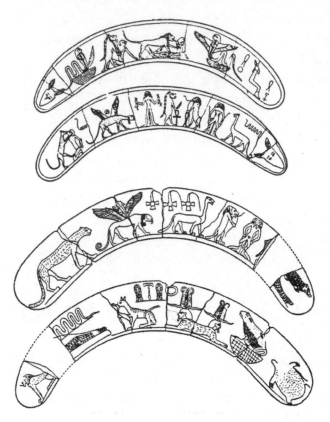

Figure 30. The frog shown on one of these ivory wands may represent Heqet. The creatures on the wands acted as magical protectors for women and young children. (The Metropolitan Museum of Art)

followers of the inundation god Hapy when he brought new life to Egypt each year. The Roman writer Pliny the Elder noted an Egyptian belief that frogs were spontaneously generated from the mud left by the receding Nile flood. Heqet came to be worshipped as a goddess of the primeval slime who gave birth to the sun god.

Heqet was regarded as the female counterpart of the creator god Khnum, and the two are linked in a Middle Kingdom royal-birth myth. The sun god Ra sends a group of deities to assist a woman called Ruddedet giving birth to three children who are destined to be kings. Four goddesses—Isis, Nephthys, Meskhenet, and Heqet—disguise themselves as dancing girls while Khnum pretends to be their servant. At the house of Ruddedet, her distraught husband asks them for help because his wife's labor is so painful and difficult. The deities lock themselves in the room with Ruddedet, and Heqet "hastens the birth" of the royal triplets. Isis names the children, Meskhenet predicts their fate, and Khnum makes them strong and healthy. The deities create three crowns for the triplets and hide them in a sack of barley before returning to the divine realm. The story implies that the children were sired by Ra, and they grow up to be the sun-worshipping kings of the Fifth Dynasty.

In New Kingdom royal-birth myths, Heqet gives life to the body and *ka* of the royal infant shaped on the potter's wheel of Khnum. In temples of the first millennium BCE, Heqet is shown assisting goddesses give birth to divine children. At Abydos, Heqet was revered for helping Isis bring Horus into the world and for assisting the murdered god Osiris to be reborn. All Egyptians hoped that after they died Heqet would act as a divine midwife at their rebirth.

See also Khnum; Ogdoad of Hermopolis

References and further reading:
J. D. Cooney and W. K. Simpson. "An Early Dynastic Statue of the Goddess Heqat." *Bulletin of the Cleveland Museum of Arts* 63 (1976).
Primary sources:
PT 539; CT 175, 258; P. Westcar; RBM; Hapy hymns

HERYSHEF (ARSAPHES, HARSAPHES)

Heryshef was a ram god who was the local deity of the important town of Herakleopolis Magna (Hnes). His name means "he who is upon his lake." From early times Heryshef was worshipped as a creator god rising out of the *nun*. Like some other ram gods, he could be regarded as a manifestation of Osiris.

The Coffin Texts refer to Heryshef as Lord of Blood and Butchery. He is shown on ivory wands among the fearsome deities who can act as magical protectors. During the first millennium BCE, Heryshef was revered as a cosmic deity whose eyes were the sun and the moon.

In one text, Osiris-Heryshef is crowned king at Herakleopolis. He sits on the throne of Ra to receive the homage of all the other deities. Even his rival, Seth, bows down to him, though it makes his nose bleed with rage. Osiris-Heryshef falls ill because he cannot control the power of the headdress of Ra, and his head swells painfully. Ra cures him by letting out the pus and blood, and this is said to be the origin of the famous sacred lake at Herakleopolis.

A fragmentary New Kingdom tale has Heryshef appear to the hero Meryra to ask for his help in a fight against a divine falcon. In a later text, an Egyptian priest living among the Persians claims to have been summoned back to Egypt by a dream-vision of Heryshef. The priest credits Heryshef with helping Alexander the Great to conquer the Persians. When the Greeks settled in Egypt, they identified Heryshef with their deified hero Herakles (Hercules).

See also Banebdjedet; Osiris
References and further reading:
H. Kees. "Heracleopolis and the Fayum." In *Ancient Egypt: A Cultural Topography.* London: 1961, 212–230.
Primary sources:
CT 420; BD 175; Stela of Somtutefnakht

HIPPOPOTAMUS GODDESSES

The male hippopotamus was feared by the Egyptians as a destructive force, but the female hippopotamus was respected as a fierce protector of her young and the embodiment of the life-giving power of water. Several hippopotamus goddesses are known, such as Ipet (Opet), Reret, and Taweret (Taurt, Thoeris), but they are probably just aspects of the same goddess. This goddess could also manifest herself in dual or group forms. As Taweret (the Great One) she was usually shown with a combination of hippopotamus, lion, crocodile, and human features. This monstrous form was a popular type of amulet for 2,000 years and passed into other cultures as a protective genie.

The Egyptians saw hippopotami as water pigs rather than water horses, so Reret means "the sow." This provides a link with the sky goddess Nut, who also had a sow form. All manifestations of the hippopotamus goddess were associated with the watery regions of the sky, the earth, and the underworld. She was sometimes equated with Hathor Mehet-Weret, the cow goddess who represented the fertile aspect of the primeval waters (the *nun*). Mehet-Weret, Nut, and the hippopotamus goddess could all be thought of as giving birth to the creator sun god. In the secret crypts of the Temple of Ipet at Karnak, the hippopotamus goddess was said to give birth to a solar form of Osiris who rose again as Amun-Ra. In the Pyramid Texts, the reborn king is nourished by the sweet milk of Ipy (Ipet). During the Middle Kingdom and Second Intermediate Periods, model hippopotami decorated with marsh flora were placed in tombs and temples. These may represent Ipet or Taweret as the goddess of the primeval marsh where all life began and the dead hoped to be reborn. The full breasts and belly on composite figures of Taweret are probably those of the inundation god Hapy, rather than those of a pregnant woman. By the New Kingdom, Taweret "Mistress of Pure Water" purified, revived, and nourished the dead. The annual Nile flood performed a similar service for the land of Egypt. A group of Reret goddesses were among the exotic beings who celebrated the return of the Distant Goddess who brought the inundation with her. In some versions of this myth the returning solar lioness can be transformed into a hippopotamus goddess when she reaches the marshy boundaries of Egypt.

Images on hippopotamus-ivory wands of the second millennium BCE may allude to this myth and its aftermath when the goddess gives birth to a divine child who is destined to rule. Taweret is shown among other "fighters" savaging foreign captives, brandishing knives or torches, or holding the *sa* symbol of protection (see Figure 30). Her role as protector of the divine child is repeated in later temple reliefs showing the birth and upbringing of kings and gods. She usually appears in the birth chamber with the lion-dwarf Bes. On a magical stela, Isis tells her son Horus that "a sow and a dwarf" were the protectors of his infant body. By the Ptolemaic Period, Taweret had the title Lady of the Birth House. Even great goddesses such as Hathor, Mut, and Isis sometimes took the grotesque form of the Great One when they acted as saviors of the innocent.

The guilty, however, could expect no mercy from hippopotamus goddesses. The female monster Ammut who devoured the souls of those who failed the judgment of Osiris was a mixture of hippopotamus, lion, and crocodile. In the

Hippopotamus constellation shown in Egyptian sky maps, Taweret and other ferocious deities eternally stand guard over Seth's evil bull form. This stellar role may lie behind Plutarch's statement that Thoeris (Taweret) was a concubine of Seth who deserted him to fight on behalf of his rival Horus.

See also Bes and Beset; Eye of Ra; Hapy; Mehet-Weret; Seth; Stars and Planets

References and further reading:

I. Nagy. "La statue de Thouéris au Caire (CG 39145) et la légende de la dèsse lointaine." In *The Intellectual Heritage of Ancient Egypt,* edited by U. Luft. Studia Aegyptica 14. Budapest: 1992, 449–456.

M. Verner. "A Statue of Tweret (Cairo Museum no. 39145) Dedicated by Pabesi and Several Remarks on the Role of the Hippopotamus Goddess." *Zeitschrift für Ägyptische Sprache und Alterumskunde* 96 (1969): 52–63

Primary sources:

PT 269; BD 137, 186; Medamud hymn; Astronomical ceilings; Metternich Stela; I&O 19

HOREMAKHET (HARMACHIS)

Horemakhet was Horus in the Horizon, a solar form of the celestial falcon.

See under Horus; Sphinx

HORUS (HOR)

Horus was the celestial falcon and the embodiment of kingship. The conflict between Horus and Seth, the Two Lords, was an enduring theme in Egyptian myth. The name Horus probably means the "Distant One." Two main forms of Horus appear in the sources. These are sometimes regarded as separate gods, belonging to different epochs, and sometimes as aspects of the same deity. Horus the Great or Horus the Elder (Harwer/Haroeris) was a primeval being who initiated creation. As Lord of the Sky, his wings spanned the heavens, and his eyes were the sun and the moon. This Horus is the son of a sky goddess, either Nut or Hathor. Horus the Younger was the son of Isis who grew up to avenge his murdered father, Osiris, and take his place as ruler of Egypt. He was usually shown as a falcon-headed man. Each king of Egypt was acclaimed as a "living Horus."

Egypt's earliest kings were shown as hawks preying on their enemies. Many Egyptian deities could be represented by birds of the hawk family. The cults of some of these gods, such as Nekheny of Hierakonpolis and Khenty-Khety of Athribis, were gradually assimilated with that of Horus. One of the earliest divine images known from Egypt is that of a falcon in a barque. This probably represents Horus as a star or planet crossing the Winding Waterway of the sky. Later texts paint a dazzling picture of the One of Dappled Plumage who opened his eyes to dispel darkness and chaos.

Figure 31. Horus and Isis triumph over the Seth hippopotamus before the gods. Ptolemaic Relief depicting the Festival of Victory in the temple of Horus at Edfu. (Courtesy of Geraldine Pinch)

Like other primeval deities, the celestial falcon coalesced with the creator sun god. He then became Ra-Horakhty (Ra-Horus of the Double Horizon) who triumphed over his enemies to rise in the east. The union of these two powers could be symbolized by a falcon crowned with a sun disk or a sun disk with falcon's wings. When a king appeared to his subjects, it was compared with the glorious rising of Horemakhet (Horus in the Horizon). The Two Lords, Horus and Seth, were either named as brothers or as nephew and uncle. Many theories have been advanced to explain the origins of their combat, from memories of an ancient civil war to observations of storms or astronomical phenomena. When the combatants are Horus the Elder, the celestial falcon, and Seth, the chaotic god of storms, the conflict seems to belong to the primeval age when opposing elements had to come together to create the divine order.

The necessity of Horus and Seth being reconciled is stressed in many sources. One of the key images of royal art was Horus the Uniter and Seth tying together the heraldic plants of Upper and Lower Egypt to symbolize the union of the Two Lands into one perfect kingdom. The figure of Seth is sometimes replaced by Thoth, an indication that Seth's role as the slayer of Osiris could not always be overlooked. When the great conflict is presented as a dynastic feud between young Horus and his usurper uncle, Horus must triumph and Seth must be punished so that justice and kingship can be established for humanity.

Harsiese (Horus, son of Isis) was destined to be king from the moment of conception. His epithet, "Horus who is upon the papyrus," alludes to the myth that Isis hid the infant Horus in the papyrus thickets of Akh-bit (Chemmis), an island among the marshes. This "nest of Horus" was guarded by divine beings such as cow and scorpion goddesses. The young Horus grew up to become "the Pillar of his Mother" and the "Avenger of his Father." Advised by Isis, Horus fought Seth in many different ways. He turned Seth's sexual aggression to his own advantage and overcame the temporary loss of the power inherent in his eye (see "The Struggles of Horus and Seth" under "Linear Time" in "Mythical Time Lines"). Horus argued his father's case before the Divine Tribunal led by Geb or the sun god Ra. Osiris is granted sovereignty over the dead and Horus over the living. Horus, the devoted son, becomes the prototype for all funerary priests when he performs a series of rituals to "raise up" Osiris. He also becomes an intermediary between the worlds of the living and the dead. Horus is shown in the Book of the Dead presenting deceased souls before the throne of Osiris.

The reign of Horus as king of Egypt was considered the model for all subsequent reigns. The semidivine kings who came after him in mythical history were called the Followers of Horus. In a few magical texts a scorpion goddess called Ta-Bitjet is called the wife of Horus. A passage in the Coffin Texts makes Horus the Elder and his sister, Isis, the parents of the four protective deities known as the Sons of Horus. A festival at Edfu temple celebrated the "Beautiful Union" between Horus and Hathor, Lady of Dendara. Here, Horus is an aspect of the sun god uniting with the goddess who was his mother, his consort, and his daughter to renew the cosmos.

Texts and scenes at Edfu illustrate the diversity of myths centered on Horus. A mythical history of the temple relates how two mysterious beings subdued the primeval swamp by cutting down reeds. When they stuck a reed in the ground, it became a perch for the celestial falcon. The reed hut built to house the falcon was said to be the center of the world and the first temple. In the Legend of the Winged Disk, Horus (the Distant One) takes the role usually given to the Distant Goddess and transforms himself into a fiery disk to blind and destroy the sun god's enemies. In the ritual drama known as the Triumph of Horus, Horus, son of Isis, harpoons Seth in hippopotamus form. After a series of battles by land and water, he drives Seth and his followers out of Egypt, just as Egyptian kings hoped to drive out foreign invaders.

See also Birds; Cattle; *Djed* Pillar; Eyes of Horus; Hathor; Horus the Child; Isis; Kings and Princes; Min; Osiris; Serqet; Seth; Sons of Horus; Sopdu; Stars and Planets

References and further reading:

H. Frankfort. *Kingship and the Gods: A Study of Ancient Near Eastern Religion as the Integration of Society and Nature.* Chicago: 1948, 36–50.

J. G. Griffiths. *The Conflict of Horus and Seth from Egyptian and Classical Sources.* Liverpool: 1960.

B. Watterson. *The House of Horus at Edfu.* Stroud, England: 1998.

Primary sources:

PT 364, 540, 670; CT 148; RDP; BD 17, 78, 185a; H&S; Solar hymns; HMP; PJ; Triumph of Horus; LWD; Edfu cosmology

HORUS THE CHILD (HARPOKRATES, HARPOCRATES)

The posthumous son of the murdered Osiris by his sister-wife Isis was known as Horus the Child. The Egyptian phrase *Hor pa khered* ("Horus the Child") was transliterated by the Greeks as Harpokrates. In Egyptian art little boys were traditionally shown naked, with a shaven head and one plaited sidelock of hair, so this is how Horus the Child appears. He was the most important of the child gods who formed the third member of divine triads in many temples. Such child gods had two main functions in Egyptian myth and iconography. The first was to symbolize the renewal of the cosmos. The second was to overcome the wild creatures who threatened the cosmic order. In both roles, child gods could be interchangeable with dwarf gods.

The pregnancy of Isis was said to have been unusually long and her labor painful and hard. Isis had to hide her infant in the papyrus thickets of the Delta to preserve him from Seth, the killer of Osiris. This mirrored an earlier mythical event: the emergence of the sun child in the lotus who had to be protected from the monstrous inhabitants of the waters of chaos by a primeval goddess. The sun child was destined to begin the work of creation during the first sunrise, and the Horus child was destined to establish the divine order on earth when he grew up to be Egypt's rightful king. Both children were powerful symbols of hope for the future, and imagery passed freely between them.

A spell in the Pyramid Texts for repelling snakes refers to Horus, "the infant with a finger in his mouth." Egyptian kings were closely identified with the infant and youthful stages of the life cycle of Horus. Pepy II (c. 2278–2184 BCE) seems to have been the first king to be shown as the Horus child, either squatting naked with his finger to his lips or sitting on his mother's lap. Powerful rulers of the Middle and New Kingdoms acknowledged their dependence on the gods by depicting themselves as the young Horus suckling from the divine cow in the papyrus thicket. During the first millennium BCE, child gods were often shown seated on the lap of a divine mother who could be identified with many different goddesses. At Dendara, Ihy and Harsomatus ("Horus, Uniter of the Two Lands") were children of Hathor. At Medamud, Horus the Child was the son of the solar goddess Raet-tawy. Such child gods had to propitiate or overcome their terrifying mothers before they could assume power in their own right.

The more forceful aspect of these child gods could be represented by a form of Horus known as Shed (the Savior). He appeared on stelae of the late New Kingdom dressed as a prince who vanquished dangerous animals with his bow or curved sword. This was a forerunner of the type of magical stela known as a cippus. On these, the naked Horus child tramples on crocodiles and squeezes the life out of other dangerous creatures such as snakes, lions, and antelopes (see Figure 16). When the Greeks saw such objects, they identified Horus the Child/Harpokrates with the infant Herakles (Hercules) who strangled two snakes that attacked him in his cradle. In the Roman Period, Harpokrates became a popular amuletic symbol, often carved on magical gems. He was revered as a god of dawn, which was thought to be the most effective time to perform magical spells.

Plutarch (c. 46–126 CE) thought that Harpokrates was a second son of Isis who had been born prematurely with deformed legs. The Horus figures on cippi often have a body that resembles that of the bandy-legged dwarf god Bes. A mask of Bes is found on most cippi, and Horus the Child seems to have taken over Bes's role as one who drove off demons and protected women and children. In spite of the triumphant visual image of the Horus child overcoming chaotic animals, the texts on cippi and magical statues usually describe how Horus was poisoned by a snake or a scorpion. His mother, Isis, has to use her magic or call on the power of the creator sun god to heal him. The healing of Horus the Child came to represent a promise by the gods to take care of suffering humanity.

See also Bes and Beset; Cattle; Hathor; Horus; Lotus; Mehet-Weret; Ra; Shai; Serqet
References and further reading:
D. Meeks. "Harpokrates." In *Lexikon der Ägyptologie II.* Wiesbaden: 1977, 1004–1011 (in French).
K. C. Seele. "Oriental Institute Museum Notes: Horus on the Crocodiles." *Journal of Near Eastern Studies* 5 (1947): 43–53.
Primary sources:
PT 378; RBM; PPB 10059; Metternich Stela; Magical statue texts; I&O 19

HU

See Sia and Hu

Figure 32. The ritual of 'cutting up the hippopotamus' at Edfu. The figure holding a book scroll may represent a priest playing the role of Imhotep. (Courtesy of Richard Pinch)

IHY

Ihy was a child god who played the **sistrum** to propitiate his mother, Hathor.

> ***See also*** Hathor; Horus the Child; Lotus

IMHOTEP (IMOUTHES)

Imhotep was a high official of the twenty-seventh century BCE who was later deified as a god of knowledge and healing. Imhotep is mentioned in a Middle Kingdom text as one of the sages whose memory lives on through their writings. He became a role model for scribes and was credited with the invention of architecture in stone. Imhotep was usually represented as a man in priestly costume with an open book-scroll on his lap.

In the Late Period, a mythology grew up to explain Imhotep's extraordinary talents. His mother, Kheredankhw (Kherduankh), described in one text as a beautiful singer, was said to have conceived Imhotep by the god Ptah. Son of Ptah became a standard epithet for Imhotep, though normally only kings were called "sons" of gods. By the Ptolemaic Period, Kheredankhw is occasionally referred to as a daughter of Banebdjedet, the ram god of Mendes. There was probably a story cycle about Imhotep's birth that is now lost. An inscription from

Saqqara gives the main events of Imhotep's story as: his birth; being presented as a child to his father, Ptah, and his divine stepmother, Sekhmet; defeating the Asiatics with the help of Sekhmet; his death and mummification; and his appearance as a god.

The Greeks identified Imhotep with their god of medicine, Asclepius. The supposed tomb of Imhotep in the desert near Memphis and a nearby temple, the Asklepion, became places of pilgrimage for sick people and childless couples. Hippocrates, the founder of Greek medicine, is said to have been inspired by books kept in the temple of Imhotep at Memphis. Priests of Imhotep were consulted about the meaning of dreams. Imhotep was said to appear to dreamers as a shining human figure or as a **scarab**. In a story inscribed on a Ptolemaic stela, it is not clear whether it is Imhotep himself or a priest of Imhotep who interprets King Djoser's dream of seven fat and seven thin cattle and discovers the origins of the Nile.

Imhotep remained a popular deity in the Roman Period. A surviving fragment from a story cycle has Imhotep use magic to defeat an Assyrian queen. His association with architecture was remembered by calling him the skillful-fingered one "who fixed the plans of the mansions of the gods." The philosophical text known as the Asclepius is a dialogue between Imhotep/Asclepius and Thoth/Hermes about the secrets of the universe. Three thousand years after his death, Imhotep was still celebrated as the embodiment of Egyptian wisdom.

> *See also* Khnum; Magicians; Ptah
> *References and further reading:*
> D. J. Thompson. *Memphis under the Ptolemies.* Princeton: 1988, 24–25, 205, 209–211.
> D. Wildung. *Egyptian Saints: Deification in Pharaonic Egypt.* New York: 1977.
> *Primary sources:*
> Famine stela; Imhotep hymn; Asclepius

IPET (OPET)

Ipet was a goddess who mothered the king and Osiris.

> *See also* Hippopotamus Goddesses

ISIS

The protective mother of Horus and the loyal wife of Osiris, Isis was part of the fourth generation in the Ennead of Heliopolis: the children of Geb and Nut. She was most commonly shown as a woman wearing the throne symbol that helps to write her name. As the "throne goddess," she was the mother of each Egyptian king. Her maternal tenderness eventually included all humanity, and Isis became more widely worshipped than any other Egyptian deity.

Figure 33. Isis in human and bird form mourns her husband Osiris and brings his body back to life. Line drawing of reliefs in the Temple of Hibis. (Metropolitan Museum of Art)

It is not clear whether Isis featured in the earliest myths about Osiris and Horus. At some important cult centers of Osiris, such as Abydos, her role was a marginal one until the New Kingdom. By that era, Osiris, Isis, and Horus had developed into a true divine family, if a markedly dysfunctional one. The kind of unselfish love that Isis displays toward Osiris and Horus is rare in Egyptian myth.

The Pyramid Texts do allude to Isis searching Egypt for the body of Osiris after he had been struck down by his brother Seth. Some of the spells promise that Isis will save the dead king's body from putrefaction or reassemble his scattered bones, just as she had the corpse of Osiris. Isis and her sister, Nephthys, kept a long vigil over the restored corpse and became the prototypes for all mourners. A New Kingdom hymn tells of Isis using spoken magic to drive away "the disturber" (Seth) and protect her husband's body. Like the creator deity Atum, she is able to produce life without an active partner. She stimulates the "inertness" of Osiris and takes his seed into her body to conceive a son.

An earlier version of this event in Coffin Texts spell 148 has Horus conceived by a flash of divine fire. Isis knows at once that she is carrying a son who will overcome Seth. She hides Horus in the marshes of Chemmis and brings him up to avenge his father. The conflicting ties of love and kinship suffered by Isis are described in the New Kingdom narrative, the Contendings of Horus and Seth. Isis intervenes when Horus and Seth fight in the form of hippopotami. She stabs Seth with her magical harpoon but spares him when he reminds her that they are brother and sister. Angered by this betrayal, Horus cuts his mother's head off. It takes more than this to kill Isis. The gods give her a new head, sometimes that of a cow.

By contrast, most sources of the first millennium BCE make Isis the implacable enemy of Seth. She takes many forms to lure, hunt down, and destroy Seth and his followers. The joy of Isis when the Divine Tribunal finally made Horus king became proverbial. The myth that Horus repaid his mother by raping her seems strange, but each king had to take possession of the throne goddess and beget a repeat of himself.

Magical and literary texts stress the cunning and determination of Isis. As Weret-Hekau (the Great of Magic) she could be shown as a cobra suckling and protecting kings. She was "cleverer than millions of gods" and a better guardian of Egypt's borders "than millions of soldiers." In the Contendings of Horus and Seth, Isis transforms herself into an old woman to fool the divine ferryman and a young girl to trick Seth into making damaging admissions. In the story known as the True Name of Ra (see "Period of Direct Rule by the Creator Sun God" under "Linear Time" in "Mythical Time Lines"), Isis is able to turn the sun god's own power against him to get what she wants. In several dramatic spells Isis is reimagined as an ordinary woman forced to leave her child alone in the marshes while she begs for food. When Horus is poisoned, she stops the progress of the solar barque across the heavens until he is cured.

By the later New Kingdom, Isis was often shown in the solar barque with Ra. This was one of the roles she took over from the goddess Hathor. The cult of Isis became more and more prominent during the first millennium BCE. She began to be honored as the goddess of the sea, responsible for bringing ships safely to harbor. The Greeks identified Isis with Demeter, the harvest goddess who perpetually searched for a lost child. In her stellar form of Sopdet/Sothis, Isis had always been linked with the coming of the inundation that made the harvest possible. She was now credited with inventing agriculture and all manner of useful crafts and institutions.

According to hymns of the Greco-Roman Period, it was Isis who made the world and decreed that men should love women and children should love their parents. All other goddesses became merely "names" of Isis. In his book "Concerning Isis and Osiris," Plutarch suggested that the all-powerful Isis allowed herself to be portrayed as a woman of sorrows to console suffering humanity. This, and her promise to believers of a happy afterlife, made the Isis cult the closest rival to Christianity in the early centuries of the first millennium CE.

See also Anti; Birds; Cattle; Eyes of Horus; Horus; Horus the Child; Min; Nephthys; Osiris; Stars and Planets

References and further reading:

C. J. Bleeker. "Isis as a Saviour-Goddess." In *The Saviour God*, edited by S. G. F. Brandon. Manchester: 1963, 1–16.

B. S. Lesko. "Isis, Great of Magic." In *The Great Goddesses of Egypt*. Norman, OK: 1999, 155–202.

R. E. Wit. *Isis in the Graeco-Roman World*. Ithaca, NY: 1971.

Primary sources:

PT 482, 535; CT 74, 148; BD 15, 151; Amenmose stela; H&S; True Name; HMP; PBM 9997 + 1039; PJ; Magical statue texts; Metternich Stela; Isis hymns; Triumph of Horus; Lamentations; I&O

IUSAAS

Iusaas was a female counterpart of Atum, shown as a woman with a scarab on her head.

See also Atum; Hand of Atum

KHENTAMENTIU (KHENTAMENTI)

Khentamentiu was the Foremost of the Westerners, a funerary god who came to be regarded as an aspect of Osiris.

KHENTY-KHETY

Khenty-Khety was a creator deity who came to be regarded as a form of Horus.

KHEPRI (KHEPRY, KHOPRI)

The dawn manifestation of the sun god; usually shown as a scarab beetle, Khepri was one of the four main forms of the sun god, Ra. His name derives from the Ancient Egyptian word *kheper* meaning "to become" or "to be transformed." *Kheperu* were changes or transformations, and Khepri was the one who transformed or "created himself."

Khepri appears as an irridescent beetle, a beetle-headed hawk, or a beetle-headed man seated on a throne. The scarab beetle's habit of pushing a large ball of dung was transformed into the image of a giant beetle pushing the sun and other celestial bodies across the sky. Young beetles hatch out of buried dung balls and fly off. Their apparently miraculous emergence from the ground may have given rise to the idea of Khepri as a self-generated deity.

As early as the Pyramid Texts, Khepri is given as one of the names of the sun god. He is addressed as "the shining one" and the one "who is in the *nun*." Khepri was linked with the creative power of the heart and identified with the infant sun god who began creation by rising out of the primeval waters or the primeval lotus.

The miracle of that first sunrise was repeated every day. In the myth, the True Name of Ra, the wounded sun god tells Isis that he is "Khepri in the morning, Ra at noon, Atum in the evening." Khepri, the young sun of dawn, often formed a pair with Ra-Atum, the old sun of evening. The Night Boat of the sun was associated with Atum and the Day Boat with Khepri. At Heliopolis, Atum-Khepri was worshipped as one god who daily underwent a series of transformations. In the Book of What Is in the Underworld, the corpse of Khepri is divided and buried during the night, but he rises again triumphantly at dawn.

Human life was seen as a series of *kheperu*, such as child into adult or old person into corpse. Khepri could help the final transformation from mummy to **akh** (transfigured spirit). In the Book of the Dead, Khepri is invoked to overcome the intense fear of putrefaction. The deceased declares that his corpse will not decay because "I am Khepri. My body parts will continue to exist." This promise of a permanently renewable life after death made the scarab form of Khepri the most popular of all Egyptian symbols. Millions of scarabs were made as amulets over a period of 2,500 years.

Khepri had no temples of his own, but giant stone scarabs were set up in some temple complexes. The famous example by the sacred lake at Karnak is close to an underground chapel that represented the *Duat* (the Underworld). In a very secret ritual, the cult image of Amun-Ra would descend into this chapel and return transformed into Khepri, "who emerges from the earth." This Khepri statue has generated its own mythology. Local women touch it when they hope to conceive, and tourists are told that the statue has the power to make wishes come true if you walk round it three times.

See also Atum; Boats; Lotus; Ra

References and further reading:

J. Bergman. "Ancient Egyptian Theogony in a Greek Magical Papyrus." In *Studies in Egyptian Religion Dedicated to Professor Jan Zandee*, edited by M. Heema Van Voss et al. Leiden: 1982, 28–37.

D. Meeks and C. Favard-Meeks. *Daily Life of the Egyptian Gods.* Translated by G. M. Goshgarian. London: 1997, 54–55, 159, 195.

Primary sources:

PT 587; BD 83, 153b–154; Ad; Solar hymns; True Name; PGM VII

KHNUM (CHNUM)

The god Khnum was usually shown as a man with the head of a long-horned ram. He was thought to control the Nile inundation, and he embodied the dangerous but life-giving power of this annual flood. As a creator deity, Khnum shaped people and animals on his potter's wheel and put life and health into their bodies. He was sometimes paired with the frog goddess, Heqet, but in his main temple on the island of Elephantine at Aswan, Khnum formed a **triad** with the goddesses Satet and Anuket.

Khnum was one of the chief deities of the First Cataract, an area of rocky rapids on the southern border of Egypt. An inscribed stela found on one of the small islands in this region of the Nile relates an interesting tradition about Khnum. The inscription purports to be a decree of King Djoser (c. 2667–2648 BCE) but was actually composed about 2,500 years after his reign. It tells how Egypt suffered seven terrible years of famine, because the Nile did not rise high enough to flood the agricultural land. Djoser summoned the wisest of the priests who could read the sacred books and ordered him to discover the source of the inundation. The priest consulted ancient books and discovered that the inundation came from twin caverns under the island of Elephantine. He told the king that only the god Khnum had the power to unbolt the doors and release the flood from these caverns. Djoser hastily made offerings to the deities of Elephantine. Then Khnum "the maker of every body" appeared to the king in a dream and promised to let the flood gush again so that the years of hunger would be ended.

It was probably the fertile mud spread by the inundation that Khnum was thought to use as a "potter god." In the Pyramid Texts and the Coffin Texts he mainly seems to make objects, such as boats. One story set in the Old Kingdom tells how Khnum was one of a group of deities who visited Egypt in disguise to assist at the birth of three children destined to be kings. Khnum's particular role was to make their bodies healthy. Later texts and scenes that describe the conception and birth of divine kings show Khnum making the royal body and its *ka* or double on his potter's wheel. This seems to be taking place in the celestial realm as a necessary prelude to the king's physical birth.

In temples of the first millennium BCE, the births of gods were celebrated in similar scenes. Khnum creates and animates the physical forms of these baby gods, starting with shaping the egg in the womb. At the Roman Period temple of Esna, Khnum's role as maker of bodies was celebrated at the Festival of the Potter's Wheel. Hymns sung at this festival praised "the lord of the wheel" as the one "who fashioned gods and men." When Khnum was viewed as a universal creator, his name was joined with those of other creator deities such as Amun, Ptah, or Ra. His wheel was spun to remake the cosmos every morning. The Egyptian word for ram sounded similar to the word for soul or manifestation (*ba*). This may be why Khnum was sometimes identified with the soul of other deities such as Geb, Osiris, and Ra. Most Underworld Books show the nocturnal sun as a man with a ram's head, because it is the soul of Ra that is passing through the underworld.

See also Heqet; Imhotep; Ra; Satet and Anuket

References and further reading:
A. M. Badawi. *Der Gott Chnum*. Glückstadt: 1937.
P. F. Dorman. "Creation on the Potter's Wheel at the Eastern Horizon of Heaven." In *Gold of Praise: Studies on Ancient Egypt in Honor of Edward F. Wente*, edited by E. Teeter and J. A. Larson. Chicago: 1999, 83–100.
Primary sources:
PT 522; CT 214; Famine stela; P. Westcar; Esna hymns

KHONSU (KHONS, CHONS)

Khonsu was a moon god whose name means "the Traveler." In the south of Egypt he was said to be the son of Amun and Mut. In the north, he was the son of Ptah and Sekhmet. He could be shown as a falcon-headed man or as child wearing the sidelock of youth. His usual headdress represented a full moon above a crescent moon.

The earliest references to Khonsu make him a terrifying figure. He was the "angry one of the gods" who strangled lesser deities and ate the hearts of the dead. Later he was associated with fate, judgment, and punishment. A baboon form of Khonsu was feared as the Keeper of the Books of the End of Year. These were the books in which the gods wrote the names of those who were going to die during the year. People appealed to a gentler aspect of the god, "Khonsu the Merciful," to alter the decrees of fate.

It was mainly for his ferocious qualities that Khonsu was invoked in spells to oppose powerful demons. An inscription dating to around the fourth century BCE relates how a statue of Khonsu was sent to help a foreign princess who was possessed by a spirit. The story is set 900 years earlier in the reign of Rameses II. It tells how Rameses married a princess of the distant land of Bakhtan. While the king and queen were celebrating a festival in Thebes, news came that the queen's sister, Bentresh, was very ill.

King Rameses sent a learned **scribe** to Bakhtan. He diagnosed that the princess's illness was caused by a spirit that was too powerful for him to fight. The prince of Bakhtan asked the king of Egypt to send him a god who could fight this spirit. Rameses consulted the oracle of Khonsu at Karnak and was told to send a statue that was inhabited by a special manifestation known as "Khonsu who determines Fate, the great god who drives out disease demons."

The divine statue arrived in Bakhtan after a journey of seventeen months. The god created magical protection for the princess, and "she became well at once." The prince of Bakhtan and his soldiers watched in terror as Khonsu conversed with the spirit he had driven out. Khonsu ordered the prince to make offerings to placate the spirit so that it would never return. The prince was so impressed by the power of the divine statue that he decided to keep it in Bakhtan.

After several years, the god appeared to the prince in a dream making it clear that he wanted to go home. The prince did not dare to keep the statue any longer and sent it back to Egypt with many rich gifts for the temple of Khonsu.

The temple of Khonsu at Karnak is very well preserved. On one of its walls is a text known as the Khonsu cosmogony. This type of text tries to explain the origins of the world. In this version, Khonsu is identified with the great snake who fertilized the cosmic egg and "traveled to Thebes in his name of Khonsu (the Traveler)."

See also Amun; Baboons; Moon; Mut

References and further reading:

G. Hart. "Khonsu." In *A Dictionary of Egyptian Gods and Goddesses.* London and Boston: 1986, 112–115.

R. A. Parker and L. H. Lesko. "The Khonsu Cosmogony." In *Pyramid Studies and Other Essays Presented to I. E. S. Edwards,* edited by J. Baines. London: 1988, 168–175.

Primary sources:

PT 273–274; CT 311; Bentresh Stela; Khonsu Cosmogony

KINGS AND PRINCES

Kingship was a sacred institution, established in the First Time as part of the divine order (*maat*). This did not mean that individual kings were always considered infallible. Mythical history included a long period when individual deities ruled as kings or queens of Egypt. A number of myths center on disputes over the royal succession. The most important of these was the sixty-year conflict between Horus and Seth. When Horus was acclaimed as the rightful ruler, he became the model for all Egyptian kings.

It was an Egyptian king's duty to please the gods, give justice to humanity, and make offerings to the spirits of the dead. Kings and princes were praised as champions of *maat* when they led the armies of Egypt into battle (see "Period of Rule by Kings" under "Linear Time" in "Mythical Time Lines"). Kings could be shown literally upholding the divine order by taking on the Heh gods' task of supporting the sky. In the Pyramid Texts of the Old Kingdom, the king can be identified with the creator who swallows up all the other deities each night. Dead kings were also assimilated to Osiris, the murdered god who rose again as ruler of the dead. In New Kingdom Underworld Books, the king sometimes joins the sun god in his barque to fight the nightly battle against chaos.

Living kings could be credited with divine qualities. The boy king Tutankhamun was optimistically described as having the courage of Seth, the strength of Horus, the knowledge of Ra, the skill of Ptah, and the discernment of Thoth. Royal-birth myths gave some rulers a divine parent. Inscriptions in Luxor temple tell how the god Amun transformed himself into a likeness of

King Thutmose IV (c. 1400–1390 BCE) (see Figure 20). He entered the palace where Thutmose's queen Mutemwiya was sleeping. She was woken by his pervading scent and was overcome by desire. Amun then did "everything that he wished with her." He promised the queen that their son (Amenhotep III) would rule Egypt "like Ra for ever."

Such myths were sometimes used to justify a change of dynasty. The climax of a cycle of stories set in the reign of King Khufu (c. 2589–2566 BCE) is the birth of three "sons of Ra" who will replace Khufu's dynasty as rulers of Egypt. This Middle Kingdom story cycle portrays Khufu as a tyrannical monarch who needs to be told what is right by a wise peasant. His bad reputation survived right down to the fifth century BCE when Herodotus was told that Cheops (Khufu) had set his own daughter to work as a prostitute to help pay for his pyramid building.

Weak or unjust rulers feature in tales of many different periods. In the New Kingdom tale The Two Brothers, a King of Egypt has the husband of a woman he wants to marry slaughtered and gives in to all this evil woman's whims. In the Late Period story of Meryra, a king learns that he is going to die unless someone enters the underworld for him. Meryra agrees to die in the king's place. He plots a dreadful revenge from the underworld when he learns that the ungrateful king has seized his widow.

Greco-Roman Period stories about a prince called Setna describe him stealing a magic book from a tomb. He fails to learn from the example of an earlier prince who was killed by Thoth for using the forbidden book. In another of the stories, an Egyptian king called Siamun is snatched from his bed every night and beaten by wax figures brought to life by a Nubian sorcerer. The king is only saved from this humiliating treatment by the wisdom of a priest-magician. Later in the same story, Setna and his father, King Rameses II, are powerless against Nubian sorcery until the spirit of the priest-magician returns to help them.

Herodotus tells a story about an Egyptian king called Rhampsinitus, who may be partly based on Rameses II. Rhampsinitus is unable to protect his royal treasure from a clever thief. In the end he has to accept the thief as his son-in-law. As in earlier Egyptian tales, intelligence and courage come off best against hereditary power.

See also Bastet; Cattle; Heqet; Horus; Magicians; Montu; Osiris; Ra
References and further reading:

H. Frankfort. *Kingship and the Gods.* Chicago: 1948.

D. O'Connor and D. Silverman (eds.). *Ancient Egyptian Kingship.* Leiden: 1995.

Primary sources:

PT 273–274; RDP; Loyalist Instruction; Ad; RBM; Sphinx stela of Amenhotep II; Karnak stela; KASP; BON; TB; PV; Herodotus H II.120–121; Setna cycle

LOTUS

In some versions of the Egyptian creation story, the sun god was born from a blue lotus that emerged from the primeval waters. The flower itself could be identified with the great goddess who gave birth to the sun. The blue lotus came to be a general symbol of rebirth. It was also the emblem of the god Nefertem.

The sweetly scented blue lotus (*nymphea caerulea*) grows in still water. Its flower buds only rise above the water and open their petals when the sun is shining. This lotus is pollinated by beetles, which links it with Khepri, the beetle god of dawn. The image of the first sunrise as a lotus emerging from the dark waters and opening to reveal its golden stamens seems to be an ancient one.

From around the fourteenth century BCE on, the newly risen sun could be pictured as a naked child sitting inside the lotus and holding one finger to his lips. In hymns intended to be sung at dawn, the sun god Ra is "the child of gold who issues from the lotus." Ra was thought to age during the course of the day, so the infant god became an old man by sunset.

In some accounts the lotus comes into being after the eight primeval beings known as the Ogdoad of Hermopolis fertilized the waters of chaos. These fertile waters might be thought of as a great primeval goddess who, in the form of a cow or a lotus, gives birth to the creator sun god. This goddess can be named as Mehet-Weret, Hathor, or Neith. Various child gods such as Horus the Child, Ihy, and Nefertem could all be identified with the solar child in the lotus. Ihy, a son of Hathor, was called "the child who shines in the lotus."

Nefertem was occasionally shown as a child seated on the lotus but more often as a man or a lion-headed man wearing a lotus headdress. His epithets, such as "the Great Lotus" and "the lotus-flower at the nose of Ra," identify him with the lotus itself. A sweet and powerful scent was a distinguishing characteristic of Egyptian deities, and Nefertem was the god who presided over perfume making. In Egyptian funerary art, the dead were often shown holding a blue lotus to their noses. Breathing in the perfume of the lotus gave them new life as followers of Ra.

See also Horus the Child; Khepri; Ogdoad of Hermopolis; Ra; Sons of Horus

References and further reading:

M. Lurker. "Lotus." In *The Gods and Symbols of Ancient Egypt.* Translated by Barbara Cumming and revised by Peter Clayton. London: 1980, 77–78.

M-L. Ryhiner. *L'Offerande du lotus dans les temples égyptiens de l'épopque tardive.* Rites Égyptiens VI. Brussels: 1986.

Primary sources:

PT 249, 512; CT 80; BD 15, 81

Figure 34. Painted relief from a Nineteenth Dynasty royal tomb showing the goddess Maat. Museo Archeologico, Florence, Italy. (Scala/Art Resource, New York)

MAAT (MA'ET)

The central concept of Egyptian cosmology and ethics was personified as the goddess Maat wearing an ostrich feather on her head. The word *maat* can mean truth, justice, righteousness, order, balance, and cosmic law. The goddess Maat was the beloved daughter of Ra, the creator sun god. She traveled with him in the sun barque, delighting his heart and giving "life to his nostrils." The primary duty of an Egyptian king was to be the champion of *maat*. In the afterlife, the dead were judged on whether they had done and spoken *maat*.

From the Old Kingdom onward, Maat's presence was thought to be vital to the daily regeneration of the sun god. In Underworld Books she is often shown standing close to Ra in both the Day and Night Boats of the sun. This, or the dual nature of Egypt as two kingdoms, may explain why Maat can appear as two identical goddesses.

Maat shares her feather emblem with the air god Shu. She was sometimes equated with Shu's sister, Tefnut. The gods were said to "live on *maat,*" and the goddess was identified with the basics of life: air to breathe, bread to eat, and beer to drink. From the fourteenth century BCE onward, Maat was often shown as a winged goddess. Like Isis, she could revive the dead with the air generated by her beating wings. Another emblem of Maat was a plinth sign that was used in the writing of her name. Such plinths are shown below the thrones of deities who act as divine judges. This depiction has been interpreted as a symbol that *maat* was the base on which Egyptian society was built.

Kings were frequently shown offering a miniature figure of Maat to the chief deity of a temple. All the daily rituals and sacrifices would be deemed meaningless unless the king and his people were living righteous lives. Judges and high officials wore images of the goddess to signify that they were enforcing her laws. Maat was often linked with Thoth, the impartial judge, who was said to have put the laws of *maat* into writing. This gave a divine precedent for the many works of Egyptian literature that teach or debate how to "live in *maat*" in the real world.

Egyptian myths of a golden age included a period when Maat was ruler of earth. She was sometimes said to have withdrawn to the heavens because she was grieved by the wicked behavior of humanity. Maat could still be thought of as living with an individual like his or her good angel and accompanying that person into the afterlife. Eventually "joining Maat" became a euphemism for dying.

In the Book of the Dead, the Hall of the Two Truths (or the Double *Maat*) is the place where the souls of the dead come to be judged. The hearts of the dead were weighed against the feather of Maat, and her image sometimes surmounts the scales. If, like Ra, the dead person had Maat in his or her heart, the scales would balance and the deceased would be declared "true of voice" or "justified" (see Figure 7).

A hymn from the time when Egypt was occupied by the Persians evokes "the beautiful face of Maat" shining from the heart of Ra. The goddess is urged to reside in the tongue and the head of the Persian king, so that he will do *maat.* During the Greco-Roman Period, Maat seems to have lost her central place in Egyptian religion, and some of her functions were taken over by Isis.

See also Birds; Isis; Kings and Princes; Shu and Tefnut; Thoth

References and further reading:

E. Hornung. "The Concept of Maat." In *Idea into Image: Essays on Ancient Egyptian Thought.* Translated by Elizabeth Bredeck. Princeton: 1992, 131–145.

E. Teeter. *The Presentation of Maat: The Iconography and Theology of an Ancient Egyptian Offering Ritual.* Chicago: 1990.

Primary sources:

CT 80; BD 125; Eloquent Peasant; Solar hymns; Amenemope; Hibis hymn (to Maat)

MAFDET

Mafdet was a goddess who butchered the enemies of Ra.

See also Feline Deities

MAGICIANS

Ancient Egyptian heroes were usually magicians rather than warriors. Deities such as Isis and Thoth were presented as powerful magicians, and the dead needed to use spells and amulets to survive in the afterlife. At a time when reading was a rare skill, book learning of all kinds was associated with magic. Historical figures with a scholarly reputation, such as the Third Dynasty official Imhotep, became magicians in legend. The amazing powers attributed to the ritual specialists known as lector priests were the subject of many tales.

A cycle of Middle Kingdom stories set in the reign of King Khufu (c. 2589–2566 BCE) tells of great magicians of the past. The first story in the sequence probably featured Imhotep, but only the last few lines are preserved. The second story concerns the chief lector priest Webaoner (Ubainer) and his wife. This lector priest discovers that his wife is meeting a lover in a lakeside pavilion. He consults his magic scrolls and makes a crocodile of wax "seven fingers long." This wax crocodile is thrown into the lake when his wife's lover is bathing. It becomes a crocodile 7 cubits long (about 3.5 meters) that seizes the lover and keeps him at the bottom of the lake for seven days. Webaoner shows his king what he has done and turns the terrible crocodile back into a wax model. The king condemns Webaoner's wife and her lover to death. The wife is burned and the lover is given up to the magic crocodile, who drags him down into the underworld.

A lake is also the main setting for the third story, but this is much more cheerful in tone. King Sneferu is bored, so the wise lector priest Djadjaemankh advises him to go for a trip on the palace lake in a barge rowed by twenty beautiful girls. When one of the rowers loses her favorite turquoise pendant, Djadjaemankh uses his magic to roll back the waters and recover the jewel from the bottom.

One of Khufu's sons then promises to bring him a 110-year-old peasant who is more skilled in magic than all these priest-magicians of the past. The peasant Djedi can tame lions with his magic, an ominous prospect for King Khufu, as this animal traditionally represented the power of the king. Khufu wants to behead a criminal and have Djedi bring him back to life. Fear of losing your head in the afterlife is mentioned in many spells, so this may be Khufu's motive. Djedi rebukes the king for wanting to experiment on people and restores the severed heads of two geese and a bull. Finally, Khufu asks Djedi for what he really wants: the number of the chambers in the mansion of Thoth. This secret knowledge would probably allow Khufu to build the perfect tomb for himself. Djedi warns him that this knowledge is destined to be revealed only to the eldest of three kings who will replace Khufu's dynasty.

Secret knowledge is a central theme in the stories told about Setna, a character based on a prince of the thirteenth century BCE who is known to have done much restoration work in the cemeteries and temples of Memphis. In legend, he was transformed into a tomb robber, determined to steal a copy of the Book of Thoth. Setna meets the ghosts of an earlier prince and his wife. They warn him that if he takes the Book of Thoth and tries to use the spells it contains, the gods will punish him. Setna ignores their warnings, but he is forced to return the book after a series of uncanny experiences.

In one of these, Setna agrees to the murder of his own children. This turns out to be an illusion, and Setna's son Sa-Osiris grows up to be a great magician. He takes his father on a magical journey through the underworld and shows him the very different fates of the evil and the good after death. When Setna and his father (Rameses II) are challenged by a Nubian sorcerer to read a sealed letter without opening it, only Sa-Osiris can perform this feat. The letter tells how hundreds of years before, a magician called Sa-Paneshe defeated a Nubian sorceress and her son who were casting spells on a king of Egypt. Sa-Osiris then reveals that he is the spirit of Sa-Paneshe reborn to protect Egypt from the continuing threat of Nubian sorcery.

See also Baboons; Bastet; Heqet; Imhotep; Kings and Princes; Thoth

References and further reading:

S. Tower Hollis. "Tales of Magic and Wonder from Ancient Egypt." In *Civilizations of the Ancient Near East,* vol. 4, edited by J. M. Sasson. New York: 1995, 2255–2264.

W. J. Tait. "Theban Magic." In *Hundred-Gated Thebes,* edited by S. P. Vleeming. Leiden and New York: 1995, 169–182.

Primary sources:

P. Westcar; Setna cycle; Petese

MAHES (MIHOS)
Mahes was a fierce lion god.
> *See also* Bastet; Feline Deities

MEHET-WERET (MEHURIT, METHYER)
Mehet-Weret was a primeval cow goddess who gave birth to the sun god. Her name originally meant the "Great Flood" but was later reinterpreted as the "Great Swimmer." She was a female counterpart of Nun, the god of the primeval ocean, and a rival for his title of "oldest of beings." In some contexts, Mehet-Weret is merely an epithet of creator goddesses such as Hathor, Neith, or Isis.

Mehet-Weret was thought of as existing before creation as a kind of fertile current in the primeval ocean. Spell 17 of the Book of the Dead states that the sun god Ra was "born from the buttocks" of Mehet-Weret. The primeval lotus, from which the sun child is alternatively said to have emerged, was probably also a form of this goddess. After creation, Mehet-Weret was identified with the celestial waters traveled by the sun barque. In the nocturnal sky she was probably the "river" of stars we know as the Milky Way.

Mehet-Weret could be shown as a cow-headed woman, a seated cow, or a cow carrying a child. One of Mehet-Weret's titles was "mound" or "island," alluding to the idea that the newborn sun god was raised above the primeval waters on the head or back of Mehet-Weret so that he could begin his work of creation. In a variation on this myth, Neith/Mehet-Weret is said to have saved the infant sun from her children (the first crocodiles) by carrying him through the waters of chaos. This finds a parallel in later mythical history. After a revolt by humanity, Ra begins a new order by being carried up into the heavens on the back of Nut in cow form. Nut and Mehet-Weret are sometimes treated as a pair of cosmic cows with parallel myths and sometimes as the same deity. Nut has an alternative sky form as a giant nude woman stretched above the earth. Ritual spoons in the form of a nude female swimmer may depict Nut/Mehet-Weret.

The starry-patterned cows that form the sides of a golden bed from the tomb of Tutankhamun are labeled Isis-Mehet [Weret]. The purpose of such funerary beds was to help the dead king to ascend to the heavens, supported by the celestial cow. In the Book of the Dead, the cow who stands at the entrance to the realm of the dead is sometimes named as Mehet-Weret. By the New Kingdom all the elite dead could hope to be helped by the cow goddess during the vulnerable period of rebirth.
> *See also* Cattle; Hathor; Neith; Nut

References and further reading:
B. S. Lesko. *The Great Goddesses of Egypt.* Norman, OK: 1999, 17, 21–26, 62.
G. Pinch. *Votive Offerings to Hathor.* Oxford: 1993, 175–183.
Primary sources:
PT 317; BD 17, 124, 186; Esna calendar

MEHIT (MEHYT, MEKHIT)

Mehit was a lion goddess worshipped at Thinis.

> *See also* Feline Deities; Onuris

MERETSEGER

Meretseger was a Theban snake goddess.

> *See also* Snakes

MESKHENET

Meskhenet was a goddess associated with birth and fate.

> *See also* Heqet; Shai

MIN

Min was an ancient god of human and agricultural fertility. The most masculine of gods, Min was shown as a cloaked figure with a large erect penis. He wears two tall plumes on his head, and his right arm is raised in a smiting gesture. Above his right hand is a flail, which may be a herdsman's whip. These features suggest that Min could be an apotropaic deity, driving away evil with his aggressive body language. Statues of Min were carried out to protect and bless the fields, and the first fruits of the harvest were presented to him. From the Middle Kingdom onward, Min was often identified with Horus, the son of Isis. At Thebes, Min united with Amun to form a creator deity capable of generating all life through his sexual potency.

From early times, Min could be represented by a mysterious emblem that has been variously interpreted as a lightning bolt, a barbed arrow, a pair of fossilized shellfish, or a door bolt. This symbol appears on the 5,000-year-old Colossi of Min found in his temple at Coptos on the edge of the eastern desert. Min was worshipped as Lord of the Eastern Desert by the miners, quarrymen, and hunters who worked in this desolate region.

Min is mentioned in several of the Pyramid Texts. His tall plumes seem to give the dead king the power to fly up into the heavens. Spells in the Coffin Texts helped deceased men to achieve the sexual prowess of Min, "the woman hunter," in the afterlife. Coffin Texts spell 335 asks who Min is and answers: "He is Horus, the protector of his father."

A tall-growing lettuce whose juice resembled semen was Min's sacred plant. An episode in the Contendings of Horus and Seth when Seth becomes pregnant after eating "the seed of Horus" smeared on lettuce leaves illustrates the extraordinary generative powers of Min-Horus. The sacred animals of Min were a falcon and a white bull, and one of Min's most important titles was Ka-mut-ef (the Bull of his Mother). Min was said to secretly unite with his mother under cover of darkness to beget himself. During the festival of Min, the queen of Egypt took the role of the "mother of Min," probably so that the royal *ka* (vital force) could be passed intact from king to king. In narratives in which the gods are treated like people, this archaic ritual becomes the myth of the rape of Isis by her son Min-Horus-Nakht (Horus the Strong). This led to a further identification of Min with Osiris, the father of the son of Isis.

When the Greeks settled in Egypt, they saw Min as a form of the virile goat-god Pan, the protector of travelers in lonely places. One Classical writer claimed that Min was promoted to god of fertility after making love to all the women in Egypt when the men were away at war.

> ***See also*** Amun; Horus; Isis
>
> ***References and further reading:***
>
> B. Adams. "A Lettuce for Min." *Studien fur Aegyptischen Kultur* 8 (1980): 9–16.
>
> R. H. Wilkinson. "Ancient Near Eastern Raised-arm Figures and the Iconography of Min." *Bulletin of the Egyptology Seminar* 11 (1991–1992): 109–118.
>
> ***Primary sources:***
>
> PT 667a; CT 335, 649, 967; Min festival texts; Hibis texts

MONTU (MONT, MONTH)

A fierce Upper Egyptian falcon god who may have originated as a star deity, Montu was the chief god of the Theban region and had temples at Armant, Medamud, and Tod. He was usually shown as a falcon-headed man, wearing a sun disk with two plumes and holding a curved sword or a spear. Fighting was "the work of Montu." He attacked the enemies of *maat* (order) and inspired kings and warriors on the battlefield. Battleships were decorated with protective images of the "four Montus" (of Thebes, Armant, Medamud, and Tod) spearing and trampling the enemies of Egypt.

Armant (Hermonthis) was considered to be the southern equivalent of Heliopolis, the city of the sun god Ra. As early as the twentieth century BCE, Montu was worshipped as an aspect of the sun god. His chief consort was Raet-tawy, a female form of Ra usually shown wearing the sun disk and cow horns headdress of Hathor. The gods Montu-Ra and Atum-Ra could represent the kingdoms of Upper and Lower Egypt. Montu-Ra was the patron deity of King Nebhepetre Montuhotep ("Montu-is-content") who reunited Egypt at the end of the First Intermediate Period.

Egyptian kings liked to compare themselves to "strong-armed Montu." An inscription of Amenhotep II (c. 1427–1401 BCE) claims that as a youth of eighteen he was able to shoot arrows through a copper target while driving a chariot because he had the skill and strength of Montu. Rameses II (c. 1290–1224 BCE) boasted that he had turned defeat into victory at the battle of Qadesh by attacking the enemy "in the likeness of Montu," charging their ranks "like a swooping falcon."

Rameses also compared himself to an "eager bull" in battle, which was another of Montu's forms. Montu was probably associated with the fights between bulls staged at some religious festivals. From the fourth century BCE onward, a black and white bull was always kept in the Montu temple at Armant. These "Buchis bulls" were revered as manifestations of the twin souls of Ra and Osiris. Each Buchis bull had a staff of twenty. He wore crowns and necklaces and a face net to keep off flies.

> *See also* Cattle; Ra; Satet and Anuket
> *References and further reading:*
> E. K. Werner. *The God Montu: From the Earliest Attestations to the End of the Old Kingdom.* Ann Arbor, MI: 1986.
> E. K. Werner. "Montu and the 'Falcon Ships' of the Eighteenth Dynasty." *Journal of the American Research Center in Egypt* 23 (1986): 107–123.
> *Primary sources:*
> PT 503; Sphinx stela of Amenhotep II; Qadesh inscriptions

MOON

A variety of male and female deities was associated with aspects of the moon. The god who personified the moon itself was called Iah (Yah), but he never gained great importance in cult or myth. Khonsu and Thoth were major lunar deities who could be shown wearing a crescent (the new moon) and a disk (the full moon). The Egyptian equivalent of "the man in the moon" was a great white baboon. The moon was also thought of as the left eye of Horus, the heavenly falcon. The complex mythology of the moon centered on its dramatic monthly cycle of decline and renewal.

As a god of the new moon Khonsu could be shown as a child, whereas as god of the full moon he appeared as a falcon-headed man crowned with a lunar disk: "a sun that shines at night." As a god who punished the wicked, Khonsu acted like a lunar equivalent of the merciless Eye of Ra. Khonsu and Thoth were both divine reckoners who decided the length of a person's life span. Thoth was said to have invented the lunar calendar, which fixed the date of temple festivals. One myth relates how Thoth's baboon form was created to rule the night sky as the deputy of the sun god so that humanity need not fear the dark. In the Book of Two Ways, the spirits of the dead strive to join Thoth in the Mansion of the Moon.

A temporary destruction of the moon is one of the mythical events frequently mentioned but never very fully described in Egyptian texts. In some versions, the lunar eye of Horus seems to be attacked or even swallowed by the god Seth in the form of a black pig. Thoth forces him to disgorge the moon again. This is similar to the image of the sky goddess swallowing the sun every night and giving birth to it every morning, so Seth can be regarded as the "mother" of the moon.

Other texts refer to a fight in which one or both of the eyes of Horus are torn out by Seth. Thoth is usually said to be the one who finds, heals, and restores the wounded eye. From Classical times onward, these myths have been interpreted as symbolic accounts of lunar eclipses or of the monthly waxing and waning of the moon. The waxing moon was sometimes represented in temple art by a fierce young bull and the waning moon by a tame ox (castrated bull).

The lunar cycle also came to be linked with the death and revival of Osiris. The Greek writer Plutarch reported the belief that the fourteen days of the waning moon were equated with the fourteen parts of the dismembered body of Osiris, which had to be joined together to make him whole again.

Plutarch also noted that the moon was sometimes thought of as female. From early times the right or solar eye of the heavenly falcon was personified as a goddess. The liking for complementary pairs seems to have led to the creation of a lunar eye goddess. The Two Ladies, Wadjyt and Nekhbet, could sometimes stand for the fiery light of the sun and the radiant light of the moon. Goddesses such as Hathor and Bastet might play the roles of both the solar and the lunar eyes. Their terrible lion forms were usually solar, but their gentler cat forms could be lunar. The behavior of cats was believed to be influenced by the lunar cycle. When Isis became the paramount deity, she was also worshipped as a moon goddess.

> *See also* Atum; Eye of Ra; Eyes of Horus; Khonsu; Onuris; Seth; Thoth; Two Ladies
> *References and further reading:*
> P. Derchain. "Mythes et dieux lunaires en Égypte." In *La Lune, mythes et rites.* Sources Orientales 5. Paris: 1962.
> A. Roberts. "Moon and Sun." In *Hathor Rising.* Trowbridge, England: 1995, 70–115.
> *Primary sources:*
> PT 359; CT 50, 155; BD 112; I&O 12, 42–44, 63

Figure 35. A statue of Mut as Queen of the Gods and consort of Amun, found in the temple of Luxor. (Courtesy of Geraldine Pinch)

MUT (MOUT)

Little is known about the origins of this goddess, but from the New Kingdom onward she was worshipped as the Queen of the Gods. At Thebes, Mut became the chief consort of Amun-Ra and the mother of the moon god Khonsu. Her name derives from the Egyptian word for mother. Mut was most commonly shown as a mature woman wearing the vulture headdress of an Egyptian queen, but she also had lioness and cat forms.

In royal-birth myths, the reigning queen was identified with Mut uniting with her consort Amun to produce a divine child who was destined to rule Egypt. Each new king absorbed the power to rule from the milk of his mother Mut. As an emblem of sovereignty, Mut could be shown wearing the White Crown of Upper Egypt or the Double Crown of Upper and Lower Egypt and holding royal scepters. A few New Kingdom hymns name her as the leader of the gods, the female equivalent of the creator sun god. They praise her for creating the inundation from the sweat of her body and caring for all people.

Mut could also play the role of the shining first-born daughter of the sun god, the Eye of Ra. She was sometimes linked with the myth in which Ra and his daughter take the form of cats to slay the Apophis serpent under the *ished* tree. When Mut quarreled with her father, she roamed the Libyan desert in the form of a cat and had to be persuaded to come back to Egypt. Her return was greeted with wild rejoicing among gods, people, and animals.

The myth of the return of the far-wandering goddess was reenacted in temples of Mut. The important ritual of the pacification of the angry goddess took place on a crescent-shaped lake representing the mythical place, Isheru. The purpose of the ritual was to transform the destructive aspect of the solar goddess (Sekhmet) into one of her more benevolent aspects (Mut, Lady of Isheru, Hathor, or Bastet). The pacified goddess would then consent to take a husband and give birth to the divine child.

Mut-Sekhmet was credited with the power to prevent or inflict plague and other infectious diseases. The hundreds of lion-headed statues of the goddess from the temple of Mut at Karnak may have been set up to protect Egypt from the epidemics that periodically devastated the Ancient Near East.

The "flame of Mut" was one of the most feared of divine weapons, and her role as a punisher was not restricted to the mythical realm. Traitors and criminals who were considered "enemies of Ra" might be burned alive on braziers in her temples. A particularly terrifying form of Mut-Sekhmet-Bastet had wings, a penis, and three heads: human, lion. and vulture. When the souls of the dead faced judgment in the afterlife, they could invoke this deity to save them from a horrible death in the Place of Execution.

See also Amun; Bastet; Eye of Ra; Feline Deities; Khonsu; Sekhmet

References and further reading:

B. S. Lesko. "Mut and the Sacred Cats." In *The Great Goddesses of Egypt.* Norman, OK: 1999, 130–154.

L. Troy. "Mut Enthroned." In *Essays on Ancient Egypt in Honour of Herman te Velde,* edited by J. van Dijk. Groningen, Netherlands: 1997, 301–315.

Primary sources:

BD 164; RBM; Mut ritual; Crossword stela; EofS

NEFERTEM (NEFERTUM)

Nefertem was the god of the primeval lotus.

See also Lotus; Ptah

NEHEBKAU

Nehebkau was a primeval snake god who could be shown as a serpent with human arms or legs.

See also Snakes

NEITH (NEIT)

Neith was a formidable creator goddess who could be called the Great Mother. Her name may mean "the terrifying one." She was commonly shown as a woman wearing the Red Crown of the north. Her temple at Sais in the Delta was one of Ancient Egypt's most famous buildings.

Neith was a very important deity in the Early Dynastic Period. The curious symbol that represented Neith in these early times may originally have been a click beetle. Later this symbol was reinterpreted as two arrows crossing a shield. Click beetles are usually found near water, and Neith was often equated with Mehet-Weret, a primeval goddess whose name means the Great Flood. She was the mother of the creator sun god and so had claims to be considered the oldest of beings. At Sais, Neith was called "the great mother who gave birth to Ra; she instituted giving birth when there had been no childbirth before." By extension, Neith could also be regarded as the mother of that other divine child, Horus.

As early as the New Kingdom, Neith was alluded to as "the Mother and Father of all things." A text in the Roman Period temple of Esna describes how Neith created the world by speaking seven magical words. As the personification of the fertile primeval waters, she was the mother of the snakes and crocodiles "who are in the abyss." Neith, "the nurse of crocodiles," was shown as a crocodile-headed woman suckling two small crocodiles. She was often named as the mother of Sobek, the most important crocodile god. When Neith spat into the primeval waters, her spittle turned into the terrible chaos monster, Apophis, who nightly challenged the rule of the sun god. One festival at Esna commemorated Neith saving the newborn Ra from her children (the crocodiles or the chaos serpent) by carrying him across the waters.

Neith, "mistress of the bow," was depicted holding a bow and arrows. The arrows of Neith were used to strike down the enemies of the sun god, including her offspring Apophis. In the Pyramid Texts, Neith was named as one of the four goddesses who protected the royal sarcophagus and canopic chest. This protective role was later extended to all the dead.

See also Apophis; Cattle; Horus the Child; Mehet-Weret; Nun; Sobek
References and further reading:
R. El-Sayed. *Le Désse Neith de Saïs.* BiEtud 86. Cairo: 1982.B.
S. Lesko. "Neith, Lady of Sais and Creator of All." In *The Great Goddesses of Egypt.* Norman, OK: 1999 , 45–63.
Primary sources:
PT 362, 555; CT 669, 820; Ad, hours 10–11; H&S; Udjahorresne; Esna calendar; Esna Texts

NEKHBET

Nekhbet was the vulture goddess of Upper Egypt.

See also Two Ladies

NEMTY

Nemty was a divine ferryman.

> **See also** Anti

NEPER (NEPRI)

Neper was the god who personified the grain harvest.

> **See also** Osiris; Renenutet

NEPHTHYS

One of the Two Sisters who mourned for the murdered god Osiris, Nephthys was the youngest of the five children of the sky goddess and the unwilling partner of her brother Seth. She mainly features in myth as the devoted companion of her sister, Isis, but she was a popular protective goddess in funerary art. Nephthys was usually shown as a woman wearing the signs that write her name (Lady of the Mansion) on her head.

Nephthys never enjoyed the high status of her sister, Isis. In spite of her nominal pairing with Seth, Nephthys seems to have lived with Isis and her husband Osiris. Perhaps because of her sham marriage, Nephthys is described in one of the Pyramid Texts as "an imitation woman with no vagina." A few Egyptian texts allude to the distress of Isis on discovering that her husband has slept with Nephthys. The Greek writer Plutarch relates that Nephthys tricked Osiris into sleeping with her and then gave birth to a monstrous son, Anubis. Nephthys abandoned the child to die, but Isis found and saved him. Plutarch saw Osiris as representing the fertilizing Nile flood, Isis the cultivated land of the Nile valley, and Nephthys the usually barren desert.

After the murder of Osiris, Nephthys and Isis searched for his body or for the dismembered parts of that body. The two goddesses were present during the mummification of the body by Anubis. Isis and Nephthys are mentioned in the Pyramid Texts as part of the group of four goddesses who guarded the king's mummified body and organs. As one of the goddesses of weaving, Nephthys was particularly associated with the linen bandages that wrapped a mummy. These bandages were sometimes called the "tresses of Nephthys." When it became common to identify all dead persons with Osiris, Isis and Nephthys were often shown standing at either end of the funeral bier.

The sisters, sometimes in the form of two kites (small birds of prey), were said to have kept a long vigil over the mummy of Osiris to protect him from further attacks by Seth. This vigil was reenacted by two young women, who represented Isis and Nephthys, at festivals of Osiris and at the funerals of important people and sacred animals. In the passionate laments sung during this ritual, Nephthys describes herself as the "beloved sister" of the "good king" Osiris.

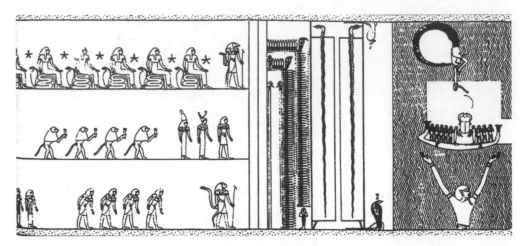

Figure 36. A scene from the last hour of the Book of Gates showing Nun lifting the sun god out of the abyss at dawn. (Art Resource)

Nephthys seems to play only a minor role in the bringing up of her nephew, Horus. She is usually shown watching in scenes in which Horus raises the *djed* pillar, a tableaux that symbolized the revival of Osiris. In the Book of the Dead, Nephthys often stands with her sister behind the throne of Osiris presiding over the judgment of the dead.

> **See also** Anubis; *Djed* Pillar; Isis; Osiris; Seshat; Seth
>
> **References and further reading:**
>
> C. J. Bleeker. "Isis and Nephthys as Wailing Women." *Numen* 5 (1958): 1–18.
>
> L. Troy. *Patterns of Queenship in Ancient Egyptian Myth and History.* Uppsala: 1986, 36–39.
>
> **Primary sources:**
>
> PT 534, 555; CT 74; BD 125; Lamentations; I&O 38

NUN (NOUN, NU)

Nun was a personification of the primeval ocean from which all life came. After creation, the watery darkness known as the *nun* continued to surround the world. It existed above the stars and as an abyss that formed the lowest depths of the underworld. As a deity, Nun was considered the oldest of beings and called the Father of the Gods. He and his female counterpart Naunet were among the eight primeval beings who made up the Ogdoad of Hermopolis.

As a member of the **Ogdoad**, Nun had a frog or frog-headed form. From the New Kingdom onward, he was also shown as a **fecundity figure** presenting the king with the gift of water, the most precious of all substances in desert countries. The Egyptians believed that all the seas and rivers had their ultimate source in the *nun*. During the annual Nile flood, Egypt seemed to revert to its primeval state, and civilization was in danger of being swept away. The creator had to intervene and send divine messengers to ask Nun to curb the destructive power of his flood.

Since the *nun* also contained the potential to create life, Nun was thought of as a **demiurge**, a kind of instinctive movement toward consciousness. At Memphis, the creator god Ptah was said to "have embodied himself as Nun" in order to make things live and grow. More often, Egyptian creation myths speak of the creator's coming into being "in the *nun*." The generative powers of the *nun* could be personified by a goddess known as Mehet-Weret (the Great Flood) who gave birth to the creator sun god.

Every night the sun god Ra returned to the watery abyss to be regenerated. Most semiconscious or unconscious states, such as dreaming, drunkenness, or death, were thought of in terms of descending into this abyss. In the Underworld Book known as the Book of Gates, Ra joins the spirits of the dead in the *nun*. At the climax of this book, the god Nun appears as a giant figure lifting the sun boat out of the depths and into the sky. More pessimistic Egyptian texts speak of the world ending when the creator chooses to return to his "father" Nun.

The chief god of any temple could be identified with Nun in order to give him seniority over other deities. Egyptian respect for the wisdom of old age led to Nun's being revered as a counselor. In one myth, Ra consults Nun when people start to rebel against the gods. Nun's advice is to send the goddess Hathor down as a lioness to punish humanity. In myths from other Near Eastern cultures, a great flood is sent to kill the wicked. The Egyptian version may not be as different as it seems, since Hathor can be both the solar lioness and the goddess known as the Great Flood.

> *See also* Hapy; Mehet-Weret; Ogdoad of Hermopolis
> **References and further reading:**
> J. P. Allen. *Genesis in Egypt: The Philosophy of Ancient Egyptian Creation Accounts.* 2d ed. Yale Egyptological Studies 2. San Antonio, TX: 1995, 4–7.
> A. Spalinger. "The Destruction of Mankind: A Transitional Literary Text." *Studien zur Altägyptischen Kultur* 28 (2000): 257–282.
> **Primary sources:**
> PT 361; CT 80, 714; BD 175; BHC; Solar hymns; BOG; BOE; BON; MT

NUT (NOUT)

Nut was the sky goddess who was the daughter of the air god Shu and his sister, Tefnut. Nut was the consort of her brother, the earth god Geb, and the mother of several important deities including Osiris, Isis, and Seth. As the sky, Nut was shown either as a giant nude woman arched above the earth or as a giant cow with starry markings. Her name probably derives from an Ancient Egyptian word for water (*nw*) and her symbol was a water pot.

Several myths deal with the separation of sky and earth. The first, which seems to be as old as the Pyramid Texts, relates how Nut and Geb embraced each other so fervently that there was no room between them for anything to exist. Either at the command of the creator or because he was jealous, Shu separated his children and held Nut and Geb permanently apart (see Figure 42). Nut could then give birth to the children she had already conceived.

In the Coffin Texts, Nut is described as the "mother of the five **epagomenal days**." A late explanation of this statement is found in Plutarch's book on Egyptian religion. It tells how Nut (whom Plutarch calls Rhea) was pregnant, but the sun god put a curse on her so that she could not give birth on any day of the year. The god Hermes (Thoth) played a board game with the moon and won enough light to make five extra days on which Nut's children could be born. The five children were Osiris, Horus the Elder, Seth, Isis, and Nephthys.

In other accounts of mythical history, there seems no permanent separation until the creator sun god Ra decides to leave the earth after a rebellion by humanity. Nut takes the form of a cow to carry Ra up into the heavens, a myth encapsulated in the image of a sun disk between cow's horns that became the insignia of several goddesses. When she was holding the sun god high above the earth, Nut's "limbs began to shake," so the eight Heh gods were created to support her.

Nut was particularly associated with the night sky, and some scholars have identified her with the Milky Way. In the Pyramid Texts, it is Nut who draws the dead king up to the heavens to live again as a star. The sky was often thought of as a watery region in which the stars and planets might swim like fish or sail in boats.

In the day, the sun god sailed along the "sea below the belly of Nut." Each evening, the sun god was swallowed by Nut and passed through a perilous inner sky inside her. At dawn, Nut gave birth to the sun, her blood turning the sky red. At the same time she would be swallowing the moon and the stars to give birth to them again at dusk. This violent imagery may have given rise to a reinterpretation of Nut's character as "the sow who eats her own piglets." From the New Kingdom onward, the solar cycle was depicted in royal tombs and in temple halls with giant figures of Nut stretching across the ceilings.

In funerary religion Nut was regarded as one of the most helpful goddesses. She was sometimes carved or painted on the underside of coffin lids, so that she could embrace the deceased for all eternity. In the Book of the Dead and in decorated tombs she was shown in a paradise garden as the goddess of the

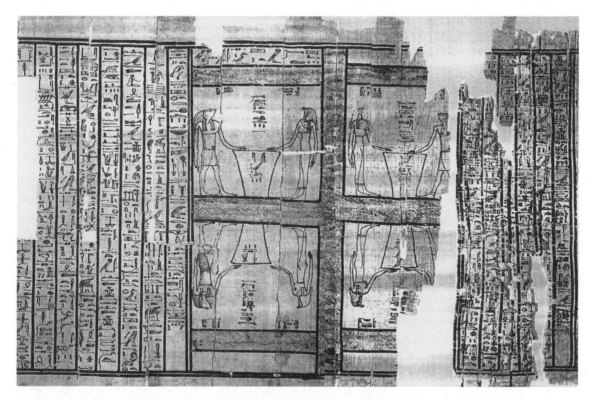

Figure 37. A rare representation of members of the Ogdoad of Hermopolis in the Book of the Fayum. (Carsten Niebur Institute of Near Eastern Studies)

sycamore-fig tree. In this role, Nut gave water and food to refresh the newly dead and strengthen them for their journey through the underworld.

> ***See also*** Cattle; Geb; Hippopotamus Goddesses; Mehet-Weret; Ra; Shu and Tefnut
>
> ***References and further reading:***
>
> B. S. Lesko. "The Sky Goddess Nut." In *The Great Goddesses of Egypt.* Norman, OK: 1999, 22–44.
>
> R. A. Wells. "The Mythology of Nut and the Birth of Ra." *Studien zur Altägyptischen Kultur* 19 (1992): 305–322.
>
> ***Primary sources:***
>
> PT 588, 606, 697; CT 76, 80; BD 59, 152; BOD; BON; BofNut; I&O 12

OGDOAD OF HERMOPOLIS

The Ogdoad of Hermopolis was a group of eight primeval deities whose chief cult center was Khenmw (Eight Town), later called Hermopolis Magna. The Ogdoad embodied the qualities of primeval matter, such as darkness, moistness, and lack of boundaries or visible powers. It usually consisted of four deities doubled to eight by including female counterparts. Obeying some primitive instinct, the eight came together to make the place (the Primeval Mound or the Island of Flame) or an object (the Primeval Lotus or the Cosmic Egg) from which the creator sun god emerged. This made the Ogdoad "the fathers and mothers" of the creator. Alternatively, creator gods such as Amun, Ptah, or Thoth were viewed as calling the eight into being. The creator was then "his" own ancestor, the "father of the fathers and mothers."

The deities who make up the Ogdoad differ from one source to another. Nun and his female counterpart Naunet, the deities of the primeval waters, are nearly always included. Naunet may be a primeval form of the sky goddess, Nut. Amun and Amunet, deities of invisible power or the breath of life, are in some of the oldest lists. When Amun was regarded as a creator separate from the eight, he and Amunet were replaced by Nia and Niat, deities of the void. Primeval darkness was represented by Kek and Keket or occasionally Gereh and Gerehet. Some lists have Tenemet, "chaos," or Heh and his female counterpart Hehet. Heh and Hehet are difficult to interpret. They may originally have embodied the strong currents in the Primeval Waters. The Ogdoad of Hermopolis was sometimes treated as identical with the group of four or eight Heh gods created by Shu to help him support the sky. They in turn were sometimes identified with the "Eastern Souls," the eight baboons who helped the sun to rise.

The Ogdoad could be represented in human form, but sometimes the males have frog or jackal heads and the females snake heads. The amphibian and snake forms of the Ogdoad were thought of as mating in and fertilizing the Primeval Waters. An image of the waters alive with glutinous frog spawn may be what the Egyptians had in mind. In some sources, the Ogdoad seem to be forces that the creator has to subdue before the work of creation can begin. In others they simply seem to die after bringing forth life. The Primeval Mound was both the place of creation and the tomb of the Ogdoad. The Heh gods could then be thought of as the shadows or heavenly souls of the Ogdoad.

The Heh gods belonged to the twilight after dusk and before dawn. This was the equivalent in the daily solar cycle to the period of precreation in the great cycle of mythical history. The Ogdoad merged in the primeval waters to allow the creator to come into being, and the Heh gods acted together to make the void in which the earth could come into being. Members of the Ogdoad such as Nun and Naunet and Kek and Keket were said to help the sun to be reborn as Khepri every morning.

> ***See also*** Amun; Baboons; Lotus; Nun; Nut; Shu and Tefnut; Thoth
> ***References and further reading:***
> S. Tower Hollis. "Otiose Deities and the Ancient Egyptian Pantheon." *Journal of the American Research Center in Egypt* 35 (1998): 61–72.

L. H. Lesko. "Ancient Egyptian Cosmogonies and Cosmology." In *Religion in Ancient Egypt*, edited by Byron E. Shafer. Ithaca, NY, and London: 1991, 88–122.

Primary sources:
PT 301; CT 76, 78–80; Leiden hymns; MT; Khonsu Cosmogony; BOF

ONURIS (ANHUR, INHUR, INHERT)

A hunter deity renowned for capturing a dangerous goddess, Onuris was the local god of Thinis (This), the home town of the kings of the First Dynasty. He was usually shown as a bearded man wearing a plumed headdress and carrying a spear and a coil of rope. As a hunter of threatening animals, Onuris could be treated as an aspect of Shu or of Horus the Harpooner. The Greeks identified Onuris with Ares, their god of war.

The epithets of Onuris characterized him as full of strength and vigor. He was the "bull of Thinis," "strong of arm" and "high of feather." Anticrocodile spells mention a great combat between Onuris-Shu and the evil crocodile Maga. Onuris, "the good warrior," was invoked as protector against demons. In royal tombs of the late New Kingdom, Sopdu and Onuris act as guardians for the dead king in the snake-infested deserts of the underworld. The name Onuris means "bringer-back of the distant one." This refers to a myth in which Onuris left Egypt to hunt in a remote desert region. His quarry was a wild lion goddess. No detailed version of this myth survives, but Onuris seems to have caught and tamed the goddess. He brought her back to Egypt, where she became his bride under the name of Mehit (Mekhit).

Originally, this Distant Goddess may simply have been a personification of the deserts of Nubia. Later, she was identified with Hathor-Tefnut, the wandering Eye of Ra, who left Egypt after quarreling with her father. In this version of the myth she was persuaded to return to Egypt and civilization by the god Thoth and her brother, Onuris-Shu. Texts in temples of the Greco-Roman Period refer to Shu "who brought back his beautiful sister to her father."

As a further complication, Shu and Tefnut could sometimes be identified with the sun and the moon, and the goddess Mehit ("the completed one") could be a personification of the full moon. Onuris then becomes the god who returned the lost lunar Eye of Horus and restored the cosmic balance.

See also Eye of Ra; Eyes of Horus; Feline Deities; Horus; Shu and Tefnut
References and further reading:
G. Hart. "Onuris." In *A Dictionary of Gods and Goddesses.* London and Boston: 1986, 148–150.
H. Junker. *Die Onurislegende.* Berlin: 1917.
Primary sources:
HMP; Cairo calendar; Mut ritual; Hibis texts

OSIRIS

Osiris, the "great god" who ruled the Egyptian underworld, was the eldest son of the earth god Geb and the sky goddess Nut. He and his sister-consort, Isis, ruled Egypt together until Osiris was struck down by his anarchical brother, Seth. Osiris died and became "the Inert One." The gods eventually decreed that Osiris should be resurrected as king and judge of the dead and that his posthumous son Horus should be made king of the living.

Osiris was usually shown as a mummified king wearing an *atef* crown and carrying a **crook** and **flail**. His skin can be black or green. These colors may originally have indicated putrefaction, but they came to symbolize the connection of Osiris with a cycle of death and regeneration based on plant life. In the Pyramid Texts, the dead king is frequently identified with Osiris or his stellar counterpart, Sah (Orion). By the second millennium BCE, this identification was nominally extended to all the dead. Every aspect of burial and mummification came to be linked to the mythology of Osiris.

Where, when, and how Osiris was first worshipped is much disputed. It has been claimed that Osiris was originally a deified Predynastic king, a primitive vegetation spirit, a jackal god of an early royal necropolis, or a mother goddess. Even the etymology of his name is uncertain, though it may simply mean the Mighty One (Death?).

The cult of Osiris only became prominent during the Fifth Dynasty (c. 2494–2345 BCE). He gradually seems to have taken over the attributes of other funerary deities, such as Andjety of Busiris and Khentamentiu of Abydos. The latter's name (Foremost of the Westerners) became an epithet of Osiris, indicating his leadership of the spirits and demons of the *Duat*. At all periods there are a few texts that describe Osiris as a terrifying figure who dispatches demon-messengers to drag the living into the gloomy realm of the dead.

In most accounts, Osiris was born wearing a crown and was chosen to succeed his father, Geb, by the sun god himself. A few sources allude to a violent dynastic struggle between Geb and Osiris. One late text from Kom Ombo even claims that Osiris was killed and born again after a union between his father, Geb, and his grandfather, Shu. No detailed accounts of the reign of Osiris or the manner of his death survive from before the Greco-Roman Period (see "The Reigns of Shu, Geb, and Osiris" under "Linear Time" in "Mythical Time Lines").

In the Pyramid Texts, Osiris is either struck down and trampled by his brother, Seth, or drowned in the Nile. A double death was probably thought necessary to kill a god permanently. The relatives of Osiris have to search for and "gather up" the body. Later sources stressed that Seth had deliberately torn up the body, but in the Pyramid Texts it is probably natural disintegration that

Isis has to reverse with her magic. With the help of the gods Anubis and Thoth, the body of Osiris is preserved and becomes the first mummy.

The sexual power of Osiris seems to be strong enough to survive his death, so he is able to make Isis pregnant. Having ensured the continuation of the cosmos through the conception of Horus, Osiris sinks back into an inert state. Other deities such as Isis, Thoth, and Horus have to argue his case before a Divine Tribunal. Osiris is vindicated as a "possessor of *maat*" (truth, justice). Since his death was unjust, the creator allows Osiris to leave his mummy and rule the kingdom of the dead as Wenenefer (Onnophris). This name originally seems to have meant "the one whose body did not decay," but it was later interpreted as "the beneficent one." The actual raising of Osiris seems to be accomplished by Horus presenting the power of his Eye to Osiris.

A Middle Kingdom royal ritual equates the body of Osiris with barley and Seth with the donkeys who thresh the grain by trampling on it. This is the earliest definite example of the death and resurrection of Osiris being linked to the annual cycle of the reaping and sowing of crops. Like the virile Min, Osiris could be worshipped as a god of agricultural fertility. Ithyphallic corn mummies were made and buried during festivals of Osiris. Their magical purpose was to give new life to the dead, just as the seed corn grew into new plants. The body of Osiris could also be shown regenerating inside a tree.

From at least as early as the New Kingdom, all the liquids that came from the body of Osiris, such as semen, sweat, and pools of putrefaction, were associated with the life-bringing flood waters of the Nile. In some accounts the body of Osiris was divided into anything from fourteen to forty-two parts. During the first millennium BCE, these body parts were said to be buried at sacred sites all over Egypt. The "tomb" of the left leg of Osiris on the island of Bigah was said to be the source of the inundation.

The body of Osiris also played an important role in some of the New Kingdom Underworld Books. In the darkest hour of the night, the soul of the sun god Ra reached the cave where the body lay and became one with the soul of Osiris. This allowed Osiris and all the dead to awake and live again. In the Book of the Dead, Osiris was shown enthroned in the Hall of the Two Truths overseeing the judgment of the dead. A New Kingdom prayer states that Osiris is the greatest of the gods because all Egyptians have to come to him in the end.

The idea of Osiris as a just judge and savior of the dead was prominent during the last stages of Pharaonic culture. In a story of the Roman Period, a prince is shown that after death, rich and poor are treated equally and only the good will survive the judgment of Osiris and enter his paradise.

See also Anubis; Banebdjedet; *Benu* Bird; *Djed* Pillar; Eyes of Horus; Heryshef; Horus; Isis; Moon; Nephthys; Primeval Mound; Ra; Seth; Sokar; Stars and Planets; Wepwawet

References and further reading:

R. T. Rundle Clarke. *Myth and Symbol in Ancient Egypt.* London: 1959, chaps. 3 to 5.

J. G. Griffiths. *The Origins of Osiris and His Cult.* Leiden: 1980.

E. Otto. *Egyptian Art and the Cults of Osiris and Amon.* Translated by K. Bosse-Griffiths. London: 1968.

Primary sources:

PT 219, 532, 576; RDP; Ikhernofret stela; Amenmose stela; BD 17, 175, 181, 185–6; Osiris hymns; H&S; Ad; BOC; BOE; BOG; Khoiak texts; P. Salt 825; Lamentations; Setna cycle; I&O

PAKHET

Pakhet was a lion goddess whose name means "the one who tears apart."

See also Feline Deities

PRIMEVAL MOUND

The Primeval Mound was the first land to rise above the primeval ocean at the dawn of time. The Primeval Mound was the place where the spirit of the creator could take on a form and begin the work of creation. The Mound remained the center of the cosmos and a place of continuous creation. It could be shown as a rounded or stepped mound. The pyramidion-shaped *benben* stone of Heliopolis may also have been an image of the Primeval Mound. The god who embodied the Mound was Tatjenen (Tatenen).

Mounds featured in many different creation myths. In Memphis, Tatjenen was worshipped as a form of the creator god Ptah. At Thebes he became a form of Amun. A high hill of sand is mentioned in the cosmology of Heliopolis. Atum, or his erect penis, was sometimes identified with this hill. At Hermopolis, the primeval forces known as the Ogdoad came together to form a mound or an island as a place for the primeval egg. Some sources imply that the broken shell of this "world egg" was used by the creator to make the first land.

When the first being was imagined as a bird, such as a phoenix, a goose, or an ibis, the Mound was its first perch. The trees that are sometimes shown growing out of the Mound may be the sacred grove from which falcon gods such as Horus and Sopdu are said to have emerged. Every major Egyptian temple claimed that its sanctuary was built on the site of the Primeval Mound. The sanctuary was the place where the god of the temple became manifest, as the creator first became manifest on the Mound.

By the New Kingdom, the god Osiris had developed strong associations with the Primeval Mound. Like the Ogdoad, he could be thought of as being buried in or under the Mound. His soul could be shown as a bird perching in a tree or grove growing from the Mound. In some Underworld Books, the souls of Ra and Osiris meet in bird form on top of the mound to bring new life to the dead. The resurrected Osiris was shown enthroned on the Mound at the center of the underworld.

>*See also* Atum; *Benu* Bird; Birds; Ogdoad of Hermopolis; Ptah
>
>***References and further reading:***
>
>R. T. Rundle Clark. *Myth and Symbol in Ancient Egypt.* London: 1959, 36–41, 170–178.
>
>A. A. Saleh. "The So-Called 'Primeval Hill' and Other Related Elevations in Ancient Egyptian Mythology." *Mitteilungen des Deutschen Archäologischen Instituts, Abteilung Kairo* 25 (1969): 110–120.
>
>***Primary sources:***
>
>PT 587, 600; BD 79, 183; BC; Leiden hymns; Ptah hymns; MT

PRIMEVAL OCEAN

The primeval ocean was made up of the waters of chaos.

>*See also* Nun

PTAH

Ptah was a creator deity who made the world with his heart and his tongue. As Ptah "South of His Wall" he was the chief god of the Egyptian capital, Memphis. He was usually shown as a bearded man wearing an artisan's skull-cap and an enveloping cloak or shroud. As "he who is beautiful of face," Ptah had skin of celestial blue. His scepter combined the *djed* symbol of stability with the **was** symbol of dominion and the *ankh* symbol of life. He bestowed these three qualities on Egyptian kings, who were often crowned in his temple at Memphis.

Ptah's consort was the solar lioness Sekhmet. Their son was Nefertem, the god of the primeval lotus. Ptah was also credited with siring Imhotep, a historical figure who was deified as god of medicine and learning. The Apis bull, the most important sacred animal in Egypt, was the earthly messenger and visible *ba* (soul or manifestation) of Ptah.

A Mansion of Ptah is mentioned twice in the Pyramid Texts. This may be the same Mansion of the *ka* of Ptah (Egyptian—*Hwt ka Ptah*; Greek—Aigyptos) that eventually gave its name to the whole country. In the Middle Kingdom, Ptah was already known as a divine craftsman who could make a new body for a dead person. Ptah became the particular patron of metalworkers and sculptors. That dwarfs were traditionally employed to make jewelry may have been a factor in the development of a dwarf form (**pataikos**) of Ptah. The Greeks later equated Ptah with their bandy-legged smith god, Hephaistos.

Ptah was said to have invented the Opening of the Mouth ritual that was used to symbolically animate cult and *ka* **statues** and reanimate mummies. Osiris was the mythical prototype for all mummies, so in Coffin Texts spell 62 Ptah helps Horus to "break open" the mouth of Osiris and let him breathe again. During the New Kingdom, Ptah acquired a reputation as a compassionate deity. As Ptah "of the Hearing Ear," he listened to the prayers of ordinary people.

The text known as the Memphite Theology may date to the late New Kingdom. In it, Ptah is acclaimed as a self-created deity who made everything that existed through the powers of thought and speech. This concept is reconciled with the theology of Heliopolis by identifying Ptah with many of the deities from the creation myths of that city. Ptah was linked with Nun and Naunet, the deities of the Primeval Waters who "gave birth" to Atum. Alternatively, Ptah was said to have shaped the creator Atum with his heart and tongue. Ptah-Tatjenen was the personification of the Primeval Mound, the place where creation began. Taking the role of Shu, Ptah was said to have made the sky and lifted it above the earth as easily as if it were a feather. He united the Two Lands (Egypt) as Horus in his "great name of Tatjenen." One of the sophisticated hymns in Papyrus Leiden I 350 reduces the Egyptian pantheon to three. Amun was hidden power, Ra the visible power in the heavens, and Ptah the power manifest on or in the earth.

Ptah was also part of the triple entity Ptah-Sokar-Osiris. This divine group has been interpreted as symbolizing the whole cycle of regeneration, with Ptah standing for creation, Sokar for death as metamorphosis, and Osiris for rebirth. Ptah-Sokar-Osiris was sometimes shown presiding over the judgment of the dead in the Hall of the Two Truths. He remained important in funerary religion right into the Roman Period.

See also Apis; *Djed* Pillar; Imhotep; Nun; Osiris; Primeval Mound; Sokar
References and further reading:
J. P. Allen. "The Means of Creation—Ptah." In *Genesis in Egypt: The Philosophy of Ancient Egyptian Creation Accounts.* 2d ed. Yale Egyptological Studies 2. San Antonio, TX: 1995, 38–47.
M. Sandman Holmberg. *The God Ptah.* Lund, Denmark, 1946.
Primary sources:
PT 345; CT 62, 187, 648; BD 82; Ptah hymns; Leiden hymns; MT

RA (RE, PRE)

The sun god who was the ultimate source of light, energy, and life. The first sunrise, when the sun emerged as a shining bird or a golden child from dark watery chaos, was the most important event in Egyptian myth. Ra merged with

Figure 38. The ram-headed night sun in his boat protected by the mehen *snake. From an Underworld Book on the walls of a royal tomb. (Courtesy of Geraldine Pinch)*

the primeval form of the creator to make the cosmos and its laws. He ruled as King of the Gods, first on earth and later from the heavens. Ra was born to his mother the sky goddess each morning. He passed through many transformations before being absorbed back into her each evening. Alternatively, the progress of the sun was pictured as a voyage across the skies above and below the earth. Each night the divine crew of the solar barque had to overcome the forces of chaos so that Ra could revive the sleeping dead and renew the world.

The name Ra is simply the Egyptian word for the sun, the most visible of the divine forces that created and sustained the world. The cult of Ra seems to have originated in the town that the Egyptians called Iunu and the Greeks Heliopolis ("city of the sun god"). From the twenty-sixth century BCE to the Roman Period, all rulers of Egypt called themselves Sons of Ra. The Enemies of Ra were the enemies of Egypt and *maat* (the divine order). The close identification between Ra and the divine order was expressed by making the goddess Maat into Ra's best-loved daughter.

In some Pyramid Texts of the Old Kingdom, the dead king claims to rest like the sun in the west and shine like the sun in the east. In others, he humbly asks for a place among the spirits who escort the "reed-float" or papyrus boat of Ra across the Winding Waterway of the sky. In the Coffin Texts of the Middle Kingdom there is an increased emphasis on the dangers of this voyage. When the Night Boat enters the caverns under the earth or within the body of the sky goddess, it is attacked by hostile forces such as the all-devouring chaos monster Apophis. Surviving temple rituals show that every Egyptian king was expected to play an active magical role to help the sun god to triumph over the forces of darkness and chaos.

The secret Underworld Books that decorate New Kingdom royal tombs link the fate of deceased kings and all the dead with the voyage of the sun (see "The Solar Cycle" under "Cyclical Time" in "Mythical Time Lines"). Just as morning light wakes sleepers in life, the passing sun god reanimated the mummies of the virtuous dead and his own mysterious nocturnal forms. In the underworld, Ra himself was mainly shown as a ram-headed man, or a scarab within a solar disk, in the cabin of the solar barque (see Figure 38). This central figure is sometimes labeled as the "flesh" of Ra. For much of the voyage the sun god is as passive as the corpse of Osiris while a huge array of other deities protect and defend him. The forceful power of the sun is concentrated in the goddess known as the Eye of Ra, who often guards the prow of the solar barque. Much solar mythology was expressed by images rather than narratives. The solar cycle could be summarized by showing Khepri (the scarab beetle), Ra-Horakhty (a falcon-headed man), and Ra-Atum (a mature man wearing the Double Crown) together in the solar barque. Khepri was the self-generating sun of dawn. Ra-Horakhty (Ra-Horus of the Double Horizon) was the triumphant sun who rose in the east as ruler. Ra-Atum was the weary setting sun whose death was an essential part of the cycle of renewal. The sun god could also be depicted with four rams' heads representing his four *bas* (souls or manifestations) (see Figure 19). The four souls are often named as Ra, Khepri, Atum, and Osiris. In some Underworld Books, Ra mysteriously merges with the corpse of Osiris, the ruler of the underworld. When they become "the United One," the dead can reawaken and the world can be remade.

The fact that the sun god was crucial to the theology of kingship may have led to a rather uncomplimentary portrayal of Ra in Egyptian literature. In some narrative myths, Ra appears as an aging king unable to prevent treachery and rebellion among his subjects (see "The True Name of Ra" and "The Destruction of Humanity" under "Linear Time" in "Mythical Time Lines"). The Book of the Heavenly Cow tells how the weary Ra withdrew to the heavens after brutally punishing the humans who had rebelled against his rule on earth. Egyptian **Instruction Texts** sometimes interpret invasions or civil strife as punishments from the angry sun god.

In the cycle of myths centered on Horus, son of Isis, Ra is a remote authority figure who does not always support the weak against the strong. When the infant Horus is poisoned, his mother's screams of anguish stop the solar barque from moving. This challenged both the power of Ra and the authority of the king, whose ritual task it was to secure a "free passage" for the sun. Ra gives in to the righteous anger of Isis and sends his deputy Thoth to heal Horus. An alternative view of the sun god is found in a Greco-Roman Period narrative about the Eye of Ra. The wise god Thoth persuades the Eye goddess to return to her father Ra by telling her fables that show that the sun god is all-seeing and frequently intervenes to establish justice on earth.

> *See also* Amun; Apophis; Aten; Atum; Boats; Eye of Ra; Feline Deities; Hathor; Horus; Horus the Child; Khepri; Lotus; Maat; Nut; Osiris; *Benu* Bird; Sia and Hu; Snakes; Thoth
>
> *References and further reading:*
>
> J. Assmann. *Egyptian Solar Religion in the New Kingdom: Re, Amun, and the Crisis of Polytheism.* Translated by A. Alcock. London and New York: 1995.
>
> E. Hornung., *The Valley of the Kings: Horizon of Eternity.* Translated by D. Warburton. New York: 1990, 71–114.
>
> S. Quirke. *The Cult of Ra Sun Worship in Ancient Egypt.* London: 2001.
>
> *Primary sources:*
>
> PT 257, 311, 334; Ipuur; KASP; Ad; BC; BOG; BOD; BOE; BHC; LofR; Solar hymns; True Name; H&S; Magical statue texts; Ankhsheshonq; LWD; EofS.

RAET-TAWY (RAIYET)

Raet-Tawy was the female sun of the Two Lands, a female counterpart of Ra.

> *See also* Horus the Child; Montu

RA-HORAKHTY

Ra-Horakhty was the solar falcon who represented the sun god at the zenith of his power.

> *See also* Horus; Ra

RENENUTET (ERNUTET, HERMOUTHIS, THERMOUTHIS)

Renenutet was a cobra goddess of fertility and luck whose name meant "the snake who nourishes." She could be represented by various combinations of snake and woman, including a cobra-headed woman suckling a child. Renenutet was associated with the nourishing and healing powers of mother's milk and with food of all kinds. As the deity who controlled the harvest, she was the mother of the corn god, Neper. In the rich farmlands of the Fayum she was worshipped as the consort of the crocodile god Sobek and the mother of Horus.

In the Pyramid Texts, Renenutet is one of the names given to the fire-breathing **uraeus** on the king's brow. She could be identified with other head gear and clothes worn by the dead king to cause gods and demons to fear him. Renenutet was also one of the divine foster mothers who nourished the royal *ka* (vital force) of each king.

Even in her cobra manifestation, Renenutet was revered by farmers and housewives as a gracious and beautiful goddess. The cobra-shaped bowls and figurines commonly found in Ancient Egyptian houses probably represented Renenutet, the Mistress of Provisions. As Lady of the Granaries, she helped to protect Egypt's vital grain supplies from rats and other vermin. In the myth Astarte and the Sea, Renenutet is chosen by the gods to present the tribute demanded by the rapacious sea. This was probably because she was responsible for the good things of the earth.

Renenutet should probably be regarded as identical with Renenet, a goddess who formed a pair with Shai, the god of fate. Renenet was said to be "on the shoulder" of deserving people from birth, bringing them good fortune. In the Greco-Roman Period, her role as goddess of fortune was gradually taken over by Isis-Thermouthis.

> ***See also*** Astarte; Shai; Snakes
> ***References and further reading:***
> G. Hart. "Renenutet." In *A Dictionary of Egyptian Gods and Goddesses.* London: 1986, 182–185.
> J. Leibovitch. "Gods of Agriculture and Welfare in Ancient Egypt." *Journal of Near Eastern Studies* 12 (1953): 73–113.
> ***Primary sources:***
> PT 256, 622; CT 575; Astarte and the Sea

SATET (SATIS) **AND ANUKET** (ANUKIS)

Satet and Anuket were two goddesses worshipped in the region of the First Cataract of the Nile. Satet, Lady of Elephantine, was shown as a mature woman wearing a version of the crown of Upper Egypt decorated with antelope horns. Anuket, Lady of Nubia, was shown as a young woman wearing a feather headdress. Her sacred animal was the gazelle, a creature admired by the Egyptians for its delicate beauty. Both goddesses are called daughters of Ra, but from the late Middle Kingdom onward they formed a triad with Khnum, the ram god of Elephantine (modern Aswan). It is not clear whether Satet and Anuket were regarded as mother and daughter or as senior and junior consorts. Khnum, Satet, and Anuket were probably treated as a group because all three were linked to the annual Nile flood.

A rock shrine on the island of Elephantine was one of Egypt's most ancient holy places. It was often thought of as the "source" of the inundation. River-worn pebbles in the forms of pregnant or nursing women found in the shrine suggest that it was dedicated to a fertility goddess. In later times the most important **nilometer** in Egypt was situated in the temple of Satet on Elephantine. This measured the height of the inundation as it reached the Egyptian border. Satet was associated with the purifying powers of Nile water and desert spring water. Her sacred animal, the antelope, was renowned for its ability to find water in the desert. The Pyramid Texts mention the four water jars of Satet that are used to purify the dead king so that he can take his place among the gods. By the Greco-Roman Period, Satet (Mistress of the Water of Life) was identified with the star goddess Sopdet-Isis. The heliacal rising of Sopdet (Sirius) coincided with the coming of the inundation.

This awe-inspiring natural phenomenon became linked to the myth of the return of the Distant Goddess, the Eye of Ra. Satet seems to have represented the ferocious aspect of this goddess. In Pyramid Text 439, Satet, the Fiery One, claims to be a deity more powerful than Ra. In the Coffin Texts, Satet defends the dead against dangers from the south with her pain-inflicting arrows. As protector of Upper Egypt, Satet was sometimes paired with the warrior god Montu. Anuket, the beloved daughter of Ra, usually represented the pacified form of the Eye goddess. She controlled the fertilizing power of the Nile flood. Her breast milk nourished and healed, and she was one of the divine foster mothers of every Egyptian king.

> *See also* Eye of Ra; Khnum; Stars and Planets
>
> *References and further reading:*
>
> H. te Velde. "Some Remarks on the Structure of Egyptian Divine Triads." *Journal of Egyptian Archaeology* 57 (1971): 80–86.
>
> D. Valbelle. *Satis et Anoukis.* Mainz: 1981.
>
> *Primary sources:*
>
> PT 439, 508; CT 313; Famine stela

SEKHMET (SAKHMET)

Sekhmet was an aggressive solar goddess who was the instrument of divine retribution. She was shown with the body of a woman and a leonine head, often surmounted by a sun disk. Death first came into the world when the Eye of Ra was sent down as Sekhmet to punish rebellious humanity. "She who dances on blood" nearly destroyed the whole human race before she was tricked into stopping. As humans were said to have sprung from the tears of the Eye of Ra, Sekhmet was slaughtering her own children. She was a more protective mother to the kings of

Figure 39. Detail of a statue of Sekhmet-Mut from a temple at Thebes. The lion-headed goddess wears a wig surmounted by a solar disk with a uraeus. (Courtesy of Geraldine Pinch)

Egypt, and in Memphis she was worshipped as the consort of Ptah and the mother of Nefertem.

In the Pyramid Texts, Sekhmet was named as a parent of the king when he was reborn into the celestial afterlife. In the Coffin Texts, she was identified with the Red Crown of Lower Egypt and with the fire-spitting uraeus: "the serpent who is upon her father." She was said to be "the one who wields the knife" on the night of the great battle between the forces of order and chaos. In New Kingdom funerary literature, Sekhmet often stands in the solar barque to defend Ra from the Apophis serpent. Users of the Book of the Dead hoped to destroy their supernatural enemies "as Sekhmet the Great would."

King Rameses II claimed that Sekhmet the Great rode with him in his chariot, ready to destroy the enemy with her fiery breath. She seems to have embodied the negative qualities of the heat of the sun that could lead to sunstroke, drought, famines, and epidemics. Of all the archer goddesses in the Egyptian pantheon, Sekhmet was the most dreaded. Her arrows came to be personified as seven messengers who inflicted plague and destruction on humanity. As the controller of disease demons, Sekhmet became a patron goddess of medicine. From the Old Kingdom onward, the priests of Sekhmet seem to have been specialists in healing magic.

Sekhmet had to be propitiated during the dangerous transition from the old to the new year, when infectious diseases were a particular danger. Spells and rituals were used to transform the raging solar lioness into a beneficent goddess. From the New Kingdom onward, Sekhmet was mainly thought of as the aggressive aspect of greater goddesses: first of Hathor, then of Mut, and finally of Isis.

See also Bastet; Eye of Ra; Feline deities; Hathor; Mut; Ptah

References and further reading:

P. Germond. *Sekhmet et la protection du monde.* Geneva: 1981.

G. Pinch. *Magic in Ancient Egypt.* Austin, TX: 1995, 37–38, 138–143.

Primary sources:

PT 248; CT 311; BD 57, 145, 179b; BHC; Qadesh inscriptions; Book of the Last Day
of the Year; Sekhmet litany; Magical statue texts

SERQET (SERKET, SELKIS)

The goddess Serqet was usually shown as a woman with a scorpion on her head
(see Figure 20) or as a scorpion with the head and torso of a woman. She controlled the breath of life and was one of the four goddesses who traditionally
protected the body and vital organs of a dead person. Serqet was also one of the
formidable deities who defended the divine mother and the boat of the sun god.
Scorpion charmers invoked the power of Serqet to drive away scorpions and
snakes.

Scorpion stings were a common hazard in Ancient Egypt. The female scorpion is larger than the male and has a greater supply of poison. Representations of
Serqet always show the tail raised in the stinging position. Scorpion stings cause a
burning pain and shortness of breath and can be fatal to young children and the
elderly. This seems to have led to the belief that Serqet could help the dead to
breathe again as part of the process of rebirth. To indicate that Serqet was a benevolent goddess, she was sometimes represented by a harmless type of water scorpion rather than the poisonous type. She was shown on the east side of coffins
and canopic chests as a guardian goddess. In the Book of Two Ways, Serqet is one
of the deities who guards a bend in the river on the watery route to paradise.

Scorpions and snakes were classed together as enemies of humanity and the
divine order, and many spells were devised to repel them. The Egyptians hoped
that by honoring the scorpion goddess, they could save themselves from all poisonous creatures. Serqet defended the sun god from the great snake Apophis,
and she appears in some narrative spells as the helper of her "sister" Isis.

One spell to drive out poison includes a story about how the pregnant Isis
fled to the marshes to hide from her brother, Seth. On her journey she was protected by seven scorpions, who were probably a sevenfold manifestation of
Serqet. Isis tried to shelter in a village. A rich woman refused to let Isis into her
house, but a poor marsh girl welcomed the goddess into her hut. The scorpions
were angry about this and decided to punish the rich woman. They placed all
their poison in the tail of Tfn, the leading scorpion. Tfn crept into the rich
woman's house and stung her baby son. Isis was wakened by the rich woman's
cries and took pity on the child. She was able to drive out the burning poison

and make the child breathe again because she knew the true names of the seven scorpions. The rich woman was so grateful that she gave all her possessions to the poor girl in order to please the goddess. Myths of this type may have been acted out at a festival known from the Roman Period during which devotees of Isis handled live scorpions.

> *See also* Horus the Child; Isis; Sons of Horus
> *References and further reading:*
> F. Känel. *"La nèpe et le scorpion": un monographie sur la désse Serket*. Paris: 1984.
> P. Vernus. *The Gods of Ancient Egypt*. Translated by Jane Marie Todd. London and New York: 1998, 35.
> *Primary sources:*
> PT 308, 362, 555; BTW; True Name; PBM 9997 + 10309; Magical statue texts; Metternich Stela

SESHAT (SECHAT)

Seshat was the goddess who measured and recorded the world. As Lady of Builders she was the patroness of architecture, astronomy, and mathematics. Known as "she who is foremost in the library," Seshat was an assistant or female counterpart of Thoth, the god of wisdom and knowledge. She and Thoth fixed the length of a king's reign by inscribing his name on the leaves of the *ished* tree at Heliopolis.

Seshat usually wears a panther skin, a symbol of priestly office. She sometimes carries a palm frond carved with notches to mark the passing years. Her mysterious headdress consists of a seven-pointed star (or seven-petaled flower) topped by an object that may be a bow or an inverted pair of horns. The goddess known as Sefkhat-abwy (the Seven-Pointed One) is probably Seshat under another name.

As goddess of writing, Seshat was the keeper of royal annals and genealogies. She was shown recording the booty gained by kings in battle, perhaps as a reminder that a share was due to the gods. Seshat was even said to descend into the underworld to record everything in the realm of the dead.

From as early as the Second Dynasty, she was shown assisting kings to lay out the foundations for temples and align them with stars and planets. In the divine realm, Seshat was in charge of building the mansions of the gods. She was sometimes assisted in this task by the gods of sight and hearing. Seshat also built "mansions in the West" for the fortunate dead.

Seshat was occasionally identified as an aspect of another helper of the dead, the goddess Nephthys. In a Coffin Texts spell, Seshat is said to be angry at a child she gives birth to, just as later tradition made Nephthys reject her son, Anubis. In other Coffin Texts, Thoth and Seshat "bring writings to a man in the

Figure 40. Seshat and Thoth inscribing a king's name on the leaves of the ished *tree. Relief in the Ramesseum at Thebes. (Courtesy of Richard Pinch)*

realm of the dead." These writings were the spells that would help the dead person to vanquish the terrors of the underworld and become a powerful spirit.

    See also Nephthys; Thoth

    References and further reading:

    G. A. Wainwright. "Seshat and the Pharaoh." *Journal of Egyptian Archaeology* 26 (1940): 30–40.

    Primary sources:

    PT 364; CT 84, 709, 849

SETH (SET, SUTEKH)

Seth, the tumultuous god who was the enemy of his brother, Osiris, and the rival of Horus, was one of the five children of Nut and Geb. Seth's sister, Nephthys, and the foreign goddesses Anat and Astarte were among his consorts. Seth acts as a catalyst in Egyptian myth. His thoughtless actions are bad in themselves but can lead to good outcomes, such as that of Osiris becoming the ruler of the underworld. The brute strength of Seth was needed by the gods to defend the solar barque from the chaos monster.

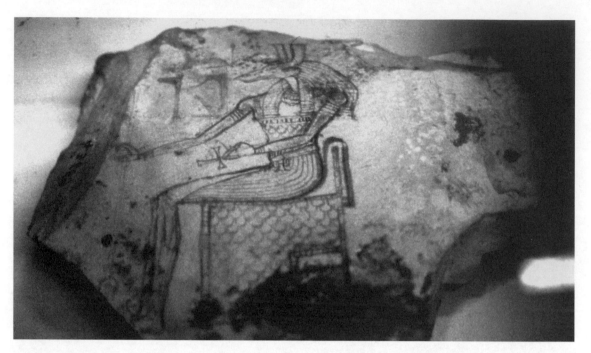

Figure 41. A votive ostracon in Cairo Museum with a drawing of Seth. He is shown with the head of an unknown animal. (Courtesy of Geraldine Pinch)

The cult of Seth seems to have originated in Upper Egypt, though he was later identified with foreign gods worshipped in the eastern Delta. In the Early Dynastic Period, Seth, Lord of Ombos, was the chief god of the eastern desert and its rich gold mines. In the western desert he remained the Lord of the Oases and their vineyards into the Greco-Roman Period. At all periods, Seth was associated with dangerous aspects of the desert such as flash floods and sandstorms. Many desert animals, particularly oryxes, wild asses, and the mythical griffin, were considered Sethian creatures. Seth himself was represented by a sinister imaginary animal. In myth, Seth takes the form of many different animals, such as bulls, pigs, hippopotami, wild asses, crocodiles, and panthers, to carry out destructive acts.

From the Pyramid Texts onward, Seth was accused of striking down Osiris. Vague allusions to Seth trampling or rending Osiris were eventually transformed into stories of complex murder plots. The two gods were often presented as opposites. Osiris could stand for order and everything that was Egyptian. Seth could stand for disorder and everything that was foreign. Osiris ruled the fertile black land of the Nile valley, and Seth the barren red land of the deserts. As the god "who causes storms and clouds," Seth was also the natural opponent of the solar sky falcon Horus the Elder. Alternatively, this conflict could be stated in terms of a dynastic feud and a struggle for justice between Seth the Usurper and Horus the Younger, the posthumous son of Osiris.

During this long struggle Seth was wounded in the testicles and Horus in the eyes. In the New Kingdom story, the Contendings of Horus and Seth, the two gods alternate between arguing their cases in front of the Divine Tribunal and fighting each other. Seth's main weapon is a gigantic mace or *was* scepter that only he can lift. He is presented as massively strong and monumentally stupid, like a giant in a fairy tale.

In temples of Horus, the story ends with a total military victory for Horus and annihilation for Seth and his followers. In other sources, terms for peace are agreed so that the Two Lords (Horus and Seth) can work together to unite Egypt and defend the cosmos. One of the secrets revealed in the royal Underworld Books was the joining of the Two Lords into one double-headed being to combat the forces of chaos in the hour of greatest danger. As "the great of strength in the Boat of Millions," Seth speared and bound Apophis every night (see Figure 43).

The concept of the perpetual struggle between Seth and Apophis was paired with a story of a single combat that took place in the mythical past. When the world was still directly ruled by the gods, Seth fought Yam, the insatiable sea, who was threatening to swallow the earth. The ending is missing in the only narrative version of this myth, but several New Kingdom spells claim that the magician will overcome demons just as Seth once overcame the sea monster.

Other New Kingdom texts describe Seth as committing a series of sacrilegious crimes such as felling sacred trees and hunting sacred fish, birds, and animals. He was also notorious for breaking sexual taboos. His lustful nature leads him into inappropriate heterosexual and homosexual encounters. In one myth he is punished for mating with the "seed goddess," who personified the semen of the creator. In another, Seth's attempt to sexually dominate his rival, Horus, leads to the unnatural birth of the moon god Thoth.

From the late New Kingdom onward, ritual scripts and narrative myths deal with attacks by Seth on the body of Osiris. Secretions from the corpse were said to play a vital role in making the Nile rise, crops grow, and women conceive children, so these were attacks on life itself. Seth disguises himself to try to steal the amulets protecting the body of Osiris. He is always recognized and brutally punished by Anubis and Thoth. At Edfu the priesthood of Horus celebrated a day of castrating Seth and "reducing him to pieces" in retaliation for Seth's mutilation of the body of Osiris and the Eye of Horus. The actual ritual involved the sacrifice and dismemberment of a wild ass in front of a cult state of Osiris.

By the Greco-Roman Period, Seth was vilified in most temples. The Greeks identified Seth with the monster Typhon, who rebelled against the gods and had to be destroyed by Zeus. Seth-Typhon was invoked in spells to kill the magician's enemies as he had killed his own brother, Osiris, or to separate lovers as he had separated Osiris and Isis.

> *See also* Anat; Anubis; Anti; Apophis; Astarte; Cattle; Eyes of Horus;
> Hippopotamus Goddesses; Horus; Isis; Moon; Nephthys; Osiris; Thoth
>
> *References and further reading:*
>
> J. G. Griffiths. *The Conflict of Horus and Seth from Egyptian and Classical Sources.* Liverpool: 1960.
>
> H. te Velde. *Seth, God of Confusion.* Leiden: 1977.
>
> *Primary sources:*
>
> PT 215, 222, 356, 359, 477; BD 39; H&S; Astarte and the Sea; P. Leiden I 343 + 345; P. Salt 825; PJ; PDM XII; PGM XXXVI; I&O

SEVEN HATHORS

The seven manifestations of Hathor presided over births and deaths. They pronounced the ultimate fate of all humans.

> *See also* Cattle; Hathor; Shai

SHAI (SHAY)

Shai was the personification of destiny. Every individual had his or her own *shai*, a personal destiny that helped to make that person unique. As a god, Shai might be shown in either human or snake form. He could be identified with any of the creator deities who shaped the destiny of the whole universe.

Shai was one of the deities credited with fixing the length of a person's life and the manner of his or her death. He also came to be associated with good or bad fortune in life. In the city of Alexandria, Shai was transformed into a snake god of fate and luck known as Agathos Daimon.

Shai was often paired with the goddesses Meskhenet or Renenutet, who presided over the vulnerable periods of a person's birth and infancy. In the Book of the Dead, Shai can be shown next to the scales in which the heart of the deceased person is weighed. Like the goddesses Meskhenet and Renenutet, he occasionally took the form of a "birth-brick" with a human head. These bricks were the supports on which Egyptian women squatted to give birth. As deities of the birth-bricks, Shai and his female counterparts helped the souls of the deceased to be reborn.

Egyptian thinkers debated how far a person's fate was predestined. Some Instruction Texts took the pessimistic view that it was impossible to evade your fate, but hymns and prayers claimed that gods such as Amun had the power to change a person's destiny and bestow extra years of life. A New Kingdom story tells how a longed-for son was born to the king and queen of Egypt. On the night of his birth, the Seven Hathors announced that the prince was destined to be killed by a snake, a crocodile, or a dog. The king tried to save his son by shutting him in a remote palace away from all animals. When he grew up, the prince begged to be released on the grounds that his fate was "in the heart of god." He traveled to the land of Naharin and married a princess who had also been imprisoned by her father. She saved the prince from his first fate, the snake. The prince managed to escape from his second fate, the dog, only to be seized by his third fate, the crocodile.

The end of the story is missing, but the last words imply that the prince may be able to save himself by fighting the crocodile's enemy. The prince in this story seems to have much in common with a god called Shed who became popular at the end of the New Kingdom. Shed, whose name means savior or protector, was shown as a young prince overcoming dangerous animals such as snakes, crocodiles, and lions. The story of the Doomed Prince seems to dramatize the Egyptian hope that human courage and divine intervention could save an individual from a bad *shai*.

> *See also* Crocodiles; Hathor; Renenutet
> *References and further reading:*
> S. Morenz. *Egyptian Religion.* London and Ithaca, NY: 1973, 66–74.
> J. Quaegebeur. *Le dieu égyptien Shai dans la religion et l'onomastique.* Orientalia Lovaniensia Analecta 2. Louvain, Belgium: 1975.
> *Primary sources:*
> BD 125; Amenemope; DP

SHED

Shed was a savior deity, shown as a prince wearing a circlet decorated with the head of an antelope.

> *See also* Horus the Child; Shai

SHENTAYET

Shentayet was a cow goddess often regarded as a form of Isis.

> *See also* Cattle; Sokar

SHEZMU

Shezmu was the wine-press god who slaughtered the enemies of the king and the sun god.

SHU (SCHU, CHOU) **AND TEFNUT** (TEFENET)

Shu and Tefnut were the children of the creator sun god. They were the first divine couple and formed the second generation in the family tree of deities known as the Ennead of Heliopolis. Shu was the god of dry, life-giving air and

Figure 42. Shu separates his children, the earth god Geb and the sky goddess Nut. Painting on a coffin from the Third Intermediate Period. (Fitzwilliam Museum, University of Cambridge)

sunlight, who first separated the earth from the sky. Tefnut may have been associated with some types of moisture, such as morning dew.

Shu and Tefnut were produced by an androgynous creator god, usually identified as Atum or Ra-Atum. He is said to have masturbated and swallowed his own semen in order to reproduce himself. As a result of this act, Shu was sneezed out and Tefnut was spat out. Atum then lovingly embraced his "fledglings."

At first, Shu and Tefnut were not fully differentiated from the creator. In the Coffin Texts they are often treated as a trinity: "the one who developed into three." This may be why the monotheistic theology of King Akhenaten found a place for Shu and Tefnut as aspects of the god of light. Some early statues of Akhenaten and his queen, Nefertiti, probably represent them as Shu and Tefnut.

In more orthodox Egyptian thought, some kind of separation was necessary for the process of creation to continue. Texts ranging in date from the Middle

Kingdom to the Greco-Roman Period describe how Shu and Tefnut left their father, either accidentally or in order to explore. They were soon lost in the darkness that surrounded the creator. The creator became lonely and anxious. He took the "sole eye from his forehead" and sent her out to seek for his lost children. Some versions imply that Shu and Tefnut were lost for a very long period. They seem to be adult when they return with the Eye of Ra.

The first sexual union of male (Shu) and female (Tefnut) produced two children, the earth god Geb and the sky goddess Nut. These two passionately embraced until they were separated by their father, Shu. This act of separation is one of the most commonly depicted mythical scenes in Egyptian art. Shu is shown in human form, with a feather on his head, trampling on the body of Geb and holding up the body of Nut. Shu becomes a cosmic giant "whose stride is the length of the sky." He was assisted by various deities known as "the supporters of Shu." The most important of these were the eight Heh gods whom Shu created out of his own bodily fluids.

By separating the earth and sky and making a void filled with air and sunlight, Shu allowed the process of creation to begin. He therefore counted as a creator deity. He was also one of the deities said to have ruled over Egypt after the departure of the sun god to the heavens. One list gives him a reign of 700 years. According to a late myth, he eventually lost his throne and his consort, Tefnut, to his son, Geb.

Tefnut, "the greatly beloved daughter," was sometimes identified with two other "daughters" of the creator sun god: Maat, the personification of the divine order, and the Eye of Ra. In some versions of the story of the Eye goddess, Hathor-Tefnut, the fiery solar eye, quarrels with her father and goes to live in the desert in the form of a savage lioness. Her brother, Shu, is sometimes named as the god who persuades her to return.

Shu and Tefnut were also identified with the twin Lions of the Horizon. They are shown as two lions or spotted great cats, facing away from each other with the sun on the horizon between them. These lions had various temporal meanings. They could represent yesterday and tomorrow or two forms of time: *nḥḥ* (eternal recurrence) and *ḏt* (eternal sameness).

See also Aten; Atum; Eye of Ra, Feline Deities; Geb; Maat; Onuris

References and further reading:

H. te Velde. "Schu." In *Lexicon der Ägyptologie V.* Wiesbaden: 1984, 735–737 (in English).

S. West. "The Greek Version of the Legend of Tefnut." *Journal of Egyptian Archaeology* 55 (1969): 161–183.

Primary sources:

PT 600; CT 76, 78, 80; BD 17; BHC; HMP; MT; BRP; Ismailia naos; EofS

SIA AND HU (HW)

Sia and Hu were the principles of creative thought and speech personified as gods. Sia has also been translated as perception or insightful planning and Hu as authority or authoritative utterance. Sia and Hu, along with a third deity, Heka (Magic), were the forces the creator used to make the world and the divine order.

As deities, Sia and Hu were said to have sprung from blood that dripped from the penis of Ra. The two gods were regarded as the constant companions of the creator sun god. In the Pyramid Texts, Sia "who is at the right hand of Ra" is in charge of wisdom and carrying the god's book. He is also described as being "in" the eye of Ra, so that the sun god can see and understand everything that happens in the world. In the Coffin Texts, Hu is called "the one who speaks in the darkness," presumably the primeval dark before light was created.

A Middle Kingdom text asks how the creator, who has Sia, Hu, and Maat (the divine order) always with him, can have allowed Egypt to descend into chaos. In New Kingdom Underworld Books, Sia and Hu are often shown standing in the solar barque with Ra. Sia acts as a spokesman for Ra during the nocturnal journey of the sun. He gives the order to open each of the twelve gates of the underworld.

> *See also* Eye of Ra; Maat; Ra
>
> *References and further reading:*
>
> S. Bickel. *La cosmogonie égyptienne avant le Nouvel Empire.* Orbis Biblicus et Orientalis 134. Fribourg, Switzerland, and Göttingen, Germany: 1994, 100–112.
>
> E. Hornung. *Conceptions of God in Ancient Egypt: The One and the Many.* Translated by J. Baines. Ithaca, NY: 1982, 76–77.
>
> *Primary sources:*
>
> PT 250; CT 261, 335, 1128, 1136; BD 174; Ipuur; BOG; BOD

SNAKES

Antisnake spells are among the oldest of all Egyptian texts, and many magical objects show deities helping humanity by overcoming poisonous snakes. Mythical snakes were found on both sides of the battle between order and chaos. Several creator deities had a primeval snake form. The ability to shed their skins made snakes an obvious symbol of eternal renewal. The cobra, who rears up and spits poison at anything that threatens her young, was adopted as a general symbol of female divinity. The uraeus on royal crowns had a mythical precedent in the cobra goddess who protected the creator sun god in the First Time. Yet the greatest enemy of the sun god was Apophis, a giant serpent with

Figure 43. Seth spears the chaos serpent Apophis when he attacks the solar barque. The barque is towed through the Underworld by jackals and cobras. Illustration from the funerary papyrus of Herweben. (Museum of Fine Arts, Boston)

crushing coils and hypnotic eyes. An Egyptian proverb states: "One should welcome the uraeus and spit on Apophis."

The Greek term *uraeus* probably comes from an Egyptian word *iaret*, which means "the one who rears up." When the creator god Ra-Atum lost his children in the dark primeval waters, he sent his Sole Eye to look for them. The Eye goddess returned with the lost children to find that Ra-Atum had grown a new eye. She was enraged, but Ra-Atum transformed her into a snake with power over all other deities. Her fiery poison destroyed anyone who challenged the sun god and his rightful heirs. All snake goddesses could be identified with this fire-spitting cobra, whatever their other functions. Isis was clever enough to turn this serpent power against Ra in order to win the throne of Egypt for her future son. When the sun god withdrew to the heavens, he charged Geb with controlling the dangerous serpents who lived under the earth.

Three important cobra goddesses were associated with the three environments where snakes were most often encountered: marshes (Wadjyt), cornfields (Renenutet), and desert hills (Meretseger). Like the divine cow, the cobra goddess could be shown protecting an infant god in a papyrus thicket. This god is sometimes named as Nefertem, the child in the lotus. Wadjyt's name links her with Egyptian words meaning papyrus and freshness or greenness. She could embody the constantly renewed vitality of the marsh vegetation.

Renenutet, "the good snake," was the goddess of fields, granaries, and kitchens. She ensured a bountiful harvest for the living and continuing nourishment for the *kas* of the dead. The snake deity, Nehebkau ("the numerous of coils"), was considered to be her son. In the Pyramid Texts, Nehebkau feeds the dead king and acts as his messenger, but only after he has been subdued by the finger of Atum.

Meretseger was another snake deity who was not always benevolent. She was the goddess of the pyramid-shaped mountain peak that overlooked the Valley of the Kings and the Valley of the Queens at Thebes (see Figure 5). Her name means "the one who loves silence." The artists who worked on the royal tombs felt that they needed to propitiate Meretseger before they could work safely in her domain. One of them describes Meretseger as striking like a lion when she was angry but coming like a sweet breeze when she was appeased.

Meretseger's mountain was one of the entrances to the underworld. Snakes were said to sleep below the earth like the dead every night and come alive again by day. The visions of the underworld painted on the walls of the royal tombs writhe with snakes. Snake-headed demons and fire-spitting snakes punish evil souls. Each of the twelve gates of the underworld has a snake guardian, and the solar barque and the corpse of Osiris were protected by the coils of the *mehen* snake, a kind of counter-Apophis (see, for example, Figure 38). Time itself was depicted as an endless snake that swallows up the hours. One of these images, the "Ouroboros" or "tail-in-mouth" serpent, passed into other cultures as a symbol of infinity (see Figure 18).

> ***See also*** Amun; Atum; Apophis; Eye of Ra; Ra; Renenutet; Shai; Two Ladies
> ***References and further reading:***
> E. Hornung. *The Valley of the Kings: Horizon of Eternity.* London and New York: 1990, 74–84, 155–163.
> A. I. Sadek. *Popular Religion in Egypt during the New Kingdom.* Hildesheim, Germany: 1987, 118–124.
> ***Primary sources:***
> Amenemope; Neferabu stela; BD 87; True Name; Ad; BOG; BOE; BHC

SOBEK (SUCHOS)

Sobek, the "raging one," was shown as a crocodile or as a man with the head of crocodile wearing an *atef* crown. He was mainly worshipped in areas of the country where the Nile crocodile was a dangerous predator. Sobek was said to be the son of Neith, a goddess who embodied the primeval waters. His consort was sometimes Hathor and sometimes the harvest goddess Renenutet. From the New Kingdom onward, he was regarded as a form of the creator sun god "in his identity of Sobek-Ra."

At Krokodilopolis in the Fayum, Sobek was praised as the one "who rose out of the primeval waters, the great male being, the lord of the floating islands." He was honored everywhere as a god of water. Sobek was the Lord of the

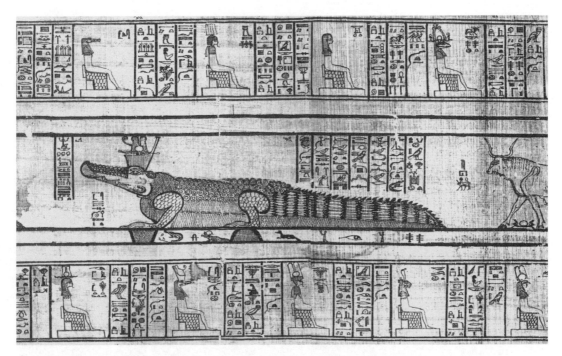

Figure 44. Sobek in crocodile form as Lord of the Fayum in the Book of the Fayum. (Carsten Niebuhr Institute of Near Eastern Studies)

Winding Waterway, the Lord of the Nile, and the one "who greens the Two Banks," an epithet he shared with the inundation god Hapy. As Lord of the Marsh, Sobek was particularly associated with the marshes that lay between the Nile valley and the edge of the desert. In the celestial realm, Sobek inhabited a glittering mansion in the liminal region of the horizon.

People who worked on the Nile had good reason to fear and respect crocodiles. Sobek seems to have become the patron god of fishermen. A myth mentioned in the Coffin Texts tells how Isis cut off the hands of her son Horus and threw them in the river. Ra ordered Sobek to retrieve the hands of Horus. Sobek was unable to do so until he invented a fish trap to catch the hands. Many fish were regarded as creatures of chaos, so as a fish eater, Sobek was helping to establish order.

On other occasions, however, Sobek was counted among the enemies of the divine order. In one spell in the Coffin Texts, Sobek "the rebel" is held responsible for mutilating the body of the good god Osiris. Sobek was sometimes identified with the crocodile form of Seth, the slayer of Osiris. The Greco-Roman Period temple of Kom Ombo was jointly dedicated to Horus the Elder and Sobek. It is possible that at this site Sobek represented an acceptable manifesta-

Figure 45. Sokar, shown as a falcon-headed god, overcomes a chaos serpent in a cave guarded by the Aker sphinx. Detail from the Amduat (Book of that which is in the Underworld) painted in the tomb of Thutmose III at Thebes. (Courtesy of Nigel Strudwick)

tion of Seth and that the whole temple celebrated the reconciliation of the Two Lords for the good of Egypt.

See also Crocodiles; Hapy; Neith; Renenutet; Seth

References and further reading:

A. H. Gardiner. "Hymns to Sobek in a Ramesseum Papyrus." *Revue d'Egyptologie* 11 (1957): 43–56.

Primary sources:

PT 317; CT 158, 160, 268, 285, 991; BD 113; Kom Ombo texts; BOF

SOKAR (SOKER, SOKARIS)

The ancient god of the cemeteries of Memphis, Sokar became the god of death as a transformative process. His qualities were often combined with those of the chief god of Memphis and the god of the dead to form the tripartite deity Ptah-Sokar-Osiris. The annual Festival of Sokar was one of the great events of the Egyptian ritual calendar.

Sokar could be represented by a human or hawk head emerging from a mound or chest. He could also be shown as a shrouded hawk or as a hawk-headed man or mummy. The silver hawk-headed **anthropoid coffin** of Sheshonq I (c. 945–924 BCE) was probably intended to transform the dead king into Sokar.

As a chthonic deity, Sokar had to be appeased when canals were dug, fields were plowed, or underground tombs were built. He was also a divine craftsman, responsible for making the silver bowls in which the feet of the dead were washed. At some point this aspect of Sokar seems to have been transferred to Ptah. Ptah and Sokar could be paired as creator deity and god of the dead as Ra and Osiris often were.

As early as the Old Kingdom, Sokar was said to be the name of Osiris after he was murdered by his brother Seth. In the Book of What Is in the Underworld, Sokar presides over a snake-infested desert region that must be crossed by the sun god and the royal dead. Sokar, Lord of the Mysterious Region, dwells in a cavern guarded by the two-headed Aker-sphinx. There he repeatedly overcomes a multiheaded chaos serpent. In later Underworld Books, it is the body of Sokar-Osiris that lies in this mysterious cavern waiting for the reviving light of the sun. The spirits of the dead were thought to join in the Festival of Sokar, which seems to have celebrated the power to journey between the realms of the living and the dead. The image of the god was dragged through the necropolis in his *henu* barque, a special boat decorated with images of fish and antelopes. Sokar was accompanied by five daughters of Ra in the forms of geese.

Statuettes of Ptah-Sokar-Osiris placed in tombs sometimes contain copies of the Book of the Dead. Others conceal **corn mummies**, symbolic bodies of Sokar-Osiris, to help the tomb owner attain resurrection. Figures of Sokar were prepared as part of the month-long Khoiak Festival, the annual reenactment of the mysteries of Osiris. The instructions for making these figures were said to be based on a divine prototype. The goddess Shentayet of Busiris made a new body for Sokar out of clay, dates, sweet-smelling spices, and precious stones and metals. The mixture was shaped into an egg and then divided among fourteen vessels. This links Sokar to lunar myths of destruction and renewal.

See also Cattle; Moon; Osiris; Ptah

References and further reading:

G. A. Gaballa and K. A. Kitchen. "The Festival of Sokar." *Orientalia* 38 (1969): 1–76.

C. Graindorge. "Sokar." In *The Oxford Encyclopaedia of Ancient Egypt III*, edited by D. B. Redford. Oxford and New York: 2001, 305–307.

Primary sources:

PT 532; CT 590; BD 185L; Ad 4th–5th hours; Khoiak texts

SONS OF HORUS

The four gods Imsety, Hapy (not the same as the inundation god), Duamutef, and Qebehsenuef were known collectively as the Sons of Horus. They were the traditional guardians of the four canopic jars used to hold mummified organs. Imsety generally protected the liver, Hapy the lungs, Duamutef the stomach, and Qebehsenuef the intestines. The four sons were also associated with the four directions (south, north, east, and west) and with four vital components for survival after death: the heart, the *ba,* the *ka,* and the mummy. Imsety is usually shown in full human form, but Hapy sometimes has the head of a baboon, Duamutef that of a jackal, and Qebehsenuef that of a hawk.

In the Pyramid Texts, the Children of Horus are invoked to protect "Osiris the king," support his body, and beat up his "great enemy." These roles are repeated in a Middle Kingdom ritual drama in which the Sons of Horus fight the Followers of Seth and then lift the body of Osiris into the heavens. Imsety, Hapy, Duamutef, and Qebehsenuef were sometimes identified with the four pillars that held up the sky.

Obscure passages in the Coffin Texts seem to name Isis and Horus the Elder as the parents of these four deities. Kinship terms were often used very loosely in Ancient Egypt, so son can just mean descendant. The Sons of Horus were sometimes treated as identical with the group of royal demigods known as the Souls of Pe and Nekhen. After the reign of Horus, the Souls ruled the kingdoms of Upper or Lower Egypt. According to one spell, the Souls of Nekhen (Hierakonpolis) could be quarrelsome and were not always willing to obey Horus.

From the New Kingdom onward, the Sons of Horus formed part of a group of seven star gods who helped Anubis to protect the body of Osiris. In the Book of the Dead, the sons are present when the dead are judged before Osiris. They were often shown standing on a blue lotus, like a fourfold version of the infant sun god who emerged from the primeval lotus (Figure 7).

The four sons came to be regarded as powerful protectors for all the dead. Pallbearers at funerals played the roles of the Sons of Horus carrying the corpse of Osiris. The sons were often named or shown on coffins and canopic chests, paired with the four protective goddesses: Isis, Nephthys, Neith, and Serqet. The heads of the four sons formed the stoppers for sets of canopic jars. If the internal organs were returned to a mummy, figures of the Sons of Horus were sewn to the mummy wrappings or placed inside the body cavity. Their function was to prevent any parts of the body being lost. The terrible fate of the body of Osiris was never to be repeated.

    See also Anubis; Horus; Osiris; Seth

References and further reading:
S. D'Auria et al. *Mummies and Magic.* Boston: 1988, 91–92, 117, 172.
J. H. Taylor. *Death and the Afterlife in Ancient Egypt.* London: 2001, 65–75.
Primary sources:
PT 541, 688; RDM; CT 157–158, 520–523; BD 112–113, 151; Triumph of Horus

SOPDET (SOTHIS)

Sopdet was the goddess of the Dog Star that heralded the inundation.

See also Isis; Satet and Anuket; Sopdu; Stars and Planets

SOPDU (SOPEDU, SOPED)

The warrior god Sopdu presided over the harsh environment of the eastern desert. Sopdu, Lord of the East, was one of the guardians of the four directions. As the "sharp-toothed one" he protected the dead from attackers from the east or southeast. He could be shown as a falcon perched on a standard or as a bearded man wearing a plumed headdress and carrying a battle-ax.

Some representations of Sopdu, Lord of the Foreign Lands, resemble the no-madic Bedouin tribesmen of the eastern desert and Sinai peninsula. From early times, Sopdu was revered as a protector of the turquoise mines of Sinai, where he was paired with Hathor, Lady of Turquoise.

Sopdu was sometimes called "the eastern Horus." In the Pyramid Texts, Horus-Sopdu is said to be the son of Sopdet and Sah, the astral forms of Isis and Osiris. Sopdu "of the shining plumes" was a form of the cosmic falcon who could be addressed as the oldest of beings. This Sopdu falcon dwelled in a sacred grove, which probably grew on the Primeval Mound.

Like other warrior deities, Sopdu had the epithet "great of strength." He habitually raised his hand in a threatening gesture to drive off supernatural foes such as the fearsome Crocodile of the South. The messengers of Sopdu were dreaded by the living. The evil dead could expect to be butchered in the Slaughter Yard of Sopdu.

See also Horus; Primeval Mound; Stars and Planets

References and further reading:
R. Giveon. "Soped in Sinai." In *Studien zu Sprache und Religion Ägyptens zu Ehren von Wolfhart Westendorf,* edited by F. Junge. Göttingen, Germany: 1984, 777–784.
I. W. Schumacher. *Der Gott Spodu, der Herr der Fremdländer.* Freiburg, Switzerland: 1988.
Primary sources:
PT 306; CT 270, 783; BD 130; HMP

SOTHIS

See Sopdet

SOULS OF PE AND NEKHEN

The Souls of Pe and Nekhen were two groups of demigods regarded as the divine ancestors of Egyptian kings. The Souls of Pe (Buto) have the heads of falcons, and the Souls of Nekhen (Hierakonpolis) have the heads of jackals.

See also Sons of Horus

SPHINX

The **sphinx** was a mythical beast with the body of a lion or lioness and the head of a different creature. The most common combination was the body of a lion and a human head with the face of a reigning king or queen. These sphinxes embodied the power and duty of the ruler to defend Egypt. Other sphinxes had the heads of rams, hawks, or even the Seth monster. These served as terrifying animated guardians for temples or tombs.

Standing sphinxes were usually shown trampling the enemies of Egypt and the divine order. Female sphinxes sometimes had wings, and it may be this form that influenced the development of the female sphinx of Greek mythology. A double sphinx known as the Aker was the guardian of the two horizons, the entrance and exit to the *Duat*, the Egyptian underworld. During the first millennium BCE, a sphinx god called Tutu became popular. He was usually shown as a standing sphinx with wings and a tail in the form of a snake. Tutu was one of the monstrous offspring of the goddess Neith. He was invoked to keep enemies at a safe distance.

The best known of all Egyptian sphinxes is the Great Sphinx of Giza. This was carved out of an extremely faulty piece of an outcrop of rock during the twenty-sixth century BCE to act as a gigantic guardian for the royal cemeteries of Memphis. Both in ancient and modern times the Great Sphinx has generated a mythology of its own. From the New Kingdom onward, it was identified with a Caananite desert god called Hauron or Hwl and worshipped as a solar deity. The two great pyramids built for Khufu and Khephren came to be thought of as the mountains of the horizon with the sphinx as the sun rising between them.

A granite stela found between the front paws of the Great Sphinx describes how a prince named Thutmose once visited Giza to hunt desert animals. In his time (early fourteenth century BCE) the statue seems to have buried in the sand up to its head. Looking for shade in the heat of the day, Thutmose lay down in front of the statue and went to sleep. He dreamed that the Great Sphinx spoke to him "as a father speaks to his son," naming itself as Horemakhet (Horus of the Horizon) Khepri-Ra-Atum. The god complained that he was "ailing in all his limbs" because the sand had overwhelmed him. He promised that if the prince would free him from the encroaching sand, Thutmose would enjoy a long life and one day be king. When he awoke, Thutmose sent for numerous workers.

The remainder of the inscription is badly damaged, but we know that the helpful prince did become King Thutmose IV. Mud-brick walls that may have been intended to keep sand away from the Great Sphinx bear his **cartouches**. Thutmose's inscription uses the traditional motif of the creator sun god (the sphinx) under attack by the forces of chaos (the desert sands) and needing to be helped to a rebirth.

To the Arab inhabitants of medieval Egypt, the Great Sphinx became known as the Father of Terror. The statue was believed to guard hidden treasure, which it sometimes revealed to the deserving. According to one legend, the Great Sphinx kept the sand from overwhelming Giza until a zealous holy man destroyed its power by mutilating the statue's face. In modern times, the Great Sphinx has been seen as the guardian of the hidden wisdom of the lost kingdom of Atlantis or as the symbol of an ancient galactic master race who built a second sphinx on Mars.

> **See also** Feline Deities; Horus; Montu; Ra; Seth
>
> **References and further reading:**
> P. Jordan., *Riddles of the Sphinx.* Stroud, England: 1998.
> G. Posener (ed.). "Sphinx." In *A Dictionary of Egyptian Civilization.* Translated by A. MacFarlane. Paris: 1962, 267–268.
>
> **Primary sources:**
> Sphinx stela of Amenhotep II; Sphinx stela of Thutmose IV

STARS AND PLANETS

Individual stars and planets were considered to be celestial manifestations of major deities, such as Horus, whereas the **circumpolar stars** were the glittering, unchanging spirits of the vindicated dead. The Pyramid Texts contain many references to the dead king becoming a star. Some Egyptologists believe that this "stellar afterlife" was older than the "solar afterlife," in which the fate of the king and humanity was tied up with the sun god. Others argue that the sun, the moon, and the stars all formed part of a great celestial circuit in which the dead took part in various ways.

In Pyramid Texts spell 245, the sky goddess Nut assigns the dead king a place in heaven as the Lone Star (Venus?). The image of Nut as a naked woman stretched above the earth has recently been interpreted as a representation of the Milky Way rather than of the sky in general. Some Egyptian texts refer to stars sailing on the sea below the belly of Nut. The belly or flanks of Nut in cow form can be patterned with stars. The markings of the celestial cow some-times resemble those of a leopard. In the Predynastic Period the sky may have been imagined as a giant panther or leopardess who devoured the stars each morning. In the theology of the Pyramid Texts, the creator god could be thought of as absorbing the power of the stars (all the other gods) each dawn to create one celestial power, the sun. This process was reversed each evening when the sun set and the one god became many again.

The Egyptians were aware that not all stars held a fixed place in the sky. Observations of the procession of the equinoxes may have had a profound im-pact on the formative period for Egyptian myth. A few scholars even trace all conflicts and fatalities among the gods to this origin. The **Decan stars** were thought of as joining Osiris in the underworld before rising from the dead when they became visible again above the horizon at dawn. Star clocks were painted inside some Middle Kingdom coffins. Their main purpose was to incorporate the spirit of the coffin owner into this stellar cycle of death and regeneration.

The most important of the Decan stars was Sirius. This star was repre-sented by a goddess known to the Egyptians as Sopdet and to the Greeks as Sothis. She was shown as a woman wearing a crown surmounted by a five-pointed star. Each year the period when Sirius rose above the horizon at dawn coincided with the coming of the inundation. This event also marked the start of the Egyptian year. In the Pyramid Texts, Sopdet is named as a manifestation of the goddess Isis. Later in Egyptian history, Sopdet was equated with the Eye of Ra and the heliacal rising of her star was linked to the myth of the return of the Distant Goddess.

Sopdet formed a triad with the star gods Sah and Sopdu-Hor. Sah is almost certainly the great southern constellation known to the Greeks as Orion. The Pyramid Texts describe Sah "of the long stride" as a stellar manifestation of Osiris. As the Lone Star, Sopdu-Hor acted as the herald of the sun god morning and evening. Various forms of Horus were equated with other planets such as Mars, Jupiter, and Saturn. It is possible that the planet Mercury was associated with Seth.

The constellation we know as the Great Bear was interpreted by the Egyptians as several deities guarding Seth's bull form or its severed leg. This is one of the few recognizable parts of the star maps that decorate the ceilings of some royal tombs. The Babylonian concept of the stars of the zodiac was intro-duced into Egypt by the Greeks. Three Decan stars were assigned to each zodia-cal sign. Nut could be shown on coffins or temple ceilings surrounded by the hours of the day and night and the twelve signs of the zodiac.

See also Boats; Eye of Ra; Feline Deities; Hippopotamus Goddesses; Horus; Isis; Moon; Nut; Osiris; Satet and Anuket; Seshat

References and further reading:

J. P. Allen. "Cosmology of the Pyramid Texts." In J. P. Allen et al. *Religion and Philosophy in Ancient Egypt.* Yale Egyptological Studies 3. New Haven: 1989, 1–28.

Jane B. Sellars. *The Death of the Gods in Ancient Egypt* (Ebook). Mighty Words Ebook: 2000.

Primary sources:

PT 219, 245, 273–274, 422, 466, 670; BD 17; BofNut; Astronomical ceilings

TATJENEN (TATENEN)

Tatjenen was the god of the Primeval Mound and the depths of the earth.

> *See also* Primeval Mound; Ptah

TAWERET (TWERET, TAURT, THOERIS)

Taweret was an apotropaic goddess often shown with the head and body of a hippopotamus, the breasts of a fecundity figure, the paws of a lion, and the tail of a crocodile.

> *See also* Hippopotamus Goddesses

TAYET

Tayet was the goddess of weaving and mummy wrappings.

TEFNUT (TEFENET)

Tefnut was the daughter of Atum and the twin sister of Shu.

> *See also* Shu and Tefnut

THOTH

Thoth was the god of wisdom and secret knowledge who invented writing and the different languages of humanity. As a lunar deity, Thoth was the deputy of the sun god, Ra. He mediated between the Two Fighters, Horus and Seth, and returned the estranged Eye of Ra to her father. As the divine physician, Thoth used his magical powers to heal the wounded Eye of Horus. Thoth could be shown as a "beautiful" baboon or as an ibis or an ibis-headed man. Ra was said to have created the baboon form of Thoth to shine in the night sky and the ibis form to act as a messenger between earth and heaven.

Thoth was sometimes called the god "without a mother." One text states that Thoth came "from the lips of Ra" to uphold *maat,* the divine order. He was also said to have sprung from the forehead of Seth after this god swallowed some of the semen of his rival, Horus. At his main cult center of Hermopolis Magna, Thoth, Lord of the Ogdoad, was worshipped as a self-creating deity who produced the cosmic egg on the Island of Flame. As a moon god he was pictured crossing the night sky in a boat, but Thoth could also be the navigator of the boat of the sun god.

Thoth, the "excellent of understanding," observed and wrote down everything that happened and reported it to Ra every morning. As the record keeper of the gods he was paired with the librarian goddess Seshat. Thoth and Seshat knew the future as well as the past. They inscribed a person's fate on the bricks on which their mother gave birth and the length of a king's reign on the leaves of the *ished* tree (see Figure 40).

Thoth set a divine example as a just judge and an incorruptible official. He lifted Maat, the goddess of justice, to her father, Ra. Thoth was responsible for framing and enforcing the laws of *maat*. In this role he could be either a gracious peacemaker or a merciless executioner. During the conflict between Seth and Osiris, Thoth acted as the advocate of the murdered Osiris before the Divine Tribunal. His spells and amulets prevented Seth from destroying the mummy of Osiris in its eternal resting place. Thoth gave his protection to Isis and healed her infant son, Horus, in the marshes of Chemmis.

The New Kingdom story, The Contendings of Horus and Seth, pictures Thoth as the secretary of the Ennead of Heliopolis. He writes several letters on behalf of the Ennead as they struggle to decide between Horus and Seth, and he offers sensible advice to the sun god. When Isis literally loses her head at one point in the conflict, it is Thoth who gives her a new one. In earlier sources it is the damaged Eye of Horus that Thoth "makes new." Thoth's offering of the whole eye (the *wedjat*) to Horus and Horus's offering of it to Osiris became the precedent for all offerings to gods and spirits.

From the Middle Kingdom onward, Thoth was shown as an ape or an ibis-headed man holding out the *wedjat* eye. In some cases this eye should be interpreted as the Eye of Ra rather than the Eye of Horus. The Eye goddess who was the estranged daughter of Ra was too powerful to be overcome by force. Ra chose Thoth to fetch this Distant Goddess back from a remote desert. Disguised as a baboon or monkey, Thoth accomplished his task through humility, cunning, and perseverance. According to one account he had to ask the goddess to come home 1,077 times. Thoth was given Nehemtawy, a pacified version of the Distant Goddess, as his consort.

Thoth played an important role in everyone's afterlife. In the Pyramid Texts the dead kings fly up to the heavens on the wings of Thoth. In the Middle Kingdom Book of Two Ways, the Mansion of Thoth provides a safe haven for spirits who can use his magic to get past the demons of the underworld. Some of the royal Underworld Books of the New Kingdom name Thoth as presiding over the mystical union of Ra and Osiris that allowed the dead to reawaken each night. In the Book of the Dead, Thoth stands ready to record the verdict when the heart of the deceased is weighed against the feather of *maat* (see Figure 7). Those who feared failure asked Thoth to plead for them as he had once pleaded for Osiris. All funerary spells could be regarded as works of Thoth. A tradition grew up that Thoth had written forty-two books containing all the knowledge needed by humanity. Some of this was occult knowledge to be revealed only to initiates who would not misuse the power it gave them. The Greeks identified Thoth with their messenger god, Hermes. The body of literature known as the Hermetica claimed to preserve the teachings of Hermes Trismegistus (Thoth the Thrice Great). Hermes Trismegistus was eventually reinterpreted as a great thinker who had lived thousands of years in the past.

See also Anubis; Baboons; Birds; Eye of Ra; Eyes of Horus; Horus; Isis; Maat; Magicians; Moon; Ogdoad of Hermopolis; Osiris; Ra; Seshat; Wepwawet

References and further readings:

J. C. Bleeker. *Hathor and Thoth.* Leiden: 1973.

D. M. Doxey. "Thoth." In *The Oxford Encyclopaedia of Ancient Egypt,* vol. 3, edited by D. B. Redford. Oxford and New York: 2001, 398–400.

Primary sources:

PT 359; BTW; CT 277; BD 17–18, 20, 125, 182; Ad; BOE; H&S; Magical statue texts; PJ; Metternich Stela; Setna cycle; EofS; Asclepius

TWO LADIES

The Two Ladies were Nekhbet (Nechbet), the vulture goddess of Upper Egypt (the south), and Wadjyt (Wadjet, Ouadjet, Uto), the cobra goddess of Lower Egypt (the north). From the Early Dynastic Period onward, the Two Ladies were the chief divine protectors of the king. As vulture and cobra, or as twin cobras, they were often featured on royal headdresses, jewelry, and furniture. Nekhbet was identified with the White Crown of Upper Egypt and Wadjyt with the Red (sometimes green) Crown of Lower Egypt.

Nekhbet's name means "she of Nekheb," an ancient town in the south of Egypt now known as El-Kab. Wadjyt may mean "the green or fresh one" or "she of the papyrus." The first **papyrus** plant was said to have come from the body of Wadjyt. Her chief cult area was the twin towns of Pe and Dep, home of legendary early kings of Egypt. These towns were later known as "the house of Wadjyt," a name rendered by the Greeks as Buto.

At his accession, each king was given the title He of the Two Ladies. In coronation scenes, the goddesses were often shown in human form on either side of the king. Wadjyt often appeared as the uraeus cobra on the king's forehead, and Nekhbet hovered above the king, shading and fanning him with her wings. The male equivalent was the Two Lords, Horus and Seth, who could also represent north and south. These two gods violently oppose each other in myth but periodically come together to support the king or the creator sun god. These

Figure 46. A king protected by the Two Ladies (Wadjyt and Nekhbet) and the Two Lords (Seth and Horus). Line drawing of a late New Kingdom relief in the temple of Khonsu at Karnak. (Art Resource)

moments of reconciliation could be symbolized in the form of a single deity with two heads. The Two Ladies have similar forms in royal jewelry. This suggests that Nekhbet and Wadjyt might once have been thought of as warring opposites, but no specific myths relating to their conflict survive.

Both goddesses were represented by dangerous creatures who needed to be appeased. Nekhbet took the form of the largest flying bird known to the Egyptians. There was a general fear of vultures devouring or dispersing bodies buried in the desert. Nekhbet could also appear as another dangerous animal, the long-horned wild cow of the marshlands. She was one of a group of cow deities who wet-nursed and protected the divine child in the marshes of Chemmis and the newly reborn king in the afterlife. This eventually led the Greeks to identify Nekhbet with their goddess of childbirth, Eileithyia. Statue groups show either a cow or a cobra in a papyrus thicket protecting the king as divine child.

As well as appearing as a cobra, Wadjyt could be shown as a woman with the head of a lioness. She was one of the goddesses identified with the destructive power of the solar Eye of Ra. Perhaps to balance this concept, Nekhbet could be associated with the light of the moon.

> *See also* Birds; Eye of Ra; Horus the Child; Moon; Seth; Snakes
> *References and further reading:*
> S. Johnson. *The Cobra Goddess of Ancient Egypt.* London: 1990.
> B. S. Lesko. "The Two Ladies: Vestiges of the Remote Past." In *The Great Goddesses of Egypt.* Norman, OK: 1999, 64–80.
> *Primary sources:*
> PT 44, 662; CT 952; BD 15

WADJYT (WADJET, OUADJET, UTO)

Wadjyt was the cobra goddess of Lower Egypt.

> *See also* Two Ladies

WEPWAWET (UPWAUT)

Wepwawet was a jackal god whose name means the Opener of the Ways. He was most commonly shown as a standing jackal on a standard. Standards of this type were carried before the king on ceremonial occasions and into battle. Wepwawet's animal form was later reinterpreted as a wolf, and his cult center at modern Assiut was named Lykopolis (Wolf-Town) by the Greeks.

Wepwawet may originally have been a title of the archaic jackal god Sed. The Heb Sed, the great festival at which the king of Egypt renewed his strength and power, was named after this deity. Egyptian kings were identified with Wepwawet, "the swift-roving jackal," when they defended their borders, so during the Heb Sed the king had to run a race to prove his fitness to rule. There was one protective Wepwawet for Upper Egypt and one for Lower Egypt.

In death, the king might become a god by assuming the jackal-face of Wepwawet. Spells in the Pyramid Texts and the Coffin Texts record Wepwawet helping the dead ascend to the heavens and opening "a good path" for them through the dangerous landscapes of the afterlife. At Abydos, he performed this service for the murdered god Osiris. There he was identified with Horus or Anubis, the loyal sons of Osiris who helped him to rise from his inert state to become the king of the underworld. Wepwawet also sniffed out and punished the enemies of Osiris.

Wepwawet's role as a kind of celestial guide dog made him a popular deity with ordinary people who faced dangerous journeys in life or death. Like Anubis, Wepwawet was Lord of the Sacred Land. This meant that he was a supernatural guardian of the desert cemeteries. In the Book of the Dead, Wepwawet is one of the council of seven gods who guard the twenty-first and final gate on the road to the throne room of Osiris. Opener of the Ways is also said to be a name of Thoth, who makes the good things of paradise accessible to those who obey the laws of *maat*.

See also Anubis; Osiris; Thoth
References and further reading:
H. Frankfort. *Kingship and the Gods.* Chicago: 1948, 92–97, 204–205.
T. A. H. Wilkinson. *Early Dynastic Egypt.* London and New York: 1999, 198–199, 297–298.
Primary sources:
PT 21, 482, 734; CT 345, 845, 953; Ikhernofret stela; BD 145, 182

WERET-HEKAU

Weret-Hekau (the Great of Magic) was a goddess with lion and snake forms who protected and nourished the king.

See also Isis

WOSRET

Wosret was a Theban goddess whose name meant "the Female Powerful One."

See also Eye of Ra

4

EGYPTIAN MYTH: ANNOTATED PRINT AND NONPRINT RESOURCES

PRINT RESOURCES

General Works on Egyptian Culture

James P. Allen. *Middle Egyptian: An Introduction to the Language and Culture of Hieroglyphs.* Cambridge: Cambridge University Press, 2000.

> A good place to start for anyone who would like to try reading some Ancient Egyptian texts in their original language and script. The lessons on Middle Egyptian grammar are interleaved with essays on the geography, history, and culture of Ancient Egypt. Several of these essays discuss creation myths.

John Baines and Jaromir Malek. *Atlas of Ancient Egypt.* Rev. ed. New York: Checkmate Books, 2000.

> An excellent introduction to the history and geography of Ancient Egypt with a superb range of maps. The "Gazetteer of Archaeological Sites" includes concise information on all the major temples and royal tombs. There is an essay on religion and a list of important deities.

Erik Hornung. *Idea into Image: Essays on Ancient Egyptian Thought.* Translated by Elizabeth Bredeck. Princeton, NJ: Timken, 1992.

> This book makes complex ideas accessible to readers with little prior knowledge of Ancient Egypt. The nine essays explore what the Egyptians thought about time and space, the nature and origins of their world, and the elements that made up a person.

Antonio Loprieno (ed.). *Ancient Egyptian Literature: History and Forms.* Leiden and New York: E. J. Brill, 1996.

> Essays on all periods and genres of Ancient Egyptian literature. Most are in English and suitable for readers with little prior knowledge of Ancient Egypt. In the chapter "Myth and Literature," John Baines concludes that although myth was not dominant in Egyptian "high culture," it was important in literature for over 2,000 years.

Gay Robins. *The Art of Ancient Egypt.* London: British Museum Press, 1997.

> A well-illustrated introduction to Egyptian art that takes a chronological approach. Mythological themes found in the art are traced over long periods of time. This book is unusual in doing full justice to the last thousand years of Pharaonic culture.

Jack M. Sasson (ed. in chief). *Civilizations of the Ancient Near East.* 4 vols. New York: Scribners, 1995.

> These volumes cover the history and culture of all the major civilizations of the Ancient Near East. There is a chapter titled "Myth and Mythmaking" for each culture. The one for Egypt, by Jacobus van Dijk, is a model of clarity. Also of interest are the chapters "Ancient Egyptian Religious Iconography," by Erik Hornung; "Tales of Magic and Wonder from Ancient Egypt," by Susan Tower Hollis; and "Death and the Afterlife in Ancient Egyptian Thought," by Leonard H. Lesko.

Ian Shaw and Paul Nicholson. *British Museum Dictionary of Ancient Egypt.* London: British Museum Press, 1995.

> A reliable source of information on all aspects of Ancient Egypt. There are numerous entries on Egyptian deities, each with a short bibliography.

David P. Silverman (ed.). *Ancient Egypt.* London: Piatkus, 1997.

> A beautifully illustrated book written by an international team of Egyptologists. It is divided into three main sections: The Egyptian World; Belief and Ritual; and Art, Architecture, and Language. Three chapters— "The Boundaries of Knowledge," "The Celestial Realm," and "The Life of Ritual"—are outstanding.

Egyptian Religion and Myth

Many more specialized works are cited in the endnotes to "Introduction" and "Mythical Time Lines" and in the suggestions for further reading in "Deities, Themes, and Concepts."

James P. Allen. *Genesis in Egypt: The Philosophy of Ancient Egyptian Creation Accounts.* 2d ed. Yale Egyptological Studies 2. San Antonio, TX: Van Siclen Books, 1995.

> This short book is essential reading for anyone interested in ancient creation myths and cosmologies. It examines the elements of the Egyptian universe, the process and means of creation, and the nature of the creator. Annotated translations are given of sixteen key texts.

Rudolph Anthes. "Mythology in Ancient Egypt." In *Mythologies of the Ancient World,* edited by Samuel Noel Kramer. Garden City, NY: Doubleday, 1961, 15–92.

> A summary of the main sources for Egyptian myth. There are detailed discussions of a selection of myths, such as those relating to the lunar Eye of Horus. Anthes stresses that "continuous change of mythological conceptions" took place.

Jan Assmann. *Egyptian Solar Religion in the New Kingdom: Re, Amun, and the Crisis of Polytheism.* Translated by Anthony Alcock. London and New York: Kegan Paul International, 1995.

> Assmann is an influential and controversial Egyptologist. In this book he analyzes the **iconography** of the daily journey of the sun god and discusses the development of the idea of a unique creator deity within the **polytheistic** religion of Ancient Egypt. It is not aimed at beginners.

John Baines. "Egyptian Myth and Discourse: Myth, Gods, and the Early Written And Iconographic Record." *Journal of Near Eastern Studies* 50, no. 2 (1991): 81–105.

> This important article discusses the status of myth in Egyptian texts. It includes a valuable summary of the ideas of the leading German-language writers on Egyptian myth.

R. T. Rundle Clarke. *Myth and Symbol in Ancient Egypt.* London: Thames and Hudson, 1959.

> This book is primarily about developments in the mythology of Osiris from the Old Kingdom through to the end of the New Kingdom. There are summaries of some other important myths and a useful chart of religious symbols.

H. Frankfort. *Ancient Egyptian Religion*. New York: Columbia University Press, 1948.

> A short book that is still worth reading. In the section "Change and Permanence in Literature and Art," Frankfort argues that the "coherent myths preserved in writing" belong "to the repertoire of popular story-tellers."

George Hart. *A Dictionary of Egyptian Gods and Goddesses*. London and Boston: Routledge and Kegan Paul, 1986.

> The best available A–Z of Ancient Egyptian deities. The 134 entries cover all the main gods and goddesses, many of the obscure denizens of the underworld, and some foreign deities who were worshipped in Egypt. Hart is particularly good at explaining complex deities, such as Horus. Most entries are illustrated with line drawings.

Erik Hornung. *Conceptions of God in Ancient Egypt: The One and the Many*. Translated by John Baines. Ithaca, NY: Cornell University Press, 1982.

> One of the most profound books ever written on Egyptian religion. Hornung uses a wealth of primary sources, including myths, to illuminate the nature of Egypt's deities and their relationship with humanity. The last part of the book focuses on the controversial issue of whether the Egyptians ever developed a form of **monotheism**.

Erik Hornung. *The Ancient Egyptian Books of the Afterlife*. Translated by David Lorton. Ithaca, NY, and London: Cornell University Press, 1999.

> This study is the ideal place to start for anyone who wishes to explore the funerary literature of Ancient Egypt. Hornung summarizes the contents of eighteen funerary collections or books and places them in their historical context. Many of the illustrations that can form a vital part of these works are shown and discussed. There is a very comprehensive bibliography for each chapter.

Barbara S. Lesko. *The Great Goddesses of Egypt*. Norman: University of Oklahoma Press, 1999.

> The author starts with an introduction: "Early Women and the First Evidence of Faith." She goes on to describe the cults of Nut, Neith, Nekhbet and Wadjet, Hathor, Mut, and Isis. Unlike much that is published about Egyptian goddesses, these are reliable accounts closely based on primary sources.

Manfred Lurker. *The Gods and Symbols of Ancient Egypt*. Translated by Barbara Cumming and revised by Peter Clayton. London: Thames and Hudson, 1980.

> This book covers the symbolic meanings of the animals, plants, and objects that appear in Egyptian art as well as the significance of divine figures. The entries are illustrated with black and white photographs or line drawings. The book ends with a useful chronological table, which lists the main cultural and religious developments in each period.

Dimitri Meeks and Christine Favard-Meeks. *Daily Life of the Egyptian Gods*. Translated by G. M. Goshgarian. London: John Murray, 1997.

> The authors have been criticized by many scholars for choosing to treat the Egyptian pantheon as if they were a "community that has caught the interest of anthropologists." The book does contain a mass of unusual information and draws extensively on mythological texts preserved in temples of the Greco-Roman Period.

Stephen Quirke. *Ancient Egyptian Religion*. London: British Museum Press, 1992.

> Quirke argues that Ancient Egyptian religion had two main functions: to answer personal dilemmas about the nature of the world and to bind the community together. The long chapters "Power in Heaven" and "Power on Earth" deal with the mythology of Ra, Osiris, and Horus.

Byron E. Shafer (ed.). *Religion in Ancient Egypt*. Ithaca, NY: Cornell University Press; London: Routledge, 1991.

> This useful book consists of three long essays: "Divinity and Deities in Ancient Egypt," by David P. Silverman; "Ancient Egyptian Cosmogonies and Cosmology," by Leonard H. Lesko; and "Society, Morality, and Religious Practice," by John Baines. The section by Lesko looks at some of the lesser-known creation myths, such as the Khonsu Cosmogony from Thebes.

Vincent Arieh Tobin. "Mytho-Theology in Ancient Egypt." *Journal of the American Research Center in Egypt* [*JARCE*] 25 (1988): 169–184; and "Divine Conflict in the Pyramid Texts." *JARCE* 30 (1993): 93–110.

> Two articles that examine the process of myth making in Egypt and the links among myth, ritual, theology, and politics.

Pascal Vernus. *The Gods of Ancient Egypt.* Translated by Jane Marie Todd. London and New York: Tauris Park Books, 1998.

> This book has magnificent color photographs by Erich Lessing, but the text is of equal importance. The subjects covered include the organization of the Egyptian pantheon and the ways in which individuals related to their gods. Vernus writes particularly well about animal forms of deities.

Books and Articles on Egyptian Myth in Other Languages

More has been written about Egyptian myth in German than in any other language. Important or interesting works include Siegfried Schott's *Mythe und Mythenbildung im alten Ägypten* (Leipzig: J. C. Hinricks, 1945); Emma Brunner-Traut's article on myth in *Lexikon der Ägyptologie,* edited by W. Helck et al., vol. 4 (Wiesbaden, Germany: Harrassowitz, 1982), 277–286, and her *Gelebte Mythen: Beiträge zum altägyptischen Mythos* (Darmstadt: Wissenschaftliche Buchgesellschaft, 1981); Jan Assmann's "Die Verborgenheit des Mythos in Ägypten" (in *Göttingen Miszellan* 25 [1977]: 7–43]; and Heike Sternberg's *Mythische Motive und Mythenbildung in den ägyptischen Tempeln und Papyri der griechisch-römischen Zeit* (Wiesbaden, Germany: Harrassowitz, 1985). In French, Susanne Bickel's *La cosmogonie égyptienne avant le Nouvel Empire* (Orbis Biblicus et Orientalis 134; Freiburg and Göttingen, 1994) summarizes, analyzes, and interprets a range of creation myths; and Isabelle Franco's *Mythes et Dieux: Le Souffle de Soleil* (Paris: Pygmalion, 1996) is a very readable general survey of Egyptian mythology.

English Translations of Ancient Texts

This is a selection of major sources for Egyptian myth. Many more will be found in "Appendix: Primary Sources."

Thomas George Allen. *The Book of the Dead or the Book of Going Forth by Day.* Studies in Ancient Oriental Civilizations 37. Chicago: University of Chicago Press, 1974.

> Probably the best English translation of the 174 spells generally agreed to make up the Egyptian Book of the Dead. Allen does not include the vignettes for the spells, and the notes are intended for scholars. The vignettes can be found in reprints of E. A. Wallis Budge's edition of the Book of the Dead, but his translation should not be relied on.

J. F. Borghouts. *Ancient Egyptian Magical Texts*. NISABA vol. 9 Leiden: E. J. Brill, 1978.

> Translations of 146 spells from a variety of sources, ranging in date from the Middle Kingdom to the Late Period. This anthology concentrates on spells that were probably used in daily life. Many of these spells incorporate short myths. There are outstandingly helpful notes and indexes.

R. O. Faulkner. *The Ancient Egyptian Coffin Texts*. Vols.1–3. Warminster, England: Aris and Phillips, 1973–1978.

> Literal translations of 1,185 Coffin Texts, including the Book of Two Ways. The notes are mainly concerned with grammar and give the reader little help to understand these difficult texts. There are very comprehensive indexes at the end of Volume 3.

R. O. Faulkner. *The Ancient Egyptian Pyramid Texts*. Warminster, England: Aris and Phillips; Oak Park, IL: Bolchazy Carducci, n.d.

> Literal translations of 759 Pyramid Texts; the oldest of the major sources for Egyptian myth. The extensive notes are intended for Egyptologists rather than the general reader. The index of the deities mentioned in the Pyramid Texts is arranged in the traditional order of the Ancient Egyptian "alphabet." More Pyramid Texts have been discovered since this translation was first published in 1969.

John L. Foster. *Hymns, Prayers, and Songs: An Anthology of Ancient Egyptian Lyric Poetry*. Edited by Susan Tower Hollis. Atlanta, GA: Scholar's Press, 1995.

> Nine of the thirteen sections in this anthology concentrate on religious poetry. The book includes selections from the Pyramid Texts and the Book of the Dead but is most useful for the translations of a wide range of hymns to Amun and Ra. Each section has a brief introduction, and there is a helpful glossary.

Miriam Lichtheim. *Ancient Egyptian Literature*. 3 vols. Berkeley, Los Angeles, London: University of California Press, 1973–1980.

> These ground-breaking anthologies have introduced thousands of readers to Egyptian literature. They translate works ranging in date from the twenty-fourth century BCE to the first century CE. The translations include important sources for myth such as the Memphite Theology (misdated to the Old Kingdom), the Contendings of Horus and Seth, and the Setna Cycle.

R. B. Parkinson. *The Tale of Sinuhe and Other Ancient Egyptian Poems: 1940–1640 BC*. Oxford: Oxford University Press, 1997.

> The best available translations of Middle Kingdom literature. The anthology includes two magical tales and several dialogues and teachings that allude to myths. Lively introductions and detailed notes to each translation make the book ideal for the general reader.

A. Piankoff. *The Tomb of Ramesses VI*. 2 vols. Edited by N. Rambova. Bollingen Series 40/1. New York: Pantheon Books for the Bolingen Foundation, 1954.

> This magnificently produced book includes translations and interpretations of the numerous Underworld Books that decorate the walls of this royal tomb. The complex pictures that are an integral part of these works are illustrated in the plates volume.

Plutarch. *De Iside Et Osiride*. Translated and with an introduction and commentary by J. Gwyn Griffiths. Swansea: University of Wales Press, 1970.

> After 2,000 years, this is still one of the most interesting books on mythology ever written. Plutarch recorded many mythical narratives while exploring the true nature of Isis, Osiris, and Typhon (Seth). He believed that the study of mythology was important because "the longing for truth, particularly for truth about the gods, is a yearning after divinity."

A Selection of Literature Influenced by Egyptian Myth

Lucius Apuleius. *The Golden Ass*. Translated by Robert Graves. 1950.

> *The Golden Ass*, also known as *Metamorphoses*, was written in the second century CE and is the only complete Latin novel to have survived. It is the entertaining story of a sorcerer's apprentice who is turned into a donkey by a witch. After many scandalous adventures, the repentant hero is rescued from his enchantment by the goddess Isis and becomes a priest of Osiris.

William Golding. *The Scorpion God*. 1971.

> A novella that begins with a vivid recreation of the *sed* festival at which an Egyptian king tries to renew his right to rule. Golding examines the mythologies of power and the impact of doubt on a fixed world view.

Christian Jacq. *Ramses under the Western Acacia*. Translated by Dorothy S. Blair. 1998.

> The last in a series of five historical novels about Rameses II by a French Egyptologist. All the novels feature the interplay between myth and ritual in Egyptian religion. There is a glossary of the deities that are mentioned.

Norman Mailer. *Ancient Evenings*. 1983.

> A violent and erotic novel, which includes some retellings of Egyptian myth. Much of the novel is set in the reign of the charismatic Rameses II, but the hero is reincarnated three times during the story, so there are colorful descriptions of the Egyptian afterlife.

Elizabeth Peters. *The Snake, the Crocodile, and the Dog*. 1992.

> One of a series of comic mystery novels about pioneering Egyptologist Radcliffe Emerson and his formidable wife, Amelia Peabody. Several books in the series use an Egyptian myth or legend as the basis for the plot. This one is based on the Tale of the Doomed Prince. A painless way to learn about the history of Egyptian archaeology.

Tim Powers. *The Anubis Gates*. 1983.

> An ingenious fantasy novel, partly set in Egypt. The time-traveling hero has to cope with Romantic poets as well as Egyptian magicians and deities.

Saxe Rohmer. *Tales of Secret Egypt*. 1918.

> Although Rohmer is best known for his Fu Manchu stories, Egypt was his real passion. He published several collections of well-researched short stories in which tomb robbers and Egyptologists encounter ancient magic and dangerous deities.

Charles Williams. *The Greater Trumps*. 1932.

> A "theological thriller" that draws on the belief that the Tarot pack was based on esoteric knowledge from Ancient Egypt. Isis appears in an unusual guise at the climax of the story.

NONPRINT RESOURCES

Videos

Egypt Uncovered

A five-volume set (no. 639328) that looks at major aspects of Egyptian civilization in the light of recent research. Mythology is covered in the videos "Deities and Demons" and "Mummies—Into the Afterlife." Available from shopping.discovery.com.

Karnak, Temple of the Gods

A beautifully filmed account of the rituals and myths associated with Egypt's greatest surviving temple. One of many History Channel videos on Ancient Egypt available from aetv.com.

Ra: The Path of the Sun God

A full-length animated film by Lesley Keen based on Egyptian mythology. The first part, "Dawn," shows images from creation myths; the second, "Noon," follows the life cycle of an Egyptian king; and the third, "Night," animates the journey of the sun god through the underworld. A Connoisseur Video available from Argos Films and the British Film Institute.

Web Sites and CD-ROMS

A huge amount of unreliable or downright false "information" about Egyptian mythology and religion is available on line. Many web sites run by amateurs feature material from Egyptology books that are a century out of date. A selection of trustworthy sites follows.

ABZU
www.oi.uchicago.edu/OI/DEPT/RA/ABZU/

A guide to resources for the study of the Ancient Near East available on the Internet. This site, run by Charles E. Jones, has many useful links to U.S. libraries, museums, and colleges.

Annual Egyptological Bibliography

www.leidenuniv.nl/nino/aeb.html

> An essential source for the serious researcher. Every academic book or article published by Egyptologists is listed and summarized in the Annual Egyptological Bibliography. The lists, which are organized under subject headings, are available on-line from 1992 onward. The complete lists from 1822 to 1997 are on a CD-ROM, which can be ordered by e-mail from w.hovestreydt@umail.leidenuniv.nl.

Bibliography of Ancient Egypt

www.ptahhotep.com

> Frequently updated lists of books, ebooks, and videos on Ancient Egypt. The site is run by Francesca Jourdan, who makes helpful comments on many of the entries. The lists do, however, include some occult and "lunatic fringe" material.

Centre for Computer-aided Egyptological Research

www.ccer.ggl.ruu.nl/

> This organization has compiled useful databases such as a list of all known hieroglyphs (4,700). They are publishing a series of twelve multilingual CD-ROMs on Egyptian treasures in Europe. Each one illustrates and describes 1,500 objects, including numerous representations of deities. Order by e-mail from ccer@ccer.nl.

Egyptian Mythology Today

Egyptmyth.com

> This site is mainly aimed at children who need help with school projects. It has nice graphics and a good list of links to other Egyptology web sites.

Egyptology Resources

www.newton.cam.ac.uk/egypt/

> This site, run by Egyptologist Nigel Strudwick, is the best place to start for anyone with an interest in Egyptology. There are links to numerous university departments, museums, and societies as well as a frequently updated "News" section.

Encyclopedia Mythica

www.pantheon.org/mythica/areas/egyptian/

> Currently has 231 entries for Egyptian myth. The entries are brief, but there are useful lists of alternative spellings for the names of deities.

Griffith Institute

www.ashmol.ox.ac.uk/Griffith.html

> The web site of the world's largest archive of research material on Ancient Egypt. This is the best place to go for information on Tutankhamun, and there is an excellent children's section.

Mythology Gallery

members.aol.com/egyptart/

> A beautifully illustrated introduction to Egyptian mythology by artist Richard Deurer. It has a helpful glossary and good lists of deities and symbols but a poor bibliography.

SCA

guardians.net/sca/

> The website of the Supreme Council of Antiquities, the organization in charge of all archaeological sites and museums in Egypt. The site is not updated as often as it might be, but it does have interesting information on current excavations.

Tour Egypt

www.touregypt.net/gods1.htm

> The official site of the Egyptian Ministry of Tourism. Go to its "Old Egypt Mythology" section for detailed information on Egyptian deities. There are translations of original source material and some good pictures.

GLOSSARY

Ancient Egyptian words are in italics.

Akh   A transfigured and powerful spirit. The aim of most funerary rites was to transform the dead person into an *akh*.

Amulet   An object that guaranteed health, good luck, or protection to the wearer.

Ankh   A hieroglyphic sign writing the word *life* and an amuletic symbol of the gift of life.

Anthropoid coffin   A coffin shaped like a person. It usually depicted the deceased transformed into a funerary deity or a transfigured spirit.

Apotropaic   Having the power to drive away evil.

Atef Crown   A tall crown decorated with two protruding horns, two feathers, and a small disc. Mainly worn by the god Osiris.

Atonism   Worship of the light of the sun as the sole god and King Akhenaten as its manifestation on earth.

Attributes   The form, costume, or objects that characterized a deity.

Ba   The soul or identity of a person or deity. The *ba* was usually shown as a human-headed bird. A closely related word means a divine manifestation.

Barque (Bark)   A sacred boat used to carry a god (in myth) or an image of a god (in cult).

Barque of Millions   The boat of the sun god.

Benben   A sacred stone in the solar temple at Heliopolis. Probably the prototype for the first obelisks and the capstones of pyramids.

Book of the Dead   A collection of funerary texts used from the sixteenth century BCE onward.

Canopic jars   The four jars containing the viscera (usually the lungs, liver, stomach, and intestines) of a mummy. Often stored in a canopic chest (see "Sons of Horus" in "Deities, Themes, and Concepts").

Cartouche   An oval shape inside which royal names were written. It symbolized that the king ruled "everything that the sun encircles."

Cataracts   Rocky areas of the Nile that created rapids. The First Cataract formed the southern boundary of Egypt in ancient times.

Cenotaph   A funerary monument without an actual burial.

Charter myth   A myth used to justify an institution or custom.

Chthonic deity   A deity whose realm was inside or under the earth.

Cippus (pl. cippi)   A magical stela with inscriptions and images used to cure snake and scorpion bites.

Circumpolar stars   The stars that are always visible above the horizon at a fixed location.

Coffin Texts   A body of funerary texts, most commonly painted on coffins of the Middle Kingdom.

Copts   The Christian population of Egypt.

Corn mummy   A miniature mummy of the gods Osiris or Sokar-Osiris; usually made from earth containing seeds.

Cosmogony   An account of the creation of the world.

Cosmogram   A symbolic representation of the universe.

Cosmology   Theories about the structure and origins of the universe.

Crook   A symbol carried by Egyptian kings, probably derived from a staff used by shepherds to control sheep.

Cubit   An ancient unit of measurement based on the length of a man's forearm. The standard "royal cubit" was about 52.4 centimeters.

Cult image   A statue to be used as a body by a deity and worshipped in a temple or shrine.

Decan stars   Stars that represented a ten-day period. Each Egyptian month was made up of three ten-day "weeks."

Delta, the   The area of northern Egypt in which the Nile splits into several branches before reaching the Mediterranean Sea.

Demiurge   A being who begins the process of creation.

Demotic   An Egyptian script developed by the seventh century BCE and a phase of the language.

Djed **pillar**   A symbol of endurance that came to be associated with the resurrection of the god Osiris (see "Deities, Themes, and Concepts").

Double Crown   Royal headdress combining the Red Crown of Lower Egypt and the White Crown of Upper Egypt.

Duat (*Dat*)   The Egyptian underworld. A realm below or beyond the earth inhabited by gods, demons, and the dead.

Ennead   A group of deities, usually nine in number, who act together. The Great Ennead was the Ennead of Heliopolis (see "Deities, Themes, and Concepts").

Epagomenal days   Five extra days after the end of the last month of the Egyptian year.

Eschatology   Descriptions of how the world will end.

Etiological myths   Myths that explain the cause or origins of something.

Fecundity figures   Personifications of the good things brought by the inundation. Also called Nile gods.

Field of Reeds   A place in the afterlife where the blessed dead lived and worked.

Flail (Flagellum)   A ceremonial whip carried by Egyptian kings.

Gnosticism   A religious movement based on a form of self-knowledge supposed to lead to the liberation of the soul.

Heb Sed   The festival (*heb*) of the jackal god Sed. This festival was traditionally celebrated to renew a king's powers after he had reigned for thirty years.

Henotheism   The choice of one god or goddess to be an individual's personal deity.

Hermetica   A body of philosophical and magical texts composed in Egypt during the Greco-Roman Period. They claim to contain the wisdom of Hermes Trismegistus (see in "Deities, Themes, and Concepts" under "Thoth").

Hieratic   A cursive script mainly used to write literary and everyday texts.

Hieroglyphs   The elaborate symbols used to write royal and religious texts in Ancient Egyptian.

Iconography   Visual symbols expressing the essential nature of a being or concept.

Instruction Texts   Instruction or Wisdom Texts were a type of literature that offered practical and ethical advice about how to live.

Inundation, the   The floodwaters of the river Nile that covered the fields every year.

Ithyphallic   Displaying an erect penis.

Ka   The vital essence of a person that continued to need nourishment after death. Shown as a person's double.

Ka **statue**   An image of a deceased person that his or her *ka* could use as a body

Lector priest   A type of priest trained to read and recite the ancient rituals recorded on scrolls.

Lower Egypt   The north of Egypt, from above Memphis to the Mediterranean coast.

Maat   Truth, justice, and the divine order (see "Deities, Themes, and Concepts").

Mammisi (Birthhouse)   A structure within a temple precinct where the birth of a deity was celebrated.

Menat **necklace**   A necklace and counterpoise imbued with divine power.

Middle Egypt   The area of Egypt between Asyut and Memphis.

Monotheism   A belief system with only one deity.

Mummy   An artificially preserved body wrapped in linen bandages.

Naos   An inner shrine made to contain an image of a deity.

Necromancy   The practice of summoning the dead to gain knowledge or power.

Necropolis   A city for the dead with tombs and funerary shrines.

Nilometer   A set of steps used for estimating the height of the annual Nile flood.

Nomarch   The governor of a nome (province).

Nome   One of the forty-two provinces into which Egypt was divided. Each nome was represented by a symbol and had at least one patron deity.

Obelisk   A tapering pillar of stone with a pointed top. Placed in open courts in temples or tombs, obelisks were mainly associated with sun worship.

Ogdoad   A group of eight deities. The most famous example was the Ogdoad of Hermopolis (see "Deities, Themes, and Concepts").

Opening of the Mouth Ceremony   A ritual to reanimate a mummy or to animate a statue or image.

Oracle   A deity who answers questions or the place where these answers are given. Egyptian oracles usually involved the movement of a cult statue toward a particular person or between a choice of two written answers.

Ostracon (pl. ostraca)   A potsherd or flake of stone used as a surface for writing or drawing.

Papyrus   A type of reed, the paper made from its stems, or a book-scroll formed from sheets of papyrus.

Pataikos (pl. pataikoi)   A type of dwarf deity used as a protective amulet.

Pharaoh   A title meaning Great House (the Palace); a respectful way of referring to an Egyptian king.

Polytheism   The worship of many gods within a religious tradition.

Ptolemaic   Something belonging to the period when the Greek Ptolemy family ruled Egypt.

Pylon   A pair of trapezoidal towers that formed the entrance to a temple. The towers were identified with the mountains of the horizon.

Pyramid complex   A royal burial area consisting of a tomb under or inside a pyramid and two temples for the cult of the dead ruler.

Pyramid Texts   Royal funerary texts inscribed inside pyramids of the late Old Kingdom and the First Intermediate Period.

Royal titulary   The long sequence of names and titles adopted by an Egyptian king at the start of his reign.

Sarcophagus An outer coffin, usually made of stone.

Scarab A seal or amulet shaped like a dung beetle; a symbol of the perpetual renewal of life.

Scribe An official capable of reading and writing one or more of the Ancient Egyptian scripts.

Sed Festival See *Heb Sed.*

Serekh A rectangular hieroglyph symbolizing the palace as the domain of Horus. Some royal names were written inside a *serekh* instead of a cartouche.

Sistrum A rattle used in temple rituals whose sound was thought to pacify angry deities and drive away evil.

Solar barque The boat in which the sun god was said to travel across the sky or through the underworld.

Solar eye The disk of the sun, or the morning star who preceded the sun; usually manifest as a dangerous goddess.

Sphinx A mythical guardian, usually with the body of a lion and the head of a human (see "Deities, Themes, and Concepts").

Stela An inscribed slab, used to display royal decrees or commemorative or pious texts.

Syncretism An attempt to combine the characteristics of two or more deities.

Triad A group of three deities, often taking the form of father, mother, and child. Triads that were treated as a single entity can also be called trinities.

Udjat See *Wedjat* eye.

Underworld Books Illustrated funerary texts describing the voyages of the sun god.

Upper Egypt The south of Egypt, from below Memphis to the Nubian border.

Uraeus (pl. uraei) An image of the cobra goddess who guarded the king; often found on royal headdresses.

Ushabti A figurine that magically performed tasks on behalf of its owner in the afterlife.

Vignette A picture that formed part of a spell, particularly in the Book of the Dead.

Was scepter A scepter with a curved head that symbolized divine power.

Wedjat eye A part-hawk, part-human eye that was a symbol of healing, unity, and power (see in "Deities, Themes, and Concepts" under "Eyes of Horus").

APPENDIX:
PRIMARY SOURCES

Each entry in "Deities, Themes, and Concepts" is followed by a selection of primary sources cited in abbreviated form. An alphabetical list of these abbreviations is given in this appendix. Numbers refer to spell, chapter, or section numbers; for example, BD 15 is the Book of the Dead, chapter 15. For descriptions of most of the primary sources, see "History and the Sources of Egyptian Myth" in "Introduction." A literal translation is cited for each source. These translations either include the text in the original language or refer to other publications that do.

LIST OF ABBREVIATIONS

Ad   Amduat (Book of What Is in the Underworld): See A. Piankoff. *The Tomb of Ramesses VI.* Edited by N. Rambova. Bollingen Series 40.1. New York: 1954, 227–318.

Alexander Romance: See R. Stoneman. *The Greek Alexander Romance.* London: 1991.

Amenemope   Instruction of Amenemope: See M. Lichtheim. *Ancient Egyptian Literature.* Vol. 2, *New Kingdom.* Berkeley, Los Angeles, and London: 1976, 146–163.

Amenmose stela   Louvre C 286: See Lichtheim, *Ancient Egyptian Literature,* 2:81–86.

Amun prayers: See Lichtheim, *Ancient Egyptian Literature,* 2:111–112.

Ankhsheshonq   Instruction of Ankhsheshonq: See M. Lichtheim. *Ancient Egyptian Literature.* Vol. 3, *The Late Period.* Berkeley, Los Angeles, and London: 1980, 159–183.

Arrian: See *Arrian: The Life of Alexander.* Translated by A. de Sélincourt. London: 1971.

Asclepius: See B. P. Copenhaver. *Hermetica.* Cambridge: 1992, 67–92.

Astarte and the Sea: See "Astarte and the Insatiable Sea." In R. O. Faulkner, E. F. Wente, and W. K. Simpson. *The Literature of Ancient Egypt: An Anthology of Stories, Instructions, and Poetry*. New Haven and London: 1972, 133–136.

Astronomical ceilings: See Piankoff, *The Tomb of Ramesses VI*, 429–432.

Aten hymns: See William J. Murnane. *Texts from the Amarna Period in Egypt*. Atlanta, GA: 1995, nos. 58-B.4, 70.7–8, 89.7.

BC   The Book of Caverns: See Piankoff, *The Tomb of Ramesses VI*, 45–136.

BD   The Book of the Dead: See T. G. Allen. *The Book of the Dead or the Book of Going Forth by Day*. Studies in Ancient Oriental Civilization 37. Chicago: 1974; and R. O. Faulkner. *The Ancient Egyptian Book of the Dead*. Revised by C. A. Andrews. London: 1985.

Bentresh Stela: See Lichtheim, *Ancient Egyptian Literature* 3:90–94.

BHC   The Book of the Heavenly Cow: See A. Piankoff. *The Shrines of Tut-Ankh-Amon*. Edited by N. Rambova. Bollingen Series 40.2. New York: 1955, 27–34; and E. Hornung. *Der ägyptische Mythos von der Himmelskuh*. 2d ed. Orbis Biblicus et Orientalis 46. Freiburg and Göttingen: 1997, 37–50.

BOD   The Book of the Day: See Piankoff, *The Tomb of Ramesses VI*, 389–408.

BOE   The Book of the Earth/Book of Aker: See Piankoff, *The Tomb of Ramesses VI*, 327–376.

BOF   The Book of the Fayum: See H. Beinlich. *Das Buch vom Fayum*. Wiesbaden: 1991.

BofNut   The Book of Nut: See J. P. Allen. *Genesis in Egypt*. 2d ed. Yale Egyptological Studies 2. San Antonio, TX: 1995, 1–7.

BOG   The Book of Gates: See Piankoff, *The Tomb of Ramesses VI*, 137–223.

BON   The Book of the Night: See Piankoff, *The Tomb of Ramesses VI*, 409–428.

Book of the Last Day of the Year: See J. F. Borghouts. *Ancient Egyptian Magical Texts*. Leiden: 1978, no.13.

Book of Two Ways: See CT (Coffin Texts), vol. 3; or L. H. Lesko. *The Ancient Egyptian Book of Two Ways*. Berkeley: 1972.

BRP   Bremner-Rhind Papyrus (British Museum 10188): See R. O. Faulkner. "The Bremner-Rhind Papyrus I–IV." *The Journal of Egyptian Archaeology* 22–24 (1936, 1937, 1938): 121–140, 10–16, 166–185, 41–53; and J. P. Allen, *Genesis in Egypt*, 27–28.

BTE   The Book of Traversing Eternity: See F. R. Herbin. *Le Livre de parcourir l'éternité*. Leuven, Belgium: 1994.

Cairo calendar: See Abdel-Moksen Bakir. *The Cairo Calendar No. 86637*. Cairo: 1966.

Crossword stela: See H. M. Stewart. "A Crossword Hymn to Mut." *Journal of Egyptian Archaeology* 57 (1971): 87–104.

CT   The Coffin Texts: See R. O. Faulkner. *The Ancient Egypt Coffin Texts.* 3 vols. Warminster, England: 1973–1978.

Dendara calendar: See Sherif El-Sabban. *Temple Festival Calendars of Ancient Egypt.* Liverpool: 2000, 180–184.

Diodorus   Diodorus Siculus Book I: See C. H. Oldfather. *Diodorus Siculus I Books I-II, 34.* Cambridge, MA, and London: 1933.

DP   The Doomed Prince: See Lichtheim, *Ancient Egyptian Literature,* 2:200–203.

Edfu calendar: See El-Sabban, *Temple Festival Calendars of Ancient Egypt,* 169–179.

Edfu cosmology: See R. B. Finnestad. *Image of the World and Symbol of the Creator.* Wiesbaden: 1985, 26–41.

Eloquent Peasant   The Tale of the Eloquent Peasant: See R. B. Parkinson. *The Tale of Sinuhe and Other Ancient Egyptian Poems, 1940–1640 BC.* Oxford: 1997, 54–88.

EofS   Eye of Sun myth: See F. de Cenival. *Le mythe de l'Oeil du Soleil.* Demotische Studien 9. Sommerhausen: 1988.

Esna calendar: See El-Sabban, *Temple Festival Calendars of Ancient Egypt,* 159–168.

Esna hymns: See Lichtheim, *Ancient Egyptian Literature,* 3:109–115.

Esna texts: See S. Sauneron. *Le Temple d'Esna,* vol. 3. Cairo: 1968.

Famine stela: See Lichtheim, *Ancient Egyptian Literature* 3:94–103.

H&S   The Contendings of Horus and Seth (Papyrus Chester Beatty I Recto): See Lichtheim, *Ancient Egyptian Literature* 2:214–223.

Hapy hymns: See J. L. Foster. *Hymns, Prayers, and Songs: An Anthology of Ancient Egyptian Lyric Poetry.* Edited by S. Tower Hollis. Atlanta, GA: 1995, 114–122.

Herodotus H: See *The History Herodotus.* Translated by D. Grene. Chicago and London: 1987.

Hibis hymn (to Maat): See Foster, *Hymns, Prayers, and Songs,* 122–123

Hibis texts: See E. Cruz-Uribe. *Hibis Temple Project.* Vol. 1. San Antonio, TX: 1988.

HMP   Harris Magical Papyrus (BM 10042): See C. Leitz. *Magical and Medical Papyri of the New Kingdom.* Hieratic Papyri in the British Museum, 7. London: 1999, 31–50.

I&O   Plutarch's "Concerning Isis and Osiris": See Plutarch, *De Iside et Osiride.* Translated and with introduction and commentary by J. G. Griffiths. Swansea, Wales: 1970.

Ikhernofret stela: See M. Lichtheim. *Ancient Egyptian Literature*. Vol. 1: *The Old and Middle Kingdoms*. Berkeley, Los Angeles, and London, 1973, 123–125.

Imhotep hymn: See Lichtheim, *Ancient Egyptian Literature*, 3:104–107.

Ipuur   The Dialogue of Ipuur and the Lord of All: See Parkinson, *The Tale of Sinuhe*, 166–199.

Isis hymns: See L. V. Zabkar. *Hymns to Isis in Her Temple at Philae*. Hanover, NH: 1988.

Ismailia naos: See G. Goyon. "Les travaux de Chou et les tribulations de Geb d'après Le Naos 2248 d'Ismaïlia." *Kemi* 6 (1936): 1–42.

Karnak stela: See Murnane, *Texts from the Amarna Period in Egypt*, 212–214.

KASP   "King as Sun Priest" texts: See J. Assmann. *Egyptian Solar Religion in the New Kingdom*. Translated by A. Alcock. London and New York: 1995, 17–37.

Khoiak texts: See E. Chassinat. *Les Mystères d'Osiris au mois de Khoiak*. Cairo: 1966–1968.

Khonsu Cosmogony: See R. A. Parker and L. H. Lesko. "The Khonsu Cosmogony." In *Pyramid Studies and Other Essays Presented to I. E. S. Edwards*, edited by J. Baines. London: 1988, 168–175.

Kom Ombo texts: See A. Gutbub. *Textes Fondamentaux de la Theologie de Kom Ombo*. Cairo: 1973; and A. Gutbub and D. Inconnu-Boquillon. *Kom Ombo I*. Cairo: 1995.

Lamentations   The Lamentations of Isis and Nephthys: See Lichtheim, *Ancient Egyptian Literature*, 3:116–121. *See also* BRP.

Leiden hymns: See Foster, *Hymns, Prayers, and Songs*, 68–79.

LofR   Litany of Ra: See A. Piankoff. *The Litany of Re*. Bollingen Series 40.4. New York: 1964.

Loyalist Instruction: See "The Loyalist Teaching" in Parkinson, *The Tale of Sinuhe*, 235–245.

LWD   Legend of the Winged Disk: See H. W. Fairman. "The Myth of Horus at Edfu-I." *Journal of Egyptian Archaeology* 21 (1935): 26–36.

Magical statue texts: See A. Klasens. *A Magical Statue Base in the Museum of Antiquities at Leiden*. Leiden: 1952; J. F Borghouts. *Ancient Egyptian Magical Texts*. Leiden: 1978, nos. 87–88, 90–91, 101, 104, 114, 118, 139–142, 144–146; and L. Kákosy. *Egyptian Healing Statues in Three Museums in Italy*. Turin: 1999.

Medamud hymn: See J. C. Darnell. "Hathor Returns to Medamud." *Studien zur Altägyptischen Kultur* 22 (1995): 47–94.

Mendes stela: See H. De Meulenaere and P. Mackay. *Mendes II*. Warminster, England: 1976, 174–177.

Metternich Stela: See Borghouts, *Ancient Egyptian Magical Texts*, nos. 90, 91, 93–95, 104, 123.

Min festival texts: See H. Gauthier. *Les fetes du dieu Min*. Cairo: 1931.

MT   Memphite Theology (Shabaqo Stone/London BM 498): See M. Lichtheim, *Ancient Egyptian Literature* 1:51–57.

Mut ritual: See U. Verhoeven and P. Derchain. *Le voyage de la déesse libyque. Ein Text aus der "Mutritual" des Pap. Berlin 3053*. Rites égyptiens 5. Brussels: 1985.

Neferabu stela: See Lichtheim, *Ancient Egyptian Literature* 2:107–108.

Osiris hymns: See R. B. Parkinson. *Voices from Ancient Egypt*. London: 1991, 118–120; and M. Lichtheim. *Maat in Egyptian Autobiographies and Related Studies*. Orbis Biblicus et Orientalis 120. Freiburg and Gottingen: 1992, 136–140.

PBM 9997 + 1039: See Leitz, *Magical and Medical Papyri of the New Kingdom*, 3–30.

PBM 10059   London Medical Papyrus: See Leitz, *Magical and Medical Papyri of the New Kingdom*, 51–84.

P. Boulaq XVII: See Foster, *Hymns, Prayers, and Songs*, 58–65.

P. Carlsberg 180: See J. Osing. *The Carlsberg Papyri 2*. Hieratische Papyri aus Tebtunis I. Copenhagen: 1998, 166–170.

P. Chester Beatty VII   Papyrus Chester Beatty VII: See Borghouts, *Ancient Egyptian Magical Texts*, nos. 85–86, 89, 109–110, 113, 116, 119.

PDM and PDM Supp.   Demotic Magical papyri: See H. D. Betz, ed. *The Greek Magical Papyri in Translation*. Chicago: 1992, 195–251, 286–292, 323–330.

Petese: See K. S. B. Ryholt. *The Story of Petese, Son of Petetum and Seventy Other Good and Bad Stories*. Copenhagen: 1999.

PGM   Papyri Graecae Magicae (Greek magical papyri): See *The Greek Magical Papyri in Translation*. Vol. 1: *Texts*. Edited by Hans Dieter Betz. Chicago and London: 1992, 3-169, 251–323.

PJ   Papyrus Jumilhac: See J. Vandier. *Le Papyrus Jumilhac*. Paris: 1961.

P. Leiden I 343–346: See Borghouts, *Ancient Egyptian Magical Texts*, nos. 13, 23–24.

P. Leiden I 348: See J. F. Borghouts. "The Magical Texts of Papyrus Leiden I 348." *Oudheidkundige Mededelingen het Rijksmuseum van Oudheden te Leiden* 51 (1970): 1–248.

P. Salt 825: See P. Derchain. *Le Papyrus Salt 825 (BM 10051)*. Brussels: 1965.

PT   The Pyramid Texts: See R. O. Faulkner. *The Ancient Egyptian Pyramid Texts*. Oxford: 1969.

Ptah hymns: See Allen, *Genesis in Egypt*, texts 13–14.

P. Turin 1993: See Bourghouts, *Ancient Egyptian Magical Texts,* nos. 92, 102, 106, 111, 115, 138.

PV   Papyrus Vandier: See G. Posener. *Le Papyrus Vandier.* Cairo: 1985.

P. Vindob: See R. L. Vos. *The Apis Embalming Ritual: P. Vindob 3873.* Orientalia Lovaniensia Analecta 50. Louvain, Belgium: 1993.

P. Westcar: See "King Cheops and the Magicians" in Simpson, *The Literature of Ancient Egypt,* 1973, 15–30; or "The Tales of King Cheops' Court," in Parkinson, *The Tale of Sinuhe,* 102–127.

Qadesh inscriptions: See Lichtheim, *Ancient Egyptian Literature,* 2:57–72.

RBM   Royal-birth myths: See H. Brunner. *Die Geburt des Gottkönigs: Studien zur Überlieferung eines altägyptischen Mythos.* Wiesbaden: 1964.

RDP   Ramesseum Dramatic Papyrus: See K. Sethe. *Dramatische Texte zu altägyptischen Mysterienspielen.* Leipzig: 1928.

Sekhmet litany: See P. Germond. *Sekhmet et la protection du monde.* Geneva: 1981, 19–87.

Setna cycle: See F. L. Griffith. *Stories of the High Priests of Memphis.* Vols. 1–2. Oxford: 1900; and Lichtheim, *Ancient Egyptian Literature,* 3:125–151.

Sinuhe: See "The Tale of Sinuhe," in Parkinson, *The Tale of Sinuhe,* 21–53.

Solar hymns: See Foster, *Hymns, Prayers, and Songs,* 41–47, 80–98; and S. Quirke. *The Cult of Ra Sun-worship in Ancient Egypt.* London: 2001, 66–70.

Sphinx stela of Amenhotep II: See Lichtheim, *Ancient Egyptian Literature,* 2:39–43.

Sphinx stela of Thutmose IV: See H. Breasted. *Ancient Records of Egypt.* Vol. 2. Chicago: 1906, 810–815.

Stela of Somtutefnakht: See Lichtheim, *Ancient Egyptian Literature,* 3:41–43.

Strabo G   See *The "Geography" of Strabo.* Vol. 8. Translated by H. L. Jones. London: 1949.

TB   The Two Brothers: See Lichtheim, *Ancient Egyptian Literature,* 3:203–210; or S. Tower Hollis. *The Ancient Egyptian "Tale of Two Brothers": The Oldest Fairy Tale in the World.* Norman, OK, and London: 1990.

Triumph of Horus: See H. W. Fairman. *The Triumph of Horus: An Ancient Egyptian Sacred Drama.* London: 1974, 77–122.

True Name (of Ra): See Borghouts, *Ancient Egyptian Magical Texts,* no. 84.

Udjahorresne   Statue Inscription of Udjahorresne: See Lichtheim, *Ancient Egyptian Literature,* 3:36–41.

Wenamun   The Report of Wenamun: See Lichtheim, *Ancient Egyptian Literature,* 2:224–230.

INDEX

Page numbers for main entries in 'Deities, Themes and Concepts' or 'Glossary' are in bold.

ABOUT THE AUTHOR

Geraldine Pinch, **Ph.D.**, is a member of the Faculty of Oriental Studies (Near and Middle East) at Oxford University. She is the author of *Votive Offerings to Hathor*, *Magic in Ancient Egypt*, and numerous articles on Egyptian religion and mythology.